Makoto Takamiya
Union Organization and Militancy

Band 5

SCHRIFTEN DES WISSENSCHAFTSZENTRUMS BERLIN
Internationales Institut
für Management und Verwaltung

Makoto Takamiya

Union Organization and Militancy

Conclusions from a Study of the United Mine Workers of America 1940 – 1974

Verlag Anton Hain · Meisenheim am Glan
1978

CIP-Kurztitelaufnahme der Deutschen Bibliothek

Takamiya, Makoto:
Union organisation and militancy : conclusions from a study of the United Mine Workers of America 1940 – 1974 / Makoto Takamiya. – Meisenheim am Glan : Hain 1978.
(Schriften des Wissenschaftszentrums Berlin ; Bd. 5 : Internat. Inst. für Management u. Verwaltung)
ISBN 3-445-01834-0

Umschlaggestaltung: Christian Ahlers, Berlin
Repro, Druck, Bindung: Friedrich Pustet, Regensburg
Printed in Germany
ISBN 3-445-01834-0

For my parents,
Susumu and Hiroko Takamiya,
with deep gratitude

EDITORS' FOREWORD

The Science Center (Wissenschaftzentrum) Berlin Publishers are pleased to include the present volume in their series of Dissertations, Bibliographies, etc. The monograph is based upon a manuscript submitted in partial fulfillment of the requirements for the degree of Doctor of Philosophy at the Sloan School of Management, Massachusetts Institute of Technology, under the supervision of Professors Charles Myers, Edgar Schein, John Van Maanen and Jim Driscoll.

There are several reasons why the Science Center Publishers should want to publish a report which essentially was produced before Dr. Takamiya joined the International Institute of Management (IIM) of the Science Center Berlin.

One is its character as an in-depth case study which the author analyses in a way allowing generalizations on some crucial organizational issues pertinent to voluntary organizations. Another is the insights the study renders into participation issues, as participation research has been an area of concentration within the International Institute of Management between 1973 and 1978. A third reason is the methodological approach chosen by Dr. Takamiya. Finally, the topic ought to be of interest not only to students of organizations, but also to union leaders and to business executives.

Dr. Takamiya's contribution to our series is pertinent to highly industrialized societies, where collective bargaining is conducted between large organizations. In such a context, it is important to understand internal organizational mechanisms of the bargaining parties and the impact on the bargaining process. As the author points out, academic literature provides little evidence yet on that question. Thus, the present study is an important and much needed contribution to the literature, since it generates empirically-based theories about the organizational effects on unions' official militancy.

The method used by the author is a historical analysis of organizational transitions. The approach enables the researcher to become familiar with the case and to make it comparable to other cases, thus providing a basis for hypothesis generation. The United Mine Workers Union has played an important role during the last hundred years in the development of the American economy. It has undergone remarkable and drastic changes, from boom to decline. Presently it must be regarded as one of the key unions when it comes to the realization of the energy program of the United States of America, and thus also to the repercussions of that program on the industrialized world. Dr. Takamiya's thesis thus seems to be a most timely contribution to organization research.

As is always and in principle the case in the Science Center Berlin Book Series, the responsibility for the data, results and conclusions presented rests with the authors exclusively.

Walter H. Goldberg
Director
International Institute of Management
Science Center Berlin

ACKNOWLEDGMENTS

This study bears, to its great advantage, the mark of a number of highly qualified persons. I regret that my appreciation can be expressed only by a brief listing of their names.

Most of the research work was completed during my stay at MIT. Among the faculty and colleagues who contribute to the stimulating and rigorous environment at MIT, I owe my heaviest debt to Professors Charles Myers, Edgar Schein, John van Maanen, James Driscoll and Subodh Mathur, who read through my lengthy manuscript at various stages of the draft and provided indispensible advice. It is very apparent that this research could not have been gathered into its present form of presentation had it not been for their professional support.

At various stages of the study, Professors Thomas Schelling (Harvard University), Roger Miller (University of Quebec), Daniel Quinn Mills (Harvard University), Ijaz Gilani (Islamabad University), Kenneth Mericle (MIT), Ralph Katz (MIT), Takeo Kurai (Kyushu Daiichi University), Yasuo Okamoto (University of Tokyo) and Makoto Sakurabayashi (Sophia University) either read parts of the manuscrupt or kindly spent long hours listening to my problems. I regret that my limited ability has not allowed full incorporation of all their suggestions, which undoubtedly have improved this study.

My new academic environment, the International Institute of Management in Berlin, gave another impetus to the study. Its director, Professor Walter Goldberg, provided me with the opportunity for publication and with consistent encouragement toward the improvement of the manuscript. My colleagues Drs. Roger Dunbar, Arndt Sorge and Bill England helped me with their penetrating criticisms. I was also very lucky to have Leah Ireland as my editor; her intelligence sometimes enabled her to go beyond her editorial duties and help me improve the content itself.

During my field research, Mr. Tom Shimabukuro, Miss Katherline Shimabukur-o and Miss Keiko Kakinuma generously provided with comfortable accomodations and friendly support; the weeks of staying with them were immensely enjoyable and apparently saved me from the usual tensions of field research. Dr. Thomas Woodruff (former staff member of the UMW), Mr. Harry Patrick (then Secretary-Treasurer of the UMW), Mr. Jim Hepe (then administrative assistant to Mr. Patrick), Mr. Ben Franklin (The New York Times), Mr. Peter Loewenberg (Department of Defense), and Miss Shelly Lieber (MIT) facilitated my interview research. I am deeply grateful to many officers and staff members of the UMW and the Department of Labor (who must remain anonymous), for taking the risk of providing delicate information.

Financial support came from the Ford Foundation, Japan Labor Institute, Scanllon Memorial Fellowship of Industrial Relations, and Kepner & Tregoe, Inc. I would like to express my gratitude to Vice President Marshall Robinson of the Ford Foundation, Professor Michael Y. Yoshino of Harvard Business School, Dr. Benjamin Tregoe of Kepner & Tregoe, Mr. Iikubo of the Kepner & Tregoe Tokyo office, and Professor Takeo Kurai, for their thoughtful arrangements. Mr. Tregoe also listened to the problems of my research and provided me with useful guidance.

Finally, I would like to express my sincere thanks to my friends in Cambridge and my family in Tokyo, who continuously encouraged me throughout these two years.

TABLE OF CONTENTS

List of Figures

List of Tables

CHAPTER I
INTRODUCTION

The history of collective bargaining goes back to the beginning of the 19th century.[1] Since then the characteristics of bargaining have changed, and a variety of social processes have been introduced to improve its effectiveness and efficiency. Section 7A of the Wagner Act of the NLRB election procedures, for example, has greatly reduced the violence and costly strikes which used to take place as a result of the union's struggles for recognition.[2] Professionalization of collective bargaining and the establishment of the Federal Mediation and Conciliation Service are other examples of improved effectiveness in labor negotiations. Despite these achievements, collective bargaining remains a complex phenomenon with many uncontrolled forces and much room for further improvement.

One inherent cause of the complexity is the "collective" character of bargaining. The behavior of negotiators is inevitably affected by the internal affairs of their organizations. In his highly regarded book, William E. Simkin, a former director of the Federal Mediation and Conciliation Service, emphasized that "internal stresses" within the union and management is the most important reason for impasses and one of the most difficult problems to handle in his mediation experiences.[3]

The academic literature shows a frustrating dearth of systematic studies concerning the impact of intra-organizational factors on the parties' bargaining behavior. Although there is a large number of studies on union organization (i.e. issues of union democracy), the major concern of these studies is to identify the causes of a particular organizational structure rather than to analyze its effects. On the other hand, numerous empirical studies of unions' strike activities have investigated intra-organizational factors only briefly.

With this gap in mind, we will attempt to investigate the influence of a union's intra-organizational factors on its policy, particularly on its militancy. "Militancy" in this study is a characteristic of the union's authorized policy in collective bargaining, and does not include the so-called "rank-and-file militancy" revealed in unauthorized wildcat strikes.

1. Literature on Strike Activities: A Critical Survey

Many social scientists have studied strike activities and their determinants, thereby yielding a great deal of information. Unfortunately, most of these use "work stoppage" data to measure their dependent variable, which includes both authorized and unauthorized strikes. Since very few works directly study the determinants of authorized strikes, we have no option in this survey but to use this "work stoppage" literature.

The factors identified as responsible for union strike activities in the existing literature can be classified into five categories: economic factors, community characteristics, institutional factors, plant characteristics, and organizational factors.

a. Economic Factors

Studies using external economic conditions as the major explanatory variable dominate the literature because of their long history, relatively rigorous methodology, and fairly consistent results.

The first study goes back to 1921, when Hansen found that strike data from 1881 to 1919 showed a clear pattern, in which the frequency of strikes inversely correlated with the business cycle in periods of long-run falling prices and positively correlated in periods of long-run rising prices.(4) Griffin and Yoder later analyzed the entire series of pre-World War II U.S. strike data in conjunction with other economic variables such as real and money wages, prices and unemployment. Although they failed to observe strong relationships with these variables, they found that strike activity generally varies directly with economic prosperity.(5,6) Jurhat and Jurhat also reported high positive correlation between strikes and the business cycle.(7)

Post World War II strike data were first analyzed by Rees. Using seasonally adjusted monthly data, he reported that the poor correlation during and after the war was caused only by the unusual disturbances of the war and the Taft-Hartley Act, and that had it not been for these disturbances, strike activities would have been determined basically by economic prosperity.(8) His argument was supported by Weibtraub, who found very close conformity between the business and strike cycles in the U.S. for 1949-1961.(9) Further support came from O'Brien, who extended Rees' analysis and found that the "cycle in strike series still exists and coincides fairly well with the cycle in general business activity."(10)

Ashenfelter and Johnson's work broke new ground in the area with sophisticated methods, broader consideration and strong results.(11) Their regression equations, derived from their theoretical bargaining model, included as explanatory variables the civilian unemployment rate, the difference between the annual percentage rates of change of money wages and consumer prices, the ratio of corporate profit after taxes to total compensation, and seasonal dummy variables. The results are most impressive: all the regression coefficients are highly significant with the correct signs;[(12)] the parameters are stable over the entire 1952-1967 period; and further, the equations "explain" more than 90% of the variance around the grand mean.

Ashenfelter and Johnson's work stimulated a number of studies, all of which confirmed their results. Pencavel proved the validity of their model using British data;[(13)] Skeels, using many measures of strike activity, found fairly consistent results in all his regression equations;[(14)] Hibbs compared the adequacy of various alternative models and concluded that the Ashenfelter-Johnson model was superior to the others.[(15)]

The high explanatory power and consistency of the results reported in these studies lends strong support to the economic explanation of strike activity. There are, however, important works which argue otherwise.

b. Community Characteristics

Harbison and Coleman (1951) based on their observation of a number of labor-management relations situations, concluded that small and medium-sized communities, characterized by greater mutual dependency and deeper personal relations, are more likely to have industrial harmony than are large urban centers.[(16)] Knowles, using British data, showed a clear regional difference in strike activities.[(17)]

The most persuasive finding in this area was reported by Kerr and Siegel. They observed that the strike data of four developed countries showed the same industry-wide pattern with coal mining and longshoring being the most strike-prone industries; textile, chemical, printing, manufacturing and construction coming in the middle; and railroad, agriculture and trade being the least strike-prone. They explained this pattern in terms of the degree to which the community is integrated with the larger society.[(18)]

c. Characteristics of the Plants

The large number of psychological studies relating characteristics of plants to worker's dissastisfaction have inspired several hypotheses relating the former to strike activities. Revans found a very strong positive correlation between the size of British coal pits and the production lost due to work stoppages. He speculated that the reasons were "social" but admitted the vagueness of his explanation.[19] Although Horvath's statistical analysis of 3332 work stoppages in 1960 showed no relation between plant size and the duration of strikes,[20] more recent works show the relevance of plant characteristics. For example, Ingham reported that the plant size was positively related to workers' pro-left, pro-union and pro-strike attitudes, and that this "size effect" was strong enough to override the conventional Conservative-Labor party attitude.[21] Eisele's analysis of a large number of U.S. manufacturers gave more explicit and complex results. The relation between plant size and strike frequency was found to be curvilinear with a positive correlation among the plants with less than 700-800 employees and a negative correlation among the bigger plants.[22] In his more recent study, he further discovered a complex interaction of size and technology of a plant on strike frequency, technology being categorized according to Woodward's typology. The curvilinear relation was observed only among plants with small batch and process technology, while strike frequency in those with large batch technology increased monotonically with size and was consistently higher than in those with other technologies.[23]

d. Institutional Factors

Coleman and Harbison, Sayles and Strauss, and Lester suggested that new unions which have not yet established their status against management tend to be "vehemently anti-management",[24] and that as they grow "mature",[25] they are likely to be more eager not to "upset the body of institutionalized common law which has been hammered out in years of grievance handling."[26]

On the basis of their observations and analysis of strike activities in a number of countries, Ross and Harmann proposed that multi-employer bargaining is conducive to industrial peace because of the availability of professional negotiators, reduction of emotional discussions, costliness of the strike, and reduced competition among employers as well as within a union.[27] Their argument, plausible as it sounds, is impressionistic and insufficiently validated. Snyder removed this drawback by applying a regression model to periods before and after the collective bargaining had been institutionalized in three industrialized countries. He found that strikes showed a very different pattern before collective bargaining became fully institutionalized, and that economic factors are important only after institutionalization.[28]

e. Union Organization

As Tannenbaum pointed out, this area is probably the least explored of all.[29] Ross and Hartman proposed that unions in the period of growth or decline tend to be more strike-prone than those in a stabilized period, and that high factional conflict inside the union may lead to strikes.[30] Their speculation was partially tested by Britt and Galle,[31] who analyzed strike activity according to volume, proneness, extent, and intensity.[32] By building causal diagrams tested by path analysis, they showed that a larger union has greater internal conflict, resulting in high proneness to strike, but that it also has a greater strike cost and a greater central control over locals which results in a lower extent of conflict.

Another organizational dimension proposed as a determinant of strike activity is the national leaders' control over rank and file. Tannenbaum and Kahn suggested that militant union action is associated with a relatively high level of "total control",[33] "control" being measured by the instrument developed by Tannenbaum. The recent work of Roomkin developed measures of union organization structure from content-analysis of 57 national union constitutions, and showed that "centralization at the level of the national union" reduces the strike proneness of the union.[34]

2. Critical Evaluation of the Field

The analysis of strikes has attracted a large number of leading social scientists over a long period of time. The field, however, still presents a ready target for criticism. Deficiencies of the area relevant to this study may be summarized as follows:

a. Overstress of External Economic Factors and Neglect of Intra-organizational Factors

Most of the works cited above have investigated the effects of external economic factors. Tannenbaum pointed out:

> Most of these (studies) concern what K.G.J.C. Knowles (1954) has defined as "conditioning" rather than "immediate" or underlying causes, as a large majority refer to social or economic determinants external to the union itself . . . while most students of the labor union acknowledge the basic importance of psychological determinants as "underlying causes" of the strike, little systematic research has been done with these factors.(35)

One reason lies in the characteristics of the available data. The most easily acccessible and widely used data, the annual work stoppage data published by the Bureau of Labor Statistics, are aggregate figures of annual strike activities (total number of work stoppages or total man-days lost in work stoppages, etc.), which do not reflect any within-year variation of strike activities stemming from the variation in characteristics of unions or industries.

This over-emphasis on external economic variables constitues a deficiency of the literature in two senses. First, it probably does not reflect the reality of each individual industrial dispute.[36] As every practitioner engaged in actual disputes knows, the internal politics of a union and of management are important variables in collective bargaining situations.[37] Bok and Dunlop emphasize:

> It was widely known that rivalries and tensions within the Machinists and among the six shop craft unions were major contributing factors to the national railroad crisis in 1967. Internecine warfare between pilots and light engineers gave rise to strikes and government intervention in the early sixties. New York newspaper strikes have been aggravated by internal pulling and hauling over which craft union would set the pattern for wage increases. When managements bargain together, conflicting interests among companies with different competitive markets and different spokesmen are quite often a significant deterrent to settlements. The 1959 basic steel shutdown, for instance, was complicated and prolonged by the different problems which the twelve individual companies confronted on local working conditions.(38)

Second, knowledge of economic determinants, which explain the across-year variations in overall strike activities, is of almost no use in solving industrial disputes. What can an arbitrator do when he knows that the state of the economy is healthy, and that unions thus tend to be strike prone? The variation caused by economic factors is an uncontrollable rule of the game within which negotiations are conducted.

b. Lack of Relational Investigation

Another weakness of the literature is that every study thus far has been

little is known about the interaction effect of the independent variables when they vary simultaneously. The only exception to this is Snyder's work, which showed that economic impact on militancy can be observed only when collective bargaining is well institutionalized. Since an actual bargaining process may be faced with any combination of the five variables, clarification of interaction effects is necessary in order for the field to be practically useful.

c. Lack of Sufficient Theory

The third weak point is the lack of sufficient explanation of statistical findings. Most of the studies do not go much beyond the simple reporting of statistically significant correlations, which does not establish the existence of socially meaningful causal relationships. Even the link between strike activities and economic prosperity, the most heavily studied phenomenon, for example, does not have a satisfactory explanation. Rees' well-accepted explanation was that high strike propensity during economic booms could be attributed to the union's bargaining advantage due to the "employer's reluctance to lose his share of the expanding market; his observation of rising wages elsewhere; his inability to replace strikers with non-strikers and the greater chance of the strikers to obtain employment elsewhere".[39] The problem with this explanation is that the same argument can lead to the opposite prediction: management, being aware of its disadvantageous bargaining position in a prosperous period, will concede to union demands before the strike takes place, and so strikes will be low in an economically prosperous period.

The reason for the lack of a satisfactory theory probably can be ascribed to the methodology chosen by the researchers. Most of the works attempt to discover a consistent pattern in aggregate statistical data, which prevents them from investigating in detail the process by which these diverse variables influence a union's strike decision.

The next chapter proposes a research design aimed toward elimination of these deficiencies of the field.

CHAPTER II
RESEARCH DESIGN

1. Hypothesis-Generation Approach vs. Hypothesis-Verification Approach

Any empirical research can be classified as belonging either to the theory-generation type or to the theory-verification type[1] Although the latter approach is more fashionable and has the advantage of being rigorous, it can produce meaningful results only when the hypotheses to be tested have a sound theoretical base. Since this theoretical base is exactly what the field lacks and what this study hopes to attain, the verification approach will not be appropriate for our purpose.

a. Detailed Study of a Few Cases vs. Large-Sample Quantitative Study

A large amount of very detailed information about the internal mechanisms of a union is needed in order to generate a well-grounded theory and to clarify the process by which diverse variables affect union militancy. A large-sample approach, while useful for obtaining general and clear results, does not easily allow this possibility. Because of this consideration, the detailed case study approach is chosen for this study.

b. Choice of a Case

The choice of a case is obviously the most important determinant in the success of the case-study approach. The following four methods of case sampling were carefully compared.

The first method is to choose a theoretically exceptional case. Lipset, Trow and Coleman's study of ITU, which is a clear exception to Michel's Iron Law of Oligarchy, is one of the most successful examples of this approach. Through a detailed search for the reason for the "exception", they successfully contributed an innovative insight to the theory of democracy.[2] The strength of this approach is that it allows the researcher to concentrate his effort on the weakest part of the theory and to produce the most relevant information in improving the theory. The disadvantage of this approach for our purpose is that it assumes the existence of a well-accepted and fully-developed theory from which an exception may be posited.

The second possible approach is to choose and compare a few theoretically relevant cases. This has the advantage of the first approach, but does not demand the existence of a developed theory so much as the first one. For example, the first approach requires a specific proposition, such as "a centralized union tends to be less militant", while the second approach postulates only the relevance of the centralized-decentralized dimension to union militancy, but not necessarily the direction of its influence. If the researcher knows that centralization is relevant to militancy but does not know how it affects the latter, he can choose four case-types: high-centralization-high-militancy; high-centralization-low-militancy; low-centralization-high-militancy; low centralization-low militancy. The disadvantage of this approach is that it will require much more work than the first one.

The third approach is the one proposed by Glazer and Strauss.(3) It does not make any a priori sampling plan, but flexibly adds a new case that is relevant to the theory developed in the process of the research. Unlike other approaches, the researcher will not be limited by an a priori choice of a case. It also does not require the existence of any theory with which to start the study.

The fourth approach is the selection of a particular union which has experienced organizational changes, for a historical comparison of the effects of these changes on union militancy. This approach combines the advantage of a one-case study, which allows the researcher to become very familiar with the case, and the advantage of a few-case comparison, which provides a better ground for theory-generation. In addition, since an organization changes inter-temporally only in a few dimensions, a relatively well-controlled comparison can be made. The existence of a theory is not required either. On the other hand, inter-temporal organizational differences may not provide enough variance of independent variables, which is crucial for theory-generation. In addition, there is no guarantee that the few organizational variables which have changed historically are relevant to union militancy.

The strengths and weaknesses of each approach can be summarized as in Table 2-1.

The above reasoning shows that there is no single perfect method of case sampling for our purpose. Without making a final decision about the appropriate approach, the author started a thorough exploration of national unions.(4) His encounter with the United Mine Workers of America presented the perfect case for the fourth approach and led to the author's choice of this approach. This union experienced several organizational transitions which seemed extensive enough to

Table 2 - 1

Strengths and Weaknesses of Four Case-Sampling Methods

	Possibility of obtaining the Relevant Results	Comparison	Existence of Theory	Variance of Independent Variables	Amount of Work
Theoretically exceptional case	** Very high	X None	X Fully developed	X	*
A few theoretically relevant cases	* High	*	* Partially developed theory required	*	X
No a priori plan, flexible addition of cases	* High	*	** No theory required	*	X
Historical comparison of effects of organizational changes	X Not so high	** Well-controlled	** No theory required	X	*

**: Very desirable for our research; *: Desirable; X: Not desirable

have made an important impact on various facets of union policy. Its militancy also showed a large fluctuation across time. In addition, due to its importance in American labor history, it is one of the best documented unions - a very helpful factor in a historical study. Lastly, the history of such a huge, complex organization is a rich sampling of human society, which provides an excellent learning opportunity for the social scientist.

2. Four Periods for Historical Comparison: a Brief Description of the UMW Case

An exploratory survey of the history of the UMWA indicates that the optimum study would cover the years 1940 to 1974, dividing these 35 years into four periods: 1940-1950, 1951-1959, 1960-1972, and 1972-1974. The organizational characteristics of each period can be summarized as follows:

From 1940 to 1950, John L. Lewis headed the union with extremely centralized strong-arm methods and charismatic legitimacy. The major decisions were made exclusively at the international level, but the international leaders were very sensitive to members' needs, and successfully brought great improvements into the miners' lives. The morale of the membership was very high and its loyalty was solid.

From 1951 to 1959, John L. Lewis continued to lead the union. Due to the remarkable achievements of the previous decade, Lewis' power in the union rose further, and his charistmatic legitimacy was firmly established. However, competition with oil forced the coal industry to cut back production substantially. The resulting severe unemployment spread across the coal fields, and in turn eroded members' morale.

Between 1960-1972, Thomas Kennedy and W. A. Boyle succeeded John L. Lewis.(5) The union was as centralized as in the earlier period, but ceased to be responsive to the members' needs. The union treasury and the Welfare Fund were mismanaged and embezzled; nepotism on the union pay-roll became common; corruption spread to every corner of the union. The voice of the membership was thoroughly suppressed; apathy and alienation dominated the members' attitudes.

The rank-and-file's rebellion, which had first failed with the tragic death of Yablonski in 1969, finally succeeded in 1972, when Arnold Miller won the presidential election against W. A. Boyle. Large-scale organizational changes were effected: the presidential power was reduced, and various democratic decision-making procedures were introduced. Several factional fights emerged inside the union, which the Miller administration was powerless to control.

Table 2 - 2

Number of Days Made Idle by Nation-Wide Strikes Called by the International Union

Year	Days	Year	Days	Year	Days	Year	Days
*1941	41	1951	0	1961	0	*1971	44
1942	0	*1952	8	1962	0	1972	0
*1943	16(26)	1953	0	1963	0	1973	0
1944	0	1954	0	*1964	0	*1974	24(5)
*1945	26	*1955	0	1965	0	1975	0
*1946	61	*1956	0	*1966	0	1976	0
*1947	17(9)	1957	0	1967	0		
*1948	28	*1958	0	*1968	6		
*1949	29	1959	0	1969	0		
*1950	7(42)	1960	0	1970	0		

a. Memorial stoppages assured in the contracts are not included.

b. The figures in the parentheses show the number of days made idle by "unauthorized" national stoppages which can be interpreted as being urged secretly by the International.

c. The years marked with the symbol * are those in which contract negotiations were conducted.

Source: The New York Times, 1941 - 1976.

Table 2 - 3

Militancy of the International's Policy in Each Period

Period	Total Number of Days	Number of Days per Year	Number of Contract Renewals	Number of Days Per Contract Renewal
1941 1950	225	22.5	8	28.1
1951 1960	8	0.8	4	2
1961 1972	44	3.7	4	11
1973 1974	24	12	1	24

Source: Constructed from The New York Times, 1941-1976

The militancy of union policy as measured by its strike activities also shows some periodic changes. Since the work stoppage data published by BLS contain unauthorized strikes, the number of days made idle by nationwide unauthorized strikes (a direct measure of official militancy) was calculated from reports in the New York Times. Tables 2-2 and 2-3 show that official militancy of the international union was very high in the 1940's, very low in the 1950's and very high in the 1970's. The characteristics of the four periods are summarized in Table 2-4.

3. Organization of the Study

The UMW will be analyzed according to each period. The next chapter will first provide background information about the characteristics of the three major actors in the drama: the coal industry, the union, and the miners. Knowledge of the peculiarities of the case is absolutely necessary in order to evaluate the actual analysis as well as to assess the generality of the conclusions.

Chapter IV surveys the first period in detail. Organizational characteristics and the militancy of the UMW in that period will be carefully examined in order to analyse the effect of the former on the latter. In this process, an effort will be made to take into account all the possible factors responsible for the particular behavior of the union, and then to assess how much and in what way organizational factors functioned in relation to other important variables.

Chapters V, VI and VII deal with the subsequent three periods in the same manner as in Chapter IV. The last chapter summarizes the findings and attempts to draw general conclusions.

Table 2 - 4

Comparison of the Four Historical Periods of the UMWA

	Organizational Structure	Leadership Power	Leadership Style	Membership Attachment	Intra-Organizational Conflict	Militancy
1940 1950	Centralized	Legitimate Very high	Charismatic	Strong, loyal attachment	Low	Extremely high
1951 1960	Extremely Centralized	Legitimate very high	Charismatic (stabilized)	Loyal calculative	Very low	Extremely low
1961 1972	Extremely centralized	Not legitimate, high	Dictatorial corrupt	Loyal calculative alienative	High	Extremely low, gradually higher
1972 1975	Decentralized democratic	Not legitimate very low	Bureaucratic democratic	(Loyal) calculative, alienative	Very high	High

CHAPTER III

BACKGROUND: THE INDUSTRY, THE UNION AND THE MINER

1. Characteristics of the Bituminous Coal Industry

In the 1930's and 1940's the coal industry was known as one of the nation's most problematic industries.[1] Its problems were chronic excess capacity, instability of market demand and price, and heavy labor costs.

a. Quick Entry into the Industry, Slow Withdrawal and Excess Supply

The market structure of the bituminous coal industry in this period was characterized by the existence of a large number of small firms.[2] The major reason was the relative ease of entry into and less facile withdrawal from the industry. The principal problem of going into the coal business, the initial capital outlay, varied according to which of three types of mining operation one intended to set up: deep or underground mining, surface or strip mining, or punch mining.[3] Although capital requirements for deep mines ran between $1 million and $2.5 million, a punch mine could be started with as little as $1,000, and a strip mine with $10,000.[4] With such a low initial investment, entry to the industry was virtually unrestricted.

Withdrawal from the industry, on the other hand, was not so quick. One reason may have been the stubborn self-confidence of the independent coal operators. Baratz described them:

> They maintain a perpetual air of confidence about the future. They can be likened to the motorist who insists that accidents always happen to the other fellow. (5)

A more fundamental reason for their reluctance to close down might have been solid economic calculations. An economically rational decision to leave the industry would have to take into account not only the current deficit, but also two other aspects of the industry. The first is the existence of fixed costs. If fixed costs exist, so far as variable costs are covered by production, operating under a deficit will be less costly than not operating at all.[6] Secondly, operation under deficit sacrifices future benefit by shortening the life of equipment, as compared with not operating and leaving that capacity for future use. Therefore, present value of future benefits should also be considered. Even if a coal operator stopped production, he still had to pay a large sum for precautions against deterioration of the mine: "Water seepage must be controlled; accumulations of marsh gas must be dispelled; roofs must be maintained."[8] In a large mine equipped with expensive modern equipment, the fixed cost was very high due to maintenance costs, property taxes and insurance charges, which made operation under deficit a necessity. The operator of an intermediate-sized mine had a very high discount rate because of his poor liquidity position.[9] He therefore preferred to pay less now than to gain more in the future, and therefore to operate under deficit.

The loss of the labor force and the revenues from the company store was another consideration:

> It can definitely be stated that an operator will not close a mine down as soon as he failed to cover his "out of pocket" expenses . . . The operator has 100 to 400 employees, who are dependent upon his mine for any kind of livelihood, and should the mine close up, the operator stands to lose a considerable amount in accounts receivable at the (company) store, and also stands to lose his entire working force who will have to depart for greener pastures. (10)

If prices continued to fall further, the marginal high-cost operators began dropping out. But even in such cases, the mine was often sold to a more optimistic operator who might then continue production:

> When things get so tough, the operator tries to find someone with greater optimism who will purchase the property. In this manner an operation drags along during a dull period until eventually the dividend for coal increases.(11)

The result was a large number of mining firms and a chronic excess capacity. Table 3-1 shows that in 1951 there were as many as 7004 underground bituminous mines, 72.6% of which employed less than 24 employees.

The chronic excess capacity and its trend toward increase is shown in Table 3-2.

b. Instability of Demand and Price

The second characteristic of the coal industry was instability of demand. The demand for coal was what economists termed a derived demand.[15] The "derived" character resulted in two peculiarities of the industry. First, the demand for coal showed cyclical fluctuations caused directly by the business cycle of the whole national economy; second, because of the principle of acceleration,[16] the cyclical fluctuations of demand for coal were much larger than those of the economy.

Table 3 - 1

Excess Capacity of the Bituminous Coal Industry
1810 - 1923

(13, 14)

Year	Production (Thousands of Tons)	Estimated Capacity (Thousands of tons)	Excess Capacity Thousands of Tons	Percent of Production
1890	111,302	153,030	41,728	37
1891	117,901	158,406	40,505	34
1892	126,857	174,477	47,620	38
1893	128,385	195,752	67,367	52
1894	118,820	216,695	97,875	82
1895	135,118	214,140	79,022	58
1896	137,640	220,246	82,606	60
1897	147,618	231,982	81,364	57
1898	166,594	242,725	76,131	46
1899	193,323	253,012	59,689	31
1900	212,316	279,317	67,001	32
1901	225,828	309,696	83,868	37
1902	260,217	347,341	87,124	33
1903	282,749	387,682	104,933	37
1904	278,660	426,478	147,818	53
1905	315,063	457,198	142,135	45
1906	342,875	493,671	250,796	44
1907	394,759	518,261	123,502	31
1908	332,574	533,723	201,149	60
1909	379,744	574,981	195,237	60
1910	417,111	590,965	173,854	43
1911	405,907	588,887	182,980	45
1912	450,105	604,774	154,669	34
1913	478,435	636,522	158,087	33
1914	422,704	672,083	249,379	59

This sensitive fluctuation of the coal demand, combined with the operators' reluctance to close down, produced still larger instability in coal prices. Even when demand and profits began falling, operators continued working as long as loss from operating was smaller than loss from not operating. As a result, operators responded to a drop in price by further price reductions in order to remain competitive and to keep production as high as possible.

c. Labor as the Major Cost Item

The third characteristic of the coal industry is the importance of labor costs. Table 3-3 shows that labor costs constituted more than 60% of the total operating costs, as compared with 40% in the steel industry during the same period.

2. A Brief History of the United Mine Workers of America Prior to 1940

The history of the miners' union is one of constant struggle against human misery, of passionate hopes alternating with defeat and despair. The initial drive for unionization was violent and militant, but at the same time local, spontaneous and sporadic due to the heterogenous ethnic background of the miners and the geographically dispersed nature of this work force. The first serious efforts for a nation-wide movement began in the middle of the nineteenth century, when a large number of predominantly Welsh and Scottish immigrant miners began moving into the American coal fields. They brought with them a strong tradition of national unionism and the necessary skills and motivation for the movement. After several failures and factional splits, two prominent national organizations, the National Progressive Union of Miners and Mine Laborers (of the AFL) and the Miners' Assembly of Knights of Labor, decided to merge in 1890. Thus the United Mine Workers of America was born.

As its first president, John B. Rae, soon discovered, the emergence of a national organization did not necessarily make the struggle easier. By 1896 the union had changed its president three times; its treasury had dropped to less than $600 and its membership to only about 10,000.[18] The youthful militant leaders Michael Ratchford and John Mitchell put a halt to the gradual decline of the union. Mitchell, who at the age of twenty-nine became the 5th president of the UMWA in 1899, successfully organized a few nation-wide strikes and by 1900 increased the membership to 232,289.[19] Although the union prospered on every front, dissent began to deveolop against Mitchell's increasing moderation and it finally drove him from office in 1908.

Table 3 - 2

Size Distribution of Underground Mines[12]

	Number of Workers in Underground Mines					
	1-24	25-99	100-299	30-499	500+	Total
Number of Mines Mines	5,085	989	616	181	134	7,004
% of Total	72.0	14.1	8.8	2.6	1.9	100

Table 3 - 3

Proportion of Labor Cost in Total Cost: Coal and Steel Industry

	1943	1944	1945
Coal	59.6%	60.8%	60.2%*
Steel	------	------	40.6**

Source *: U. S. Office of Price Administration, Economic Data Analysis Branch, Preliminary Survey of Operating for Commercial Bituminous Coal Mines for the Years 1943, 1944, 1945.

Source **: American Iron and Steel Institute, Annual Statistical Report, 1945, New York, 1946.

After Mitchell's departure, the union's growth was hardly less stormy. The economic depression of 1907 struck the union severely: contracts were violated, wages were cut, strikes were broken by force. Internal strife developed, and union presidents changed in quick succession. The rank-and-file, "out of their dark despair, struck down their own leaders again and again with the blind fury of their own bitterness."[20] Although economic recovery during World War I and a liberal government under Woodrow Wilson somewhat improved its gloomy situation, the union continued to be plagued by poor leadership and intense internal struggles. Hayes, who became president in 1917, was perpetually drunk and had no heart for the routine office work. His vice-president took over most of the union business and seized actual control of the headquarters. In 1920 he became president. This was the man named John Llewellyn Lewis, who was to rule the union and determine the course of its history for the next forty years.

Lewis' first decade was an exceptionally turbulent one. In 1920 he ordered that southern West Virginia be organized. As the operators were determined to crush the union, the battle ended in an open gunfight between a "citizens' army" of 6,000 armed and disciplined miners and 2,000 well-armed strike-breakers and imported thugs.[21] When the U.S. Army moved in three days later, the miners promptly gave up their guns, which also meant surrender of their hopes. In 1922, when operators rebuffed the union's wage demand, Lewis ordered a nation-wide strike. Violence broke out in Herrin County, Illinois, when the operators imported thugs from Chicago to forcibly break the strike. When one miner was shot to death, armed miners, farmers, shopkeepers and legionnaires came from all over southern Illinois, armed for retaliation. After a day of intense gunfire, the besieged strike-breakers finally surrendered. The furious miners, not satisfied with their victory, lynched the defeated strike-breakers, beating, stabbing, stoning, hanging or shooting them.

Lewis' bloody battle was not confined to warfare against the operators. He began engaging in vehement disputes with opposing leaders inside the union. In Nova Scotia district leaders were termed "Communists" and replaced with Lewis' lieutenants. In West Virginia, where the recent warfare had weakened the district, autonomy was suspended, and a ruthless purge was conducted. In Illinois, where District President Frank Farrington had his own machine, things did not go so smoothly: after being purged, Farrington allied himself with other disenchanted leaders such as John Brophy, Power Hapgood and Alex Howard, and rebelled against Lewis. The bitter infighting lasted until 1932, when Lewis finally defeated them.

The industry in the 1920's was in miserable shape, plagued by chronic excess production and cut-throat competition. UMWA contracts were breached over and over again and illegal wage cuts, blacklisting and strikebreaking were the rule. Union members were evicted from company houses and rendered homeless. In 1925, when Consolidation openly repudiated the Jacksonville Agreement (which had been reached only one year earlier), almost all the major companies followed suit. In 1926 and 1927, unemployed miners starved and begged for handouts. Union officers, on the other hand, pleaded with the government to force the operators to honor the contract. Lewis' anger and combativeness had no effect in the face of cold economic reality. In this decade he lost two thirds of his members.

The 1930's began with a crisis for American labor. The depression which struck the nation in 1929 now had its full impact. The AFL was losing more than 7,000 members each week. But while other labor leaders were contemplating further retreat, the UMWA was preparing a counterattack. As Roosevelt's new administration moved into Washington with the pledge of a "New Deal", Lewis began an intensive campaign for the inclusion of Section 7A ("Right of Labor to Organize") in the NRA. When Congress passed the NRA with this section on June 16, 1933, Lewis embarked on a full-scale organizing campaign, throwing virtually the entire treasury of the UMW into the battle. "The President wants you to join the union," shouted organizers in every coal field. Miners responded enthusiastically, jamming the union halls and deluging organizers with applications for membership. In one year, membership jumped to 400,000. Lewis also scored a major triumph when he successfully obtained the Joint Appalachia Wage Agreement which for the first time covered both northern and southern coal mines.

With the abatement of internal feuding and with his impressive success in organizing and signing the North-South pact, Lewis was rapidly becoming numbers of unskilled workers should be organized, and was fully prepared to fight for it. Leaders of the American Federation of Labor, however, were indecisive in adopting the new principle of industrial unionism. The issue came to a head at the 1935 convention of the AFL, when John L. Lewis, now vice-president of the Federation, led the minority group consisting of Sidney Hillman of the Amalgamated Clothing Workers of America, David Dubinsky of the International Ladies' Garment Workers, Charles P. Howard of the Typographical Union, Thomas F. McMahon of the United Textile Workers of America, Max Zaritsky of the Cloth, Hat, Cap and Millinery

Workers' International Union, Thomas H. Brown of the Mine, Mill and Smelter Workers' Union, and Harvey C. Fremming of the Oil Field, Gas Well and Refinery Workers of America.[22] When their minority report on industrial unionism was rejected by the convention, Lewis resigned from the executive council of the AFL, ignored the resolution of the convention and resumed his massive organizing campaign.

In 1936 the CIO won the recognition of the United Rubber Workers as the bargaining agency for the Goodyear Rubber Company. In 1937, waves of sit-down strikes began to spread in the auto industry. When General Motors refused to negotiate, 35,000 militant UAW workers staged a sitdown strike at seven GM plants. Lewis provided them with his constant support and advice. They fought an extremely tense forty-day battle and won a historic victory. Steelworkers were organized by the UMW's Vice President Phillip Murray, and obtained a contract from U.S. Steel. In a landslide of successes the CIO conquered Armstrong Cork Company, Caterpillar Tractor, Chrysler Corporation, Firestone Tire and Rubber, General Electric, B.F. Goodrich Rubber Company, Hudson Motors, Jones and Laughlin Steel, Libby-Owens Fork Glass, Pittsburgh Plate Glass, Studebaker Motors, Timken Roller Bearing, and a host of others.[23]

Lewis was now the unbeatable champion for the nation's millions of workers. No other labor leaders could match his national influence and prominence. The UMW ended a triumphal decade with Lewis at the peak of his power and prestige.

3. The Miners

a. Environment and Living Conditions

The milieu in which the miners lived was harsh by any human standard, and its peculiar roughness created some distinct characteristics in the men. In order to understand the miners, it is useful to analyze this environment and the life they led in it.

(i) Economic Instability

As we have seen, the demand and the price for coal fluctuated greatly and unexpectedly. Coal operators tended to adjust themselves to price drops by cutting labor costs. Although the miners' nominal daily wage was already among the highest paid for manual labor, they could work only seven to nine months in a normal year and as little as three to five months in a bad year, which curtailed

Table 3 - 4:

Employment History of a Coal Town, 1904-1951[24]

						Total
Average Number of Days Worked	0-129	130-169	170-209	210-249	250-289	
Number of Years in each Category	6	12	14	8	8	48

their average annual earnings drastically. Table 3-4 shows that in 18 out of the 48 years between 1904 and 1951 (38%), the average number of days worked in one coal town was below 170, and that in 32 of these years (67%) it was below 210 days.

Miners felt this economic instability to be one of the most distressing aspects of their life:

> You take the cycle of the way these mines work. It is either feast or famine. It is a period of good work and then it slacks off. It runs in cycles and your children are better off in a steady industry. (25)

In a region where the union was not strong enough, illegal wage cuts were commonly observed in times of recession. A miner described this practice and his resentment against it:

> You would come to work in the morning and the plant manager told you your wage was cut to 25 cents an hour. This stuff sticks in your craw. You don't forget that easily. The men were working then (1930's) at 30 to 45 cents an hour for a 33 hour week. The plant manager put it down and said, "If you want to work you can; if you don't, I can get plenty of men at that price." (26)

Being in debt was an ever-present problem:

> Hell, I would not be a coal miner again if I had it to do all over again. It's a hard life. It's heavy work and you lose from three to six months of the year. In addition to that you are always in debt. All they used to do was draw their little coupon books and take it to the store and they never did see any money for a long time. If I had my life to live all over again, I would be a carpenter . . . (27)

(ii) Mining

At 5:30 A.M., when many other Americans were still asleep, coal miners were busily preparing for the morning shift.[28] Their wives had been up before them, preparing a massive miner's breakfast. This might be a fried chicken or ham with potatoes, hot cakes, biscuits, and endless cups of coffee. A heavy meal was needed to fortify them against the backbreaking physical work and the threat of death which waited for them in the pit. Equipped with electric caps, they went down into the earth. In a large mine they might ride a coal train as far as six miles before they reached their work area. In complete darkness they got off the train and sloshed to their individual workrooms in ankle-deep water. The workroom might be three feet high, or five feet if they were lucky. Directly ahead was the end wall of coal known as the "face". Before they approached it, they would carefully check the timber and the roof. They knew that roof fall was the commonest cause of mining disasters.

Satisfied with the timber, they sliced a deep groove along the bottom of the face with an undercutting machine. After the undercut they drilled a small hole, choosing the depth and location on the basis of long experience. Into this hole they inserted sticks of dynamite, retreated outside the room, and touched off the explosives. This was one of the most dangerous moments.

The large chunks of coal freed by the explosion were now ready for loading. If the loading machine were available, it could load as much as a few tons of coal in a matter of minutes. If no such machine were available, miners had to hand-load. Once the coal was loaded into the railroad cars, the same cycle would be repeated until three o'clock. There was one 30-minute break for lunch in the mine, but no coffee breaks.

Mining was one of society's most dangerous jobs. Figure 3-2 shows that the fatality rate in the coal mining industry was far higher than in other industries. Yet even this formidable death rate does not fully reveal the hazards of mining. A still larger number of miners was disabled, a larger number yet again suffered light accidents which were not reported, and even the exceptionally lucky few who escaped these troubles suffered from back trouble, black lung or ulcers.

> I started out in 1956 and moved over to Big Ridge when we opened in 1958 ... First time I got hurt was 1959. I got covered by a rib roll (a collapsing wall) and got three vertebrae busted and a busted pelvis. I got a 25% disability for that, but I came back to work anyway. In 1965 or 1966, I forget which, I slipped in some grease and broke my neck and got my but I came back and worked four more years. In 1971, I hurt my right leg and right arm and was paralyzed. Oh yeah, I've also got first-stage rock-dust silicosis. I got paid a flat $3,100 but my lungs are so bad I can't hardly get around. (30)

Vecsey continues that this story was nothing exceptional in mining towns:

> His buddies half-listen to Raymond's story. Most of them can match it, fracture by fracture, wheeze by wheeze. Although it is not apparent from the way they move in their mining wear, which makes everybody seem slow, many of them have some physical disability. Seen in street clothes, a lot of them walk in the slightly disjointed fashion of something that has been broken and put back together again, like marionettes. Particularly the hands.

> Shaking hands with a coal miner is always an adventure. He slips you his hand and you sort out the damage without showing any expression. Hmm. Top joint missing on index finger. Hmm, No thumb. Hmm. Two smallest fingers gone. (31)

Miners, in spite of their awareness of these grim problems, seem to be casual about the ever-present perils of their underground work.

> A man with plenty of experience down in the coal mine, he doesn't worry about getting hurt. At least, it seems to me that he doesn't worry. I knew I never did. You see, when you're a coal miner you have to take lots of chances, and you just don't think about getting hurt... (32)

> You know, I don't think a coal miner worries. I think that it is the farthest thing from a coal miner's thoughts. If you worried about it, you couldn't go. I think he just goes to the mine as a matter of course. (33)

Some of the miners were reckless enough to go into a gassy mine or even smoke there:

> I would tell lots of men what to do. The trouble is that most of them wouldn't listen. Some of the miners didn't care. When you got marked there, "Stay out, Gas," you have to wait until the gas man comes and checks. (34)

Despite this superficial casualness, careful analysis of further data suggests that fear had penetrated deeply into the miners' minds. They knew that they had to go into the pits regardless of fear or indisposition. This necessity forced them to drive their fear into their subconscious.

> You see, these mines were filled with gas and it was really scary down there when you would see that gas around, and you would want to get out of there as fast as possible. Now, you were not supposed to smoke in the mines but I did. I just didn't give a damn about anything and many times I broke black powder with a pick and I had on an oil lamp too, and I don't know why I never did get killed or blown up. (35)

Apparently it was not fearlessness or confidence in his safety that made him behave so recklessly: he was indeed frightened. Nevertheless he had to stay and work with the constant threat of explosion from the gas. He countered his anxiety with reckless behavior, creating artificial certainty in his mind and relieving himself of fear.

> I think a miner worries a great deal about getting hurt ... The family worries too. You see, if I let myself think about it, I guess I would go crazy, but you can't do that. You can't let yourself think about what might happen to you down there because if you did you never would get anything done. I've been injured three times in the mine myself. (36)

In some cases, this fear in the subconscious self took over the conscious field and made miners totally impotent.

> I can remember some of these miners who would get scared and then they would come back and they wouldn't even go to work, and the family members did not know if the man was coming home from work after his shift or not. (37)

Thus, despite their apparent fearlessness, miners regarded their occupation as extremely hazardous and frightening. Fear tended to be suppressed into the subconscious and played a complex role in determining behavior.

(iii) Isolation: Physical, Social and Psychological

The nature of the mining industry necessitated the location of plants and associated settlements at the point of extraction in the mineral fields, were virtually no other industries existed. As a result, miners lived exclusively with themselves in small dispersed settlements, totally isolated from the rest of society.

This physical isolation was not only geographical, but also historical. Most of the initial settlers of the coal camps in the 19th century were immigrants from European coal fields, where the same isolation prevailed.[38] As in the European mine communities, the miner's son had no other thought than to work in the mine where his father worked. The miner's daughter typically married a miner in the same or a nearby settlement. Therefore very few outside elements entered the mining camps and very few inside elements went out. Due to this historical process, the geographical isolation became perpetual and developed into social as well as psychological isolation. For the people outside, the miners spoke a mysterious jargon, behaved incomprehensibly, and were like people from another world.[39] From the miners' point of view, outsiders were prejudiced and discriminatory, totally lacking understanding or sympathy toward them. The following personal testimony illustrates the psychological and social barriers between miners and the "outside world".

> They don't know if a coal miner is an elephant or monkey. One fellow tells a story that is supposed to be true about a fellow who tells his wife that he is bringing home a coal miner for dinner. She says that it's O.K., but to be sure to tie him on a leash in the yard. I'm not kidding, that's a true story. Some people don't even know if a coal miner is a human being. In the mine we say to each other, "Get out of here, you underground savage!" (40)

The psychological isolation of the miners manifested itself when they tried to live in a city. Their adjustment to urban communities was difficult and at best marginal. A miner talked about his son working in a city:

> He would like to come back. He was raised here. It is home to him. They don't any of them like to leave here. They have spent a lot of money coming back here on weekends. My boy comes home every weekend. (41)

Many miners could not adjust to urban life and returned to the mines. One recent miner reflected upon his decision:

> I always said that I would never go in the coal mines. I said that until I got 30 years old. And then all of a sudden something struck me, and I changed my mind like that. I was in Columbus, Ohio, working in an auto-parts plant, and I wanted to go back home. Go back to West Virginia. The first three hours in the mine, I was scared to death. I thought a thousand times even the first two, three shifts - the first two, three weeks - of quitting and saying the heck with it. I had heard my dad and granddad and so many other coal miners talk of how dangerous it was ... But I wouldn't go back to the city again for nothing in the world, unless it was just a have-to case. People in the city are not as nice and congenial as here. You can live in the city until you're old, and you may not even know your next-door neighbor. (42)

(iv) Dominance of Mining in Community Life

In these isolated, monolithic communities, the miner's life was totally dominated by mining. Their relatives were likely to be miners; their houses as well as the town's grocery stores were owned by the company; the sheriff and the clergymen might well be ex-miners. Even in leisure time, there was very little "nonmining" element. When the miner came home from the day's shift, he was so thoroughly exhausted that further physical exertion was out of the question.(43) In the slack season he might have an abundance of leisure, but this was so irregular and uncertain that any constructive use of the free time was difficult. In addition, his community typically offered very few opportunities for non-occupational activities. Most communities had no evening schools, libraries, or reading rooms.[44] There were movie theaters in relatively large towns, but a baseball diamond, a pool room, or in some cases ramshackle brothels summed up the resources that most mining towns could offer.[45] The union hall provided men with a place to meet, to gossip about the mine and to acquire some training for union activities.[46]

The miners' typical off-duty entertainment was drinking on weekends, but this may not properly be called "recreation". While they were drinking, their thoughts were still occupied with the mines, until they were finally completely intoxicated. One miner concluded that this self-destructive habit was a desperate effort to escape from the fear and hardship of the occupation:

> ...Drinking numbs my brain. Drinking helps me forget. I don't do it every Sunday, George, you know that, but goddamn it, it's good to get dumbed out once in a while. Look, I make coal mining sound so damn exciting, but let's face it, we're all terrified every time we go over to that place. We never know when the roof is going to fall or something is going to blow up ... You're living under constant pressure. I feel my lungs starting to give out. Goddamn it, this is no way to live. It's good to forget once in a while ... Drinking is a mountain man's right, the way I look at it. Margaret doesn't like it but she respects my right to get dumbed out. (48)

Thus the miners' environment and daily life consisted of economic instability, extremely exhausting and hazardous work, physical, psychological and social isolation from the rest of society, and lack of diversion from mining. Living in such a milieu and leading such a life, the miners developed a peculiar view of the world and a singular mode of behavior. Certain peculiarities of their behavior are particularly relevant to this study.

b. Miners

Many years in such a tenuous mode of existence, without hope of improvement, fostered deep feelings of unworthiness, self-pity and self-effacement in the mineworker. Many of the ballads that have come out of the coal fields illustrate these feelings:

> Pick! Pick! Pick!
> In the tunnel's endless gloom,
> And every blow of our strong right arm
> But helps to carve our tomb.

But what is that to thee
Who live by our blood and toil?
For mining royalties must be made
To glut the coal barons' spoils. (50)

At the same time the miner showed great pride and self-confidence.

Nay don't despise the miner lad,
Who burrows like the mole;
Buried alive from morn to night,
To delve for household coal ...

As honorable thy calling is
As that of hero lords;
They owe to the poor miner lad
The ore that steels their swords ... (51)

This complex combination of self-pity and pride seems to have important bearing on the behavior of miners. If one has perfect confidence in oneself, without any feeling of inferiority, one can quietly brush aside any ill-founded slander from others. On the other hand, if one does not have pride in oneself, but instead only self-pity, one may be resigned, apathetic, and inactive against calumny. With their mixture of pride and self-effacement, the miners were self-centered and sensitive toward the remarks of outsiders. Lantz found this to be true in the course of his interviews:

> On the whole we found the miner to be a person with marked sensitivities which became manifest whenever discussions centered around personal questions regarding self-feelings and personal worth. Any implication that mining as an occupation was inferior to other occupations or that miners were cowardly or not as fine as persons from other occupations, brought much defensiveness. (52)

When the outside world discriminated against him the miner was easily offended and turned resentful and aggressive. Bitterness toward the outside world was a common attitude of mineworkers:

> People seem to think miners are some kind of animal - underground rats they call us - but we're just like other people trying to earn a living. (53)

A significant result of this sensitivity was the miners' peculiar expectations with regard to their union leaders. For the miner, the union president was the only window to the outside world. He was in a sense an ambassador from the isolated coal camps. The leader was expected to represent their pride, dignity and resentment in his behavior. Hardman observed this phenomenon:

> ... the miner built in his mind the image of the union's national leader as one different from the ordinary leader, even as the miner himself was different from the other workers and unionists: "the miner lad whose calling is as that of hero lords".
> In that image, the miner's leader is his ambassador to the world and to all powers that be. He must be endowed with a great sense of justice and invested with power to secure justice. The image excludes self-interest, triviality, slap-on-the-back behavior. The leader must be a great man, his greatness derived from the elemental force of the earth itself which the miner penetrates, knows, lives by. (55)

c. Strong Solidarity and Devotion to the Union

The uncertainty of the future, caused by economic fluctuations and accidents, made it necessary for the miners and their families to form very close relationships for mutual aid. One recent miner, who came back from a city where he had vainly tried to settle down, said:

> The good side of mining is the people.. I've met a lot of people, but coal miners, once they go underground, are some of the most congenial people that I ever met in my life. You're dependent on me, and I'm dependent on you, so you take care of old buddy and old buddy will take care of you. (56)

This friendship was especially evident in time of need:/

> People in the mine industry build strong friendships. You will see this in a catastrophe or even in sickness. When one got hurt in the mine when I first came here, it wouldn't be half a week until a collection was taken up for him. (57)

> Men form close friendships. It is surprising that they can argue about things but when a man gets hurt, all come to do what they can. It is an unwritten law among them. You are good buddies and you never do forget them. (58)

This cohesiveness of the community, while it offered companionship for shariug the hardships, could not eliminate the fundamental ills of the situation. The rise of the union, therefore, was greeted with enthusiasm. When the organizers appeared in the 1920's in Harlan County, a traditionally anti-union region, many miners jumped at this new hope despite the personal danger.

> Mining just didn't pay nothing ... I was getting right about $2.86 a day and working only three, four days a week. I jumped at the union right quick. I tell you, though, it was a rough son of a bitch. The thugs were everywhere. If they found out you were organizing they'd come to your house and beat the hell out of you. (59)
>
> A lot of men were killed in this county over the union ... It was worth every bit. Companies just don't have any feeling for a man or his family. The union, it's the only thing a poor man's got. (60)

After a successful organizing campaign and a series of tangible achievements, the union came to be regarded as the miner's sole protector. One ballad expresses enthusiasm for what the union had brought to the miners:

> Now we don't care what the operators say,
> We're goin' to keep fightin' for that six-hour day.
>
> Lord, Lord, we're independent now.
> . . .
> Now when you meet your boss you don't have to bow,
> He ain't no king - never was nohow.
>
> Lord, Lord, we're independent now.
>
> You can't fire him and he can't fire you
> And if he don't like our union he knows what he can do.
>
> Lord, Lord, we're independent now. (61)

To the question of what would happen if the union disappeared, miners replied:

> That's like asking what would happen to us if the atomic bomb was thrown at you. I would just feel like quitting work. There would be no reason to work ... You wouldn't have no security at all. You could be a slave to the company. Everything would fall apart. They'd fire you right off the bat ... Right around here there are 1,400 men out of jobs and if there was no union some of them would work cheaper and cut the condition down to nothing. (62)

In addition to this enthusiastic acceptance, social pressure toward uniformity in the monolithic mining community helped to strengthen and protect the solidarity of the miners.

> If the majority of my buddies working with me see the reason for it and I didn't, I'd still get out with them and help. Belonging to an outfit like this, you can't do what you feel as an individual. You have to do what the majority wants. (63)

If a miner once betrayed the union, he would be ostracized socially as well as economically, and his "citizenship" would never be restored. Since the union circulated the blacklist to the local unions, it became very difficult for a miner who had once scabbed ever again to work in a mine. One folk song tells the story of a scab's life:

> Once a pretty maiden climbed an old man's knee,
> Asked for a story: "Papa, tell me,
> Why are you lonely, why are you sad,
> Why do the miners call you a scab?"
> ...
> "Brave men were striking, standing side by side,
> Striking for justice, striking with pride;
> I then was with them - with them heart and soul,
> But when the test came I left them in the cold;
> I thought best, pet, best to turn a scab,
> Best to return, pet, to the job I had:
> ...
> I have tried to tell them, tried to explain,
> But they will not listen, pleading is in vain.
> Everywhere I wander, everywhere I roam
> The story of my shame is sure to find my home. ... (64)

Thus, for the miners, the union was not merely an economically useful organization; it was "the pillar of their hopes"(65) and the sole source of protection against serfdom. Many miners were willing to throw their whole lives into work for the union when its existence was at stake. The union was also the source of social acceptance. Being so isolated from the rest of the world, miners had a strong need to be accepted by their "buddies". They often tried to prove themselves by showing blind, indiscriminate loyalty to the union out of a desperate need for social acceptance.

d.. Emotion, Direct Mode of Behavior and Violence:

Many researchers have observed that the typical miner's view of the world consists simply of what he likes or what he dislikes, with no ambiguous grey area. The miner tends to be strongly emotional; he loves impetuously or hates vehemently. Zweig writes:

> The other characteristic of the miner is his impetuosity and passion. His emotional life is very intense and sharp. Men are for him bad or good, not just average. He loves and hates. He sees white and black, but he is not very good at distinguishing shades. He is full of contrasts, and in his environment he moves from opposite to opposite almost without transition. The miner has a big heart and an even greater imagination. He sees everything with passion and fullness of heart. He is never tepid and lukewarm. (66)

Miners rarely tried to use subtle means such as persuasion, psychological, social or political influence, or court procedure to solve their personal problems.

> A man usually took care of things himself. That is, there was either individual violence or mob violence and it was a sign of weakness to call the police or to take care of your troubles in court. This was viewed a weak way out. (67)

> The group considered the most violent person the best. This is what the group believed ... The most preferred companion was one who could give and take violence. If attacked, he had to fight ... He would fit alright if he defended himself with violence. If he would not reply or wouldn't pay any attention to it, then he was held in contempt. Even though his ideas were held in contempt, if he was man enough to get up and defend himself, he was respected. (68)

e. Summary

From the foregoing it can be seen that due to their harsh and isolated life, miners developed peculiar characteristics in their view of the world and their mode of behavior.

1) These can be summarized as a complex emotional mixture of self-pity on the one hand and great pride to to their strenuous life on the other; of frustration over the apparent futility of their efforts and of isolation from the rest of society. This complex mixture fostered enormous sensitivity and aggressiveness in miners toward the "outside world" and its prejudice against them. It also made miners expect their president to be an extraordinary man and their "ambassador" to the "outside world".

2) Union organization quickly accomplished strong solidarity among miners and deep attachment to their union. The instability of their lives, the extremely hazardous work and the monolithic nature of their community made relationships among miners very close and cohesive. The union received enthusiastic support from them as a savior of their community. They tended to devote their whole personal lives to the union. The community also exercized strong social pressure on miners to be loyal to the union, and punished those whose loyalty wavered.

3) Miners tended toward emotional extremes, a naive black or white view of the world, with all the resultant behavioral manifestations. They were inclined to settle their conflicts not by persuasion but by violence, and not by compromise but by elimination of the "evil" source of the conflict.

CHAPTER IV

THE UMWA IN 1941-1951: HIGH MILITANCY, CHARISMATIC LEADER AND DEVOTED MEMBERS

In this chapter the UMWA's militancy will be analyzed. For clarity of the exposition, the 1943 contract-renewal negotiations, which typify the UMWA's behavior in that decade, will be investigated in detail. The first section examines the singular features of the UMWA organization in this period, which will serve as a setting for the following discussion (establishing the pattern of the "independent variables"). The second section describes the 1943 dispute in a quasi-analytical manner, with the intention of characterizing the union's policy and behavior in terms of its militancy (establishing the value of the "dependent variable"). In the third section an attempt will be made to explain the variables with special reference to the impact of intra-organizational factors (demonstration of the shape of the functional relation between the two variables).

1. Organizational Setting

a. Organizational Structure: Configuration and Location of the Decision-Making Authority

The UMWA in the 1940's consisted of three major hierarchical levels: international, district and local unions. The international union was headed by international officers (president, vice president, secretary-treasurer, auditors and tellers) and the International Executive Board.(1) International officers were elected every two years by a referendum vote of the members.(2) The Executive Board was constituted by one delegate from each district (amounting to 31 members).(3) The International Convention, which had supreme authority in executive, legislative and judicial decisions of the union, was held biennially.(4) Local unions sent delegates in proportion to the number of members they had (one delegate per 100 members).(5) Between the conventions, the president made the final decision in executive, legislative and judicial areas, based upon the instruction of and under the supervision of the Executive Board.(6)

Unlike other unions, whose international unions were essentially federations of local unions, all the major decisions of the UMWA (such as those concerning collective bargaining and strikes) were made exclusively by the international union. The area of local and district decisions was limited to grievance adjudication and safety inspection.

b. Power of the Leaders

The UMWA in the 1940's provided a variety of institutional mechanisms which endowed the international president with considerable power over the rank-and-file.

In the first place, in such a geographically dispersed organization as the UMWA, even widespread dissatisfaction among the members can hardly influence the international's policy decision unless scattered local unions are able to communicate with each other. In the UMWA, however, the constitution prohibited communication between locals, and could be used effectively to quash any concerted rebellion:

> Article XX, Section 3.
> Any member guilty of slandering or circulating, or causing to be circulated, false statements about any member or any members circulating or causing to be circulated any statement wrongfully condemning any decision rendered by any officer of the organization, shall, upon conviction, be suspended from membership for a period of six months and shall not be eligible to hold office in any branch of the Organization for two years thereafter. The above shall be construed as applying to any local officer or member reading such circulars to the members of a local union, or who in any way gives publicity to such ...

The terms "false statements" or "statement wrongfully condemning" in the text were so ambiguous that virtually any statement against the leaders' positions could be interpreted as such. This clause was very effectove, as shown in the following speech made by a local delegate at the 1944 Convention:

> (Delegate, Local 195, District 12:) ... How are you going to know in the rank-and-file whether or not there has been enough requests sent in for the restoration of autonomy? We never know because we are not allowed to circularize on another's locals. There is no way for us to get together ... (7)

A second method of preventing the growth of dissent was non-allocation of financial resources to the local. A comparison of three major industrial unions in 1947 as to the proportion of membership dues allocated to the international union (Table 4-1) clearly shows that a substantial proportion of dues collected in the UMWA was sent to the international.

As a result, while the international had one of the richest treasuries in the

Table 4 - 1

Amount of Membership Dues Sent to the International Union: Auto Workers, Steel Workers and Mine Workers[8]

	Dues/Month	Amount sent to the International
Auto Workers	$1.50	65¢
Steel Workers	$1.50	75¢
Mine Workers	$1.50	90¢

country, local unions were too poor to finance activities. The financial embarrassment of the local unions[9] can be seen from their frequent requests at the international conventions to increase local allocations.

> Due to the tax and expenses of local unions, we cannot have money in our treasury at fifteen cents return from dues; therefore, be it:
> Resolved, that each local be returned twenty five cents of each dollar's dues collected. (10)

An additional means of imposing financial difficulty on opposition movements was provided by the constitution:

> Article XIV, Section 20
> ... It shall be illegal to contribute funds for the promotion of the candidacy of any candidate for office within the organizations.

Thirdly, the president was empowered to revoke the charter of any disloyal district union and to appoint a provisional government.

> Article III, Section 2
> ... Charters of the Districts, Subdistricts and Local Unions may be revoked by the International President, who shall have authority to create a provisional government for the subordinate branch whose charter has been revoked...

While many other unions had granted similar powers to their international union, none had revoked charters to the extent practiced by the UMWA.[11] By 1942, 21 out of 31 districts were deprived of their autonomy. In addition, once the charter was revoked, it was never restored.

Fourth, the constitution provided the international leaders with the power to issue sanctions against the dissidents with relative ease.

> Article XVIII, Section 7
> When any officer of the International Organization, or of any District, Subdistrict or Local thereof, or when any member of the United Mine Workers of America, is charged with fomenting, leading or encouraging a dual union or a dual movement within the Organization, upon charges being filed with the International Executive Board, notice to such accused persons or persons of not less than five days of the time and place of hearing shall be given, and a hearing of said charges shall be had. If upon such hearing the International Executive Board finds such officer or officers or persons guilty, it may order the removal of such officer from office and his expulsion from the Organization or suspension from membership, and in the case of a member accused and found guilty the Board may order the expulsion of such member from the Organization or the suspension of his membership ...

The enormous powers which these consitutional provisions granted the international leaders were formally supposed to be exercised upon the request and under the supervision of the International Executive Board, which could potentially prohibit the abuse of such power by the president. In actual practice, even this last check was made ineffective by the international's successive purge of dissenting Executive Board members in the 1920's and 1930's, which was constitutionally indorsed as follows:

> Article IX, Section 3
> He (International President) may suspend or remove any International Officer (12) or appointed employee for insubordination or just and sufficient cause.

Since "insubordination or just and sufficient cause" was so ambiguous as to be amenable to broad interpretation, this provision enabled the international president to oust opposing delegates from the Executive Board and to build his own political machinery.

From the constitutional evidence, it is easy to trace the growth of the international's disproportionate power relative to that of the members during the decade under discussion.

c. Style of Leadership: Charismatic Authority of John L. Lewis

John L. Lewis was a typical example of a charistmatic leader [13] The literature offers two methods of identifying charismatic authority: One is to examine the characteristics of the leader's messages to his followers to check:

a) whether or not his speeches stress the divine or revolutionary character of his policy rather than the legal rule or tradition through which the policy has formed;[14]

b) whether or not his speeches stress his extraordinary quality in order to justify his regime;[15]

c) whether or not his speeches show thematic simplicity, use of high action-potential verbs, focus on shared identity, and reiteration and elicitation of audience response.[16]

The second method is to examine followers' interview statements and to see whether or not these show uncritical acceptance of the leader's personal ability.[17]

(i) Lewis' Speeches

Lewis' emphasis on the "divine" nature of his policy, combined with an extremely agitative rhetoric, is a common feature of his speeches. In his campaign for the mine safety legislation in 1949, he stated:

> ... while we were otherwise occupied keeping up day-by-day with the daily sensation of the press, and attempts of Congress to legislate wisely for the interests of all Americans, more than a million and a quarter Americans employed in coal mines were maimed, mangled, and butchered with impunity by those charged with the responsibility for their protection, with no redress for men so affected. A million and a quarter!
> A million and a quarter men! If I had the powers of a Merlin, I would march that million and a quarter men past the Congress of the United States. I would have the ambulatory injured drag the dead after them, so that the Congress might see; and I would have the men whose eyes were shot out and who were disemboweled in the mines crawl in that procession along the cobblestones so that the Congress might see them trailing their bowels after them.
> THOU SHALT NOT KILL!(18)

His emphasis on the capability of his regime as a justification of his rule his use of reiteration, and his ability to elicit audience response, can be seen, for example, in his speech in the 37th International Convention.

> Between that 225,000 members of that day and the 600,000 members today ... (there) are many heartbreaks and many heartburnings and a tremendous degree of human sacrifice and starvations and blacklists and boycotts, with our men driven and hunted by guards in the non-union fields in this country, and I have seen these solidly organized districts with autonomous representatives wiped out of existence by the forces arrayed against them, more often than not because the leadership that had been elected were not capable of dealing with their adversaries on equal terms. There were good men, they meant well, they believed in democracy, but ... (their) views were so provincial and so limited in the sweep and scope of their vision, their own experience was so limited and their own capabilities not sufficient properly to lead and protect the men in the mining communities... I want to ask the mine workers of Alabama, whose members have been brought from the economic bondage in which they slaved there for years, whether they want to get rid of William Mitch (District President appointed by Lewis).
> (Cries of, "No, no!")
> I want to ask the men from District 29, who have a new vision before them, whether they want to get rid of George Titler.
> (Cries of "No, no!")
> I want to ask the men from District 19 whether they want to get rid of Bill Turnblazer.
> (Cries of "No, no!")
> There is your story; there is your story. I could call the roll of the districts and receive the same reply, because these are honorable men, they are capable men, they are men capable of meeting in debate the high-priced representatives of the coal operators or government on even terms. <u>It takes something more than a mere desire to be an officer, to really be an officer</u>. (19)

Thematic simplicity, use of emotionally arousing rhetoric, focus on shared identity and reiteration and elicitation of audience response were everywhere in Lewis' speeches. Lewis' thematic simplicity can be seen in his description of his enemy, Senator Garner:

A labor-baiting, whisky-drinking, evil old man.(20)

Commenting on the NLRB's decision to rule the UMWA guilty of unfair labor practice, Lewis said:

> Denham, hatchet man for the High-profit Tong, is urged by the coal operators to lay about him and create an orgy of legal blood-letting at the expense of tax payers. (21)

Emotional rhetoric was standard practice with Lewis. For example, he responded to Governor Frank Murphy's decision to use state troopers to throw sit-down strikers out of GM plants in 1937:

> Tomorrow morning, I shall order the men to disregard your order, to stand fast. I shall then walk up to the largest window in the plant, open it, divest myself of my outer raiment, remove my shirt and bare my bosom. Then when you order your troops to fire, mine will be the first breast that those bullets will strike. And as my body falls from that window to the ground, you listen to the voice of your grandfather as he whispers in your ear, "Frank, are you sure you are doing the right thing?" (22)

Of his shared identity, he told an editor of the international's official history book:

> The thing that gives me strength is the fact that I am able correctly to interpret the aims of my people. I know the psychology of the coal miner. I know about his dreams and his ideals and trials and tribulations, I have lived with coal miners. I am one of them ...
>
> I have laid down in a mine tunnel with my face in a half inch of water and pulled my shirt up over my head, expecting to die the next minute in an explosion I heard coming toward me. And when God performed a miracle and stopped that explosion before I died, I think it gave me some understanding of what men think about and how they suffer when they are waiting to die in a coal mine explosion.
>
> ... When I speak, I speak the thoughts of the membership of the United Mine Workers of America, because I understand them. I remain true to them and they remain true to me. (23)

(ii) Members' Attitudes toward Lewis

Most of the miners showed an unconditional acceptance of Lewis' legitimacy on the basis of his capability. For example, one delegate's speech illustrates their reverence and awe:

> I want to say this as to why I am not in favor of autonomy. John Lewis -one man called him Father John - if he was good enough, and Thomas Kennedy and the other International Officers of this union were good enough to come down in the southern field in 1933 and take us miners out of bondage and were good enough to safeguard the mining industry, I am satisfied to let matters rest in their hands. I was in bondage, lived in bondage, from 1902 until 1933 ... John Lewis - I don't call him John Lewis, I call him Moses, the man that came down the southern coal fields and led the children of Israel out and put them on safe ground. Did you ever stop to think when Moses led the children of Israel out that they proceeded to backslide and went back into bondage? ... (24)

Even more cautious and skeptical members showed very little doubt about Lewis' capability:

> I don't like his strong-arm methods and power in the union. But we don't want to change him because he can get more for the miners than anybody else and he's done just that. (25)

From these considerations, it can be concluded that John L. Lewis fitted the standard description of the charismatic leader.

2. Contract Negotiations in 1943

The early 1940's saw the United States fully geared for war. The government imposed central control on all phases of American public life. On July 16, 1942, the National War Labor Board ruled on the demands of the steel workers with the so-called "Little Steel Formula", which regulated the wages of all workers based on the May, 1942, level.[(26)] All AFL and CIO leaders declared full support for the government's war effort and made a "no-strike" promise.[(27)]

After May, 1942, when the workers' wages were controlled, the Office of Price Administration granted price increases to several industries. The resulting increases lowered the workers' standard of living. The problem was especially severe in coal towns, where the only available stores were owned by the coal companies. The company store generally charged more than stores in other parts of the country.[28] In the middle of January, 1943, spontaneous strikes demanding wage increases spread throughout Pennsylvania.[29] Miners grudgingly returned to work on January 22 by order of Lewis and Roosevelt.[30] This was an omen of the storm that was to follow.

On March 10, when the first negotiations between the UMWA and Appalachian soft-coal operators began in New York, Lewis presented the union's final demand and declared its determination to break the Little Steel Formula.[31] The union's demands can be summarized as follows:

(1) Improvement in working conditions;
(2) Retention of the 35-hour 5-day work week;
(3) Establishment of a portal-to-portal practice for starting and quitting time for underground workers;
(4) Time-and-a-half for overtime, and double-time for Sundays;
(5) Elimination of existing wage differentials within and among districts, and operation of only two instead of three shifts within a given twenty-four-hour period as a means of eliminating hazards and improving safety conditions;
(6) Inclusion of 50,000 foremen, assistant foremen, and other supervisory employees of coal mines under the contract;
(7) A basic wage increase of $2 a day.[32]

Lewis' speech on the first day of the parley focused the union's demands on increasing the miner's income. When all wages were generally controlled by the Little Steel Formula, the increase which would result from demands (3), (4) and (7) was so striking as to cause one operator to call it a "ridiculous, wild statement".[33] But as the WLB and the operators soon found out, the UMWA top leaders were fully determined to fight for the demand.

Appalachian operator spokesman Charles O'Neill rejected the demands and made little effort to negotiate. On March 19, the policy committee of the UMW adopted a one-month truce starting March 31, provided that the new contract was retroactive from April 1.[34]

Since the operators made no counter proposal, the negotiations in April were utterly fruitless. On April 22, Secretary of Labor Francis Perkins certified the dispute to the WLB and ordered all parties to appear before it. This move outraged the miners; wildcat strikes began at Republic Steel Corporation in Pennsylvania, spreading over Pennsylvania, Alabama, Kentucky, West Virginia and Illinois, and finally involving 23,000 miners.[35] Roosevelt telegraphically ordered Lewis to halt the strike, threatening to "use all the power vested in me as President and Commander-in-Chief ... if the United Mine Workers' strikes continue after 10 A.M., May 1." The miners' response was not compliance, but instead more wildcat strikes. In Ohio, 9,700 more miners walked out of the pits.[36] Then came the first of May, the expiration date of the truce. With the nation watching anxiously, half-a-million miners quietly stayed home, defying their government and the Commander-in-Chief in the midst of war. Roosevelt ordered Harold L. Ickes, Solid Fuel Administrator for War, to seize all the mines. Resentment and attack against Lewis and the UMWA were heard from various parts of the country.

On May 2, Roosevelt broadcast an address criticizing Lewis and the miners. Lewis, with perfect timing, had announced a 15-day truce just before Roosevelt's speech.[37] Ickes and the UMWA began conferring, but Ickes still insisted that negotiations should be continued with the operators subject to approval by the WLB. Fifteen days passed without an agreement. The UMWA, aware that Ickes was moving toward its side, extended the truce to May 31, following Ickes' plea.[38] On May 25, the WLB denied the $2.00 rise, Sunday double-pay, and guaranteed a 52-week work year; it approved some increase in vacation allowance and occupational expenses, and remanded the portal-to-portal pay and 6-day week back to direct negotiations.[39] The UMWA ignored the WLB notice, and on June 1, as the truce expired, shut down all the mines in the nation.[40]

On the next day, a storm against the UMWA began to build up. The WLB bitterly accused Lewis, and suggested that all negotiations be stopped until the strike was called off. Roosevelt convoked an emergency conference with Ickes, J.E. Byrnes (War Mobilization Director) and eight members of the WLB, and issued a personal attack on Lewis.[41] The House of Representatives started debating the Smith-Connally Act, apparently aimed at Lewis, which provided for imprisonment of any leader conducting a strike in a government-seized industry.[42] The media branded Lewis a provocateur, a destructionist, an obstructionist, a fascist agent and a new Benedict Arnold.[43]

The UMWA turned a deaf ear to all accusations. The WLB found its no-negotiation suggestion totally ignored when Lewis began conferring with operators who were urged by Ickes to be at the table. The UMWA leaders proposed $1.50 per day as travel pay until the survey on the portal issue was completed. The operators practically agreed to the offer, but hesitated to sign on the grounds that the survey result, which might well exceed $1.50, would "constitute a contingent liability which was not a stabilizing force for the industry".[44] June 3 found negotiations progressing while the miners were still on strike.[45]

The WLB ordered the cessation of all negotiations while the strike continued in force. Lewis charged, "These little strutting men have sought to place upon the miners the responsibility for this work stoppage, which rests actually upon their smug shoulders. Fearful lest a solution be reached under auspices not compatible with the self-importance of the War Labor Board, that body maliciously commanded that these negotiations cease." On that day, in response to the WLB's order, he ordered the strike to cease, not immediately, but on June 7, four days later, setting the new deadline at June 20.[46]

In the meantime, on June 5, Congress finally passed the Smith-Connally Act, empowering the WLB with the right to subpoena witnesses (and thus to force Lewis to appear before the Board), and to imprison any leader who promoted a strike in a government-seized industry.

The operators, shaken by their miscalculation of the UMWA's determination, were seriously concerned about the return of their properties and began to shift away from the uncompromising stand of the WLB and Roosevelt. On June 7 the Illinois Operators' Association,[47] and on June 9 the Central Pennsylvania Coal Operators Association orally agreed to $1.50 portal-to-portal pay.[48] On June 18, however, the WLB rejected these agreements, demanding that Roosevelt force the UMWA to sign the WLB contract or use such strong measures as cancelling the established check-off dues, seizing the treasury of the UMWA, and civil or criminal prosecution of Lewis.[49]

Lewis did not budge. On June 20, notwithstanding these severe threats, the nation's 530,000 miners stayed out of the pits as though there were no war, no WLB and no Smith-Connally Act.[50] On June 22, through Ickes' efforts, the UMWA called off the strike and set a new deadline of October 31.[51]

On July 21, the UMWA succeeded in making the Illinois Operators Association sign a 2-year no-strike contract, with an 8-hour 6-day work week, and portal-to-portal pay to be retroactive with 50% payable from October, 1938 to April, 1943, and fully payable thereafter.[52] Several calculations (Alinsky, Southern Coal Operators Association, and the New York Times) showed that with longer hours, time-and-a-half for overtime, vacation pay and portal-to-portal pay, this contract would provide a pay increase of almost $3.00 a day for every coal miner. Lewis had not only countered the attacks but had also obtained a gain even greater than those provided for in the original demands. Furthermore, contract negotiations with the remaining operators and the WLB inevitably would be based on this new contract agreement.

The WLB promptly began hearings to investigate this contract.[53] On August 16, Roosevelt issued an Executive Order empowering the WLB to withhold dues of unions not complying with its decisions, and to cancel draft deferment of the strikers.[54] With this new power the WLB turned down the UMWA-Illinois Operators agreement on August 25.[55] This time, fully aware of the fatal blow which Roosevelt's executive order could cause to the union, Lewis did not ignore the WLB and immediately started negotiating with the Illinois operators for a revised agreement. On September 23 a new accord was reached.[56] On October 26 the WLB again rejected the revised contract, but this time offered a counter-proposal of $8 and 12.5¢ a day, a cut of 37.5¢ from the revised contract. This was very close to what the UMWA had originally asked.[57] The union leaders did not respond, and the miners in the field, angered by the WLB's rejection, began walking out on October 29.[58]

On November 1, as the deadline expired, the nation's half-million miners were once more idle. Roosevelt immediately seized the mines, but permitted Lewis to negotiate with Ickes.[59] They reached an agreement on November 3, granting the miners $8.50 for an 8-hour work day, an actual daily increase of $1.50.[60]

Having failed in spite of the emergency measures, and realizing that the anger and irritation of the miners were growing beyond the control even of their leaders, the government had no alternative but to concede. Lewis' victory came on November 20 when the final approval of the WLB was handed down.[61]

The UMWA had clearly won the battle. A calculation by the <u>New York Times</u>[62] showed that the contract would provide about $1.75 increase for a 6-day work-week of 48 hours. Most miners would probably earn in excess of this. The WLB calculated that even the settlement it proposed (37.5¢ less <u>per diem</u> than the final agreement) would bring the miners an average weekly wage of approximately $60, a 130% increase from their weekly average of $26 in January of 1941. The WLB's policies had been completely ignored. Its insistence on stopping negotiations during the strike was brushed aside; its argument that $8 and 12.5¢ a day (37.5¢ less than the Lewis-Ickes accord) was the maximum that Congress and the executive orders allowed, was also sidestepped by the Lewis-Ickes agreement, which made up this 37.5¢ by reducing the lunch break from 30 minutes to 15 minutes.

From this brief chronology of the 1943 dispute, two distinct features of the UMWA's policy and behavior can be noted:

(i) militant demand focused principally on pay increase;

(ii) militant tactics against attack by the government.

A number of questions are prompted by this history. Why did the UMWA policy-makers push a wage increase more than anything else? Why did they set the demand so high in such a difficult time, at the risk of total desctruction of the union? The following section will be devoted to finding an answer to these questions.

3. Analysis

The literature provides to explanations for the UMWA's high militancy. The first is given by McAlister Coleman, who argues that the constant retreat of labor and the UMWA's consciousness of itself as being a "spearhead" of the American labor movement constitute the major reason.(63) Although the UMWA did play the role of "shock troops" for the labor movement in the 1930's, this explanation is not very persuasive by itself. There is good evidence that (1) the UMW's involvement in the CIO campaign was motivated not by altruistic interests but by carefully calculated self-interest,(64) and that (2) the extremely high cost associated with militant policy in the 1940's (as compared to the relatively low risk in the 1930's) makes the policy untenable on rationalistic grounds. The second theory advanced to date argues that Lewis had an inexhaustible thirst for power and an inability to take second place; the union's excessively militant policy was therefore the result of his effort to come back to the national scene from the setbacks he had experienced in the early 1940's.(65) Although there may be some truth in this explanation, a collective bargaining process of this magnitude is too complicated to be explained by the effects of the personality of a single individual. Two more factors must be added in order to fully comprehend the militant stand of the UMWA.

a. Pressure toward Militancy on the International Leaders

There were three sources of pressure on the international union leaders to adopt a militant policy in the 1940's. We will examine each of them in order.

(i) Competitive Pressure from the CIO and the Steelworkers

The first source of pressure was the necessity of outdoing the CIO and the Steelworkers. There were two reasons for the competition:

(aa) Intra-Organizational Turmoil: Murray's Invasion

Although there had been virtually no significant dissensions inside the union, a new turmoil began developing which had serious implications for the future. In 1942, Lewis purged the UMWA vice-president, CIO President Phillip Murray, from the union in a humiliating trial. After the break with Lewis, Murray began infiltrating the UMWA. On July 23, 1942, a group of miners from District 2 had a meeting at the Steelworkers' building in Johnstown to organize a rebellion. James Brown, a delegate from Revlock, Pennsylvania, was named secretary. Present at the meeting were Abe Martin, a former representative of District 2, now organizing director for the Steelworkers; Nathan Cowan, a member of the Revlock local union; and Maurice, the regional director in the Johnstown area for the Steelworkers. They named their organization "the Committee for Democracy Within the United Mine Workers of America". Martin began an extensive organizing tour in Districts 2, 3, 4, and 5.[66] Murray's infiltration was not restricted to local rank-and-file members, but also extended to Lewis's lieutenants. For example, President Davis of District 31, a loyal follower of Lewis, was secretly offered a federal government position, which can be interpreted as a co-optive tactic designed by Roosevelt and Murray. In District 17, District President Van A. Bittner began openly attacking Lewis, forcing him to revoke the charter of District 17. Bittner, thrown out of office, took a job in the Steelworkers Union and continued rebel activity in the UMWA as an assistant to Murray. A similar rebellion was also observed in District 7, which resulted in another charter revocation.

The most important feature of this series of rebellions is that it stemmed from the former vice president of the union. Murray and his assistants Bittner and Brophy were still influential among the rank-and-file miners as well as among the district-level leaders. In addition, the invading leaders had access to the financial and human resources of the Steelworkers and the CIO, thus making possible simultaneous rebellions across several districts. Although the international leaders had been able to control the earlier rebellions, this invasion could easily become uncontrollable. They knew well that mere suppression would not solve the problem. They needed to prove their ability to outdo overwhelmingly the achievements of Murray and the Steelworkers.

(bb) The Failure of District 50 and the Competitive Pressure

Internal difficulty in the union also stemmed from the UMW's catch-all

District 50. District 50 was originally established in 1936 with jurisdiction over the "by-product of coal". "By-product" was so ambiguous a term that Lewis enlarged it in the early 1940's to include clerical, technical and supervisory workers, paper, pulp, sulphite or chemical industries, dairy farmers and fishermen.(67) He placed great importance on this organizing campaign and poured into it a large sum of financial and human resources.(68) To cover the heavy financial expense, a 50¢ assessment was imposed on membership dues.(69) Dissatisfaction soon spread among the rank-and-file already hurt by the ever-increasing cost of living. On September 9, 1941, miners in Edison Anthracite and Lehigh Coal and Navigation Corporation walked out from the pits in protest against the dues increase. The wildcat strike, which soon spread to all collieries in District 7 and some in District 1, lasted more than a month despite repeated return-to-work orders from the International leaders and the National Defense Mediation Board.(70)

Despite the enormous financial investment, the organizing campaign did not show any signs of progress. Although contract negotiations for District 50 were conducted separately from those of the coal industry *per se*, the initial failure of this ambitious venture placed more pressure on international leaders to secure a substantial gain in the next contract negotiations in the coal industry. The organizing campaign of District 50, whose jurisdiction overlapped with that of a number of CIO unions, resulted in harsh competition between the two parent organizations. The best weapon the UMWA could have was evidence showing its capacity to outdo the CIO in contract gains.

b. The Autonomy Movement and the International's Commitment

It will be remembered that 21 out of 31 districts had been deprived of local autonomy. The 1942 International Convention saw 108 local resolutions concerning autonomy, which was the largest number among the items discussed.(71) Content analysis of a randomly chosen sample (one fourth of the total local resolutions, cf. Table 4-2) shows that (a) in 1942 the autonomy issue collected a larger proportion of resolutions than in any other year, which can be interpreted to mean that the miners' concern over autonomy was exceptionally strong in 1942, and that (b) the overwhelming majority of these resolutions concerning autonomy demanded either complete or partial autonomy. In addition, the autonomy movement was found to be linked to Murray's invasion effort.

The international union's response was to argue the merits of the efficiency of the present scheme, as is well reflected in Lewis' speech in the 1936 convention:

Table 4 - 2

Members' Attitude on Autonomy, 1942-1960

	1942	1944	1948	1952	1956	1960
Total No. of Resolutions on Autonomy in the sample	52 (10.2%)	57 (9.5%)	8 (1.6%)	13 (2.0%)	8 (1.8%)	4 (3.5%)
No. of Resolutions for Perfect Autonomy (in the sample)	27	113	3	8	7	14
No. of Resolutions for Partial Autonomy (in the sample)	19	28	3	5	0	0
No. of Resolutions Against Autonomy (in the sample)	6	16	2	0	1	1

Note: Figures in parentheses on the first row show a percentage of resolutions on autonomy out of the total sample.

Source: Appendix 1

I trust that the Convention, in considering this matter (autonomy), will consider it for what it is really worth and what it means to the organization. It is not a fundamental principle that the Convention is discussing. It is a question of business expediency and administrative policy as affecting certain geographical areas of the Organization. It is a question of whether you desire your Organization to be the most effective instrumentality within the realm of possibility for a labor organization or whether you prefer to sacrifice the efficiency of your organization in some respects for a little more academic freedom in the selection of some local representative in a number of districts. (72)

Although the powerful Lewis machine dominated the final vote with a large margin against autonomy, the movement could potentially grow to become a threat in the future. There was no reason to suspect that the age-old argument of instrumental efficiency, which had not fully persuaded the members in the previous conventions, would be particularly convincing in 1942. The miners who demanded restoration of autonomy had heard the efficiency argument hundreds of times, and yet they had come back again with a much stronger voice. They returned to their locals with growing discontent. In some cases, they found it impossible to persuade their members.[(73)] Murray and the CIO were on the brink of exploiting this dissatisfaction across the coal fields.

To stop the growing trend for autonomy as well as Murray's infiltration, the international leaders would be forced to demonstrate the oft-touted instrumental efficiency by making a substantial contract gain. Coal miners, severely hurt by a rise in the cost of living, expected the union's help. If the international union couldn't prove its argument, the miners' discontent might possibly explode and become the ideal vehicle for Murray's invasion.

c. Poverty Across the Coal Fields

The wage-price regulation of the OPA and the WLB was patently unfair to mining labor. In coal towns, where the only retailers were company stores with their inflated prices, the problem was very serious. Even The Nation, known to be anti-UMWA, reported on the poverty spreading across the coal fields:

On the adequacy of the prevailing $7 wage, I changed my opinion after witnessing the wide-spread poverty that still exists in the mining camps. "We could buy more with $5.60 two years ago than we can with $7 today," miner after miner declared ...

The continued poverty of the miners is due in part to the numerous and sizeable deduction made from their pay by the operators. After war-bond

> allotments and Social Security and Victory taxes are taken out, there are deductions for rent, light, water and coal, and then for health, hospital, and burial benefits. The men are even required to pay rental for lamps they use in the mines and the cost of the explosives they need to get out the coal. I saw several pay slips on which gross figures of $80 or $90 for two weeks' work had been trimmed down a third or a half by these charges. "They got back that last pay raise long ago in bigger cuts and higher prices at the commissary," one miner told me. The workers are not forced to take "scrip" usable only in the company stores, but most of them are obliged to buy a large part of their supplies from the company because it is so hard to get into town. Complaints of over-charging and violations of ceiling prices in the company stores are widespread. (74)

The miners' deep concern about wage increase can also be seen in the local resolutions at the 1942 convention. A content analysis of these shows that the number of demands related to income increase totalled 205, by far the largest number for any single item, and that in comparison to other years the ratio of income-related demands to the total number of resolutions was the highest in 1942 (Appendix 1).

The strain of poverty finally exploded in early 1943, when spontaneous wildcat strikes began in Pennsylvania. On January 7, scattered strikes spread to 15 collieries in the Pennsylvania area, with the miners demanding wage-increases, overtime pay and abolition of the dues increase. On January 11, the WLB and the Anthracite Committee of Twelve, a policy-making committee of the industry, of which Lewis was a member, ordered the striking miners to return to the pits. Despite this order from Lewis and the US Government, January 12 saw the miners refusing to work, making 15,000 men idle in the fields. On January 15, the WLB issued another order to resume work, to which the miners responded by increasing the scale of the strike. The next day Roosevelt intervened, and on January 22 the strikers grudgingly returned to the pits.

The miners' walk-out in defiance of the government and of Lewis implied that their frustration over encroaching poverty was approaching the threshold of explosion. The international union realized that it would be much more difficult to control the miners later if no steps were taken to help them now. If the leaders failed to obtain a large gain, the miners would have to live with an unsatisfactory contract for another two years, which might well lead to chaos in the mine fields.

d. Combination of the Instability of Charismatic Authority and the Devotion of Members as Amplifiers of Pressure

The militant-pressure argument cannot alone explain why only the UMWA became so militant at that time. The Steelworkers Union as well as other CIO unions encroached upon by District 50 faced the same competitive pressure as the UMW. All the labor leaders in the nation experienced members' strong discontent against the "Little Steel Formula". There was a number of unions whose internal turmoil was far more threatening to the leaders than Murray's invasion and the autonomy movement. There also existed a condition peculiar to the UMWA-organization which functioned as an "amplifier", making the impact of these pressures upon leaders' decisions much larger than it would have been otherwise.

(i) Instability Caused by Characteristics of the Members: Homogenous but Isolated Community - Mass Society

"Mass society" is defined as a society containing an aggregate of "atomized" individuals who are related to one another only by their relationship to a common authority, because of the lack of independent, intervening voluntary groups capable of integrating them into the larger society.[75] The findings of studies on "mass society" can be summarized in three propositions.

1) People in a mass society tend to take very direct methods of protest, since they lack intervening organizations through which they might exercise their influence.[76]

> Mass behavior is associated with activist interpretations of democracy and with increasing reliance on force to resolve social conflict ... The breakdown of normal restraints, including internalized standards of right conduct, and established channels of action ... frees the mass to engage in direct, unmediated efforts to achieve its goals and to lay hands upon the most readily accessible instruments of action. Ordinarily, even in countries having democratic constitutional systems, the population is so structured as to inhibit direct access to the agencies of decision. The electorate participates at specified times and in defined ways; it is not free to create ad hoc methods of pressure. The citizen, even when organized in a pressure group supporting, say, a farm lobby, can vote, write letters, visit his congressman, withold funds, and engage in similar respectable actions. Other forms of activity are strange to him. But when this code has lost its power over him, he will become available for activist modes of intervention. (77)

2) The content of their behavior tends to take extreme forms because they are

not exposed to different opinions as provided by various groups, nor to debates which would force them to be more informed, realistic and rational; and because no immediate group disciplines their behavior.[78]

3) Their behavior also tends to be "highly unstable, readily shifting its focus of attention and intensity".[79]

Mining communities in the 1940's had an environment very similar to the above description of a "mass society". As shown in Chapter 2, there were very few voluntary organizations or leisure facilities, either of which could have functioned as intervening groups semi-independent of the authority in Washington. This lack of modulating organizations deprived the miners of the chance to solve grievances and differences with their companies through indirect, peaceful means. The companies which employed them were controlled in turn at headquarters far away from the mines, and had only limited right to adjust grievances. Local and district unions were solely controlled by the international union in Washington, and could not act as a channel for local grievance adjustment. Most of the officers in local government or in the courts in mining towns were either company men or union men. Under these conditions, an indirect and more democratic approach to resolving grievances on the local level was nearly impossible. In addition, due to the occupational, geographical and psychological barriers to mobility, the miners' protest could not take the form of moving to another industry. Therefore protest tended to take a direct and violent form.[80] Kerr and Siegel make this point:

> The strike for this isolated mass is a kind of colonial revolt against far-removed authority, an outlet for accumulated tensions, and a substitute for occupational and social mobility. The industrial environment places these workers in the role of members of separate classes distinct from the community at large, classes with their share of grievances. (81)

To make things more difficult, miners tended to share the same grievance. Since the community consisted completely of miners and ex-miners with the same experience and ideas, they reinforced each other's belief in the righteousness of their demand, which made even unrealistic ideas a firm "social reality".[83]

> When you go on strike, you do so knowing that you are right to do it, that conditions are intolerable - and everyone around you agrees with you! Everything about you confirms the justice of your demands and gives you moral support. There is no room left for doubt.
>
> During the war, you did hear it said that you shouldn't strike. But your reasoning seemed logical - weren't your brother and uncle or perhaps son

fighting in the Pacific or in Europe? They were fighting against Hitlerism and its oppression. You too were fighting against oppressions - in your own coal camp. (83)

> The miners, sailors, the longshoremen, the loggers, to a much lesser extent the textile workers, form isolated masses, are almost a "race apart". They live in their own separate communities; the coal patch, the ship, the waterfront district, the logging camp, the textile town. These communities have their own codes, myths, heroes, and social standards. There are few neutrals in them to mediate the conflicts and dilute the mass. All people have grievances, but what is important is that all members of each of these groups have the same grievances ... they all do about the same work and have about the same experiences. (84)

(ii) Loyalty and Personal Attachment of Members

The miners' involvement with the union organization was total, personal, and involved deep loyalty. The union was not only their economic instrument but also their protection, their pride, and the center of their social activities. In such an intense and personal relationship, hostility toward the union and union leaders was taboo. Coser pointed out in a more general context a peculiarity of intense relationships:

> The closer the relationship, the greater the affective investment, the greater also the tendency to suppress rather than express hostile feelings ... In such cases feelings of hostility tend to accumulate and hence to intensify. (85)

When this intensified latent hostility becomes manifest, the conflict tends to be violent. The local miners perceived an intra-union element which disagreed with their positions as an actual threat to their lives. This perception led to the following reactions: a) Since the disagreeing elements were their personal enemies, the miners took a passionate stand on the issues involved. b) Instead of calculating the costs and benefits of participation in the conflict, they were willing to risk their lives in removing the threat.

John L. Lewis knew this dangerous characteristic of the miners.[87] He watched the development of the miners' dissatisfaction carefully. Saul Alinsky, interviewing Lewis, observes the significance of the strike of January, 1943, upon the union leader's decision:

> ... The miners, although the most disciplined of union members, temporarily had broken out of union control. This was extremely significant, because it was clear that the miners had reached the breaking point of frustration and disgust with the wide disparity between their wages and the high living costs ... Lewis was deeply impressed by this strike. To him it spelled out two extremely important facts. First, the condition of the miners was so severe that they spontaneously struck against it, regardless of union discipline ... Second, he noted the miners' reaction during this unauthorized strike. He saw the leaderless miners of their own volition deliberately flout the authority of the National War Labor Board and even stall for two days on a direct order from the President before they finally returned to work. Lewis did not forget this lesson. He now knew that there would be no question about coal miners' going out on strike, war or no war ... (88)

(iii) Instability Caused by the Style of Leadership

In the first section of this chapter, we established that the legitimacy of the international leaders of the UMWA in the 1940's was based on the charismatic character of John L. Lewis. At this point it is useful to discuss theoretically the instabilities of such a charismatic leader, and then to examine whether such instabilities can be observed in the particular case of John L. Lewis and the UMWA.

The theory of charismatic authority argues that charisma is inherently unstable in two ways. The first is that the leader constantly faces the danger of adopting goals which do not appeal to his followers. Weber explains:

> The holder of charisma seizes the task that is adequate for him and demands obedience and a following by virtue if his mission. His success determines whether he finds them. His charismatic claim breaks down if his mission is not recognized by those to whom he feels he has been sent. (89)

The problem is that a charismatic leader can not be influenced by the members through informal recommendations, by political pressures, or by accepting the majority view when deciding the goal of the organization. Supposedly he alone sets the direction of the group. Weber observes:

> ... he (a charismatic leader) does not derive his "right" from their (followers') will, in the manner of an election. Rather, the reverse holds: it is the duty of those to whom he addresses his mission to recognize him as their charismatically qualified leader. (90)

Thus, the charismatic leader has to face a difficult task: setting goals which appeal to his followers without any concrete influence from them.

The second cause of instability is that he has to constantly prove his extraordinary ability by concrete achievement. Even a small mistake may damage the myth of his charisma. Weber argues:

> The charismatic leader gains and maintains authority solely by proving his strength in life. If he wants to be a prophet, he must perform heroic deeds. Above all, however, his divine mission must "prove" itself in that those who faithfully surrender to him must fare well. If they do not fare well, he is obviously not the master sent by the gods. (91)

John L. Lewis was no exception to this general argument. As to his goal-setting activities, there were two factors that made him sensitive to the collective will of the members. First, although he suppressed any concrete opposition to his policy, he understood from personal experience the situation of the mineworkers, though he thought of them in the collective sense.[92] Hardman observes:

> Lewis, a miner, felt for the miners, but only as a collectivity. It was not in his character to think concretely of individual miners. He considered people en masse: "fifty million shrunken bellies", the "labor movement", the "400,000 mine workers". He views individuals only as instrumentalities to be approved or found wanting and treated accordingly. (93)

Second, Lewis established communication channels outside the formal hierarchy, in order to maintain his sensitivity. He hired many local leaders as international representatives to collect information about rank-and-file members directly, bipassing the formal channels. A former high-ranking staff member revealed Lewis' mode of communication with the rank-and-file:

> Before any major step is taken by the union, hundreds of letters and telegrams are exchanged between the headquarters of the union and the district close to the roots. Policy Committees, composed of "run of the mine" workers, meet at the various headquarters and the will of the men, their attitude, their determination and their strength are ascertained beyond a doubt. (94)

As to the pressure to prove his charismatic ability, the theory also seems to apply to John L. Lewis. The pressure is known to be especially strong when the leader has experienced a failure. In 1940, Lewis staged an open fight against Roosevelt, was defeated, and resigned from the CIO presidency. After the break with Roosevelt, Lewis' prominence and influence as a national labor leader started going downhill. His anti-war stand and his defiance of government orders in a national emergency stirred outcries from all over the country. Although he made his longtime lieutenant Murray his successor at the CIO post, the CIO turned solidly anti-Lewis in less than two years, thus depriving him of all national powers he had.

One may argue that this series of failures in the political arena was not a serious challenge for his charismatic legitimacy, because the failures were in an area outside of UMWA activities. Next, however, came the failure of District 50, which was undoubtedly an internal affair of the UMWA. The impact of this failure on his charismatic legitimacy was serious, as Saul Alinsky observed:

> ... Since 1934, he (Lewis) had been beaten only by Roosevelt, and that was in the political arena. In the field of labor organization Lewis was recognized as the undefeated champion ... But Lewis failed ... Since then, the monotonous defeat of District 50 had weakened the myth of Lewis' infallibility. Millions of dollars have been poured into this amorphous structure, which has long outlived even its usefullness as a threat. District 50 and defeat have become synonymous, and outside of its being a rest haven for some worn-out organizers it would have been better for Lewis if he had abandoned it. (95)

Under these circumstances, he faced the year 1943. The encroaching impoverishment of the mineworkers, the invasion by Murray, and the autonomy movement put pressure on him to gain a substantial pay raise for the membership. The miners, who tend to take extreme and unstable positions, began showing signs of a drastic shift toward rebellion. With the increasing threat to his charismatic authority, Lewis had no other option than to respond sensitively to rank-and-file pressure.

4. Summary

Analysis of the UMWA's policies in the 1940's and especially in 1943 produces the following conclusions:

(1) The UMWA had a) a highly centralized decision-making structure; b) a high-powered leader; c) charisma as a major source of legitimacy; and d) homogenous, geographically isolated, highly devoted members.

(2) Union policies and tactics in the 1943 contract negotiations were characterized by a) substantial wage increase as its primary demand and b) militant and uncompromising tactics to secure the wage gain, even at the risk of destroying the union itself.

(3) Existing explanations attributing the militant policy of the UMWA to a decline of the labor movement, or to mere thirst for power on the part of John Lewis, are inadequate.

(4) The alternative explanation presented here asserts that two conditions were responsible: a) existence of organizational pressure to bring a substantial pay raise; b) the instability of the leader-member relationship. Condition a) was created by (i) the competition with the Steelworkers and the CIO stemming from the Murray invasion and the initial failure of District 50; (ii) the leaders' commitment to the instrumental-efficiency argument used to suppress the movement for restoration of autonomy; and (iii) the worsening impoverishment of the miners due to malfunction of the wage-price regulation. Condition b) resulted from: (i) homogeneity and isolation of the mining community, as well as the miners' loyalty to the union; and (ii) the charismatic style of leadership functioning as a "multiplier of the effects of the former condition on the UMWA's policy decision.

The structure of the alternative explanation can be expressed as in Figure 4-1. The crucial part of the explanation, the "amplifier" effect of the latter condition, may be illustrated as in Figure 4-2.

Figure 4 - 1
Structure of the Proposed Explanation

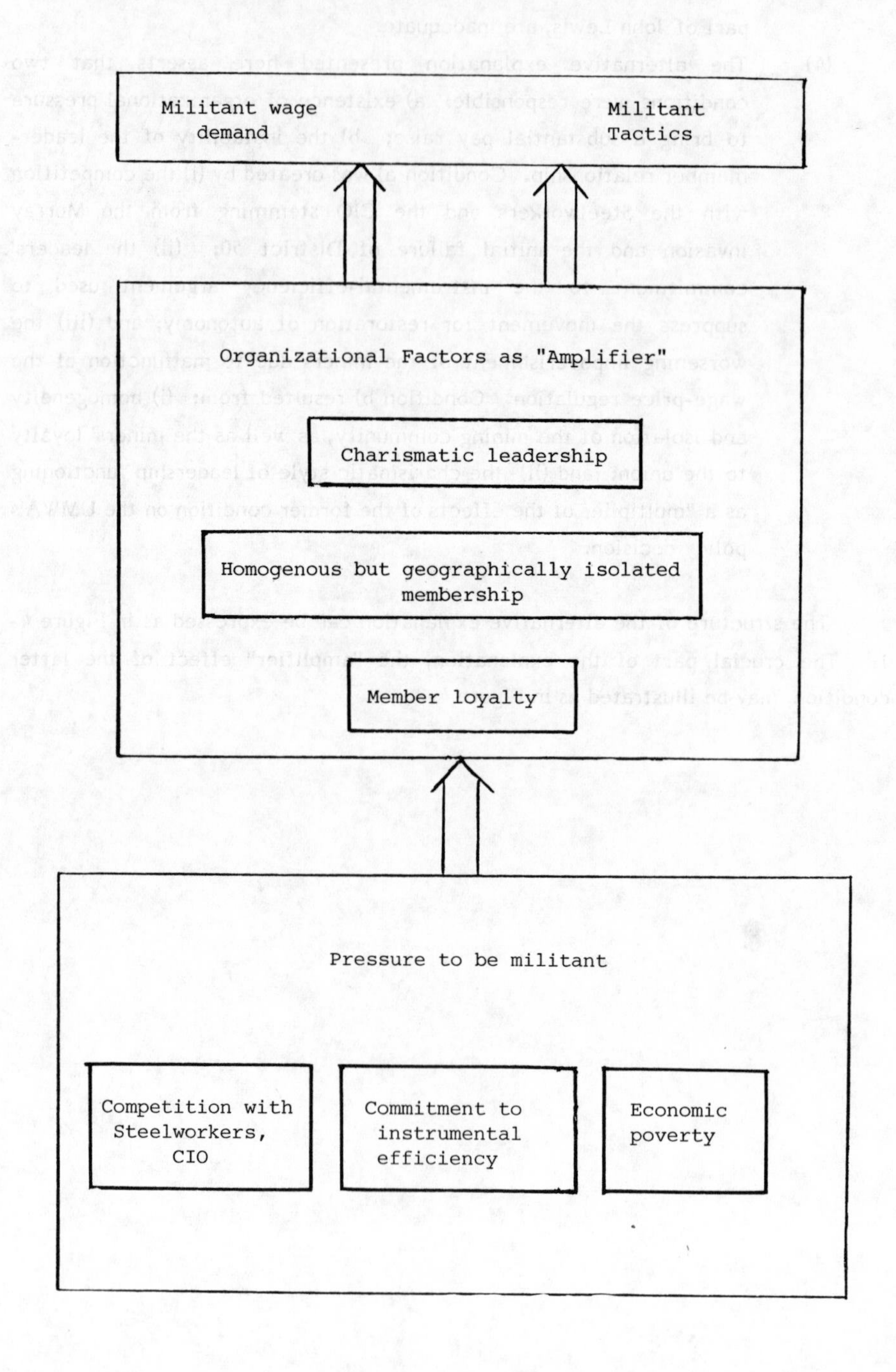

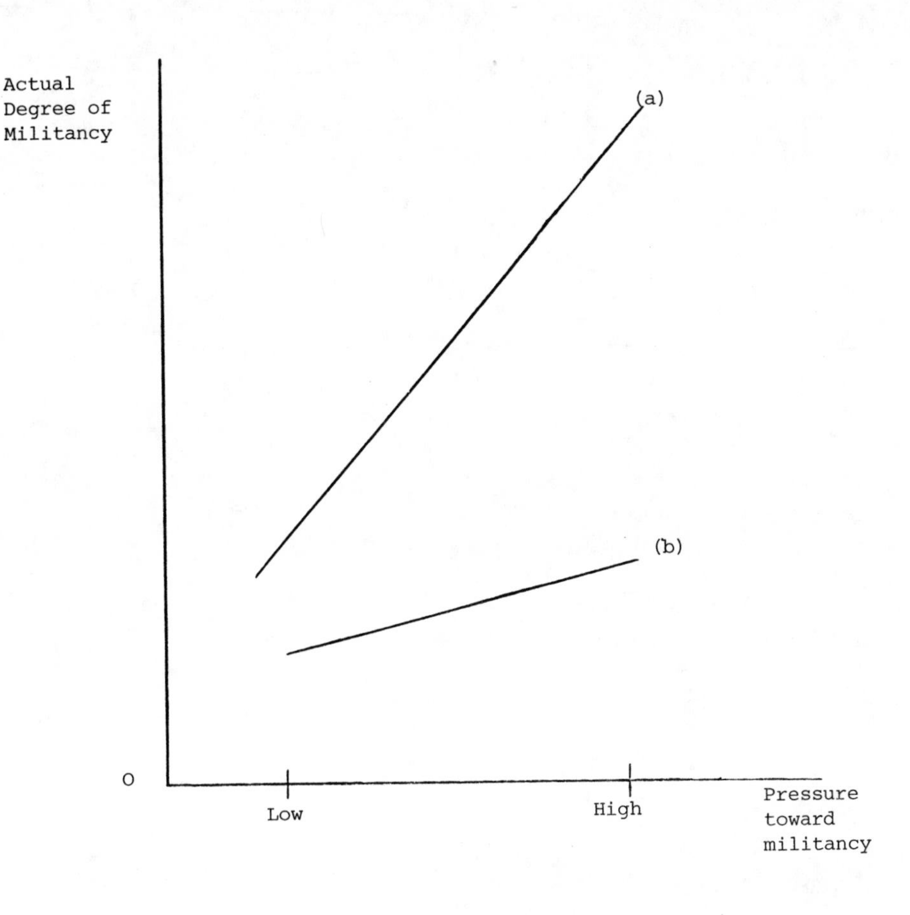

Figure 4 - 2

Charismatic Authority and Loyalty of Membership as "Amplifier"

(a) - Union with charismatic leader and very loyal members

(b) - Union with other conditions

CHAPTER V

THE UMWA IN 1950-1959: LOW MILITANCY AND A CHARISMATIC LEADER

1. Historical Prologue: Developments after 1943

The remainder of the 1940's was a near repetition of the 1943 drama. Through a series of fierce battles against many quarters of society, the UMWA continued to show extreme militancy, brilliant tactics and solid discipline. As is demonstrated in Table 5-1, the union achieved remarkable gains.

The most significant development here is the establishment of the company-financed Welfare and Retirement Fund. This was the first union fund in American labor history and had great impact not only on the miners' lives but also on the whole American union movement. The UMW fund soon began providing miners with retirement pensions and free medical care, which substantially reduced the insecurity of their lives.

2. Union Behavior in the 1950's

After the militancy of the 1940's, union policy shifted drastically during the 1950's. This section describes the new policy in three areas: collective bargaining, organizing activities, and business activities.

a. Collective Bargaining: from National Menace to Labor Statesman

On September 21, 1950, northern soft coal operators (producing 153 million tons annually, or about 34% of the industry's total output) organized the "Bituminous Coal Operators Association" in order to present a united front in negotiations with the UMWA.(1) Henry Moses, president of H.C. Frick Coke Company, was elected president. On January 17, 1951, Lewis suddenly summoned the 200-member Policy Committee, the union's contract ratification body, and the following day signed a new pact with Moses.(2) This move astonished contemporary observers because it differed markedly from previous industry practice. Since 1919, when Lewis took office, the parleys had always started with bitter exchanges of accusations before the flash bulbs and microphones of the press, followed by several months of turmoil and strikes. By September of 1951, however, Moses and Lewis had already been negotiating secretly for a month before they announced the agreement.

The second new development was that Joseph E. Moody, president of the Southern Coal Producers Association, a traditionally anti-union group, and Harry Treadwell, president of the Illinois Coal Operators' Association, joined the northern operators for the first time in the industry's history and signed the pact

Table 5 – 1

Achievement of UMW in the 1940's

Item	1940	1948
Hourly pay	85.7¢ (North) 80¢ (South)	$1.63
Travel-time pay	none	one hour a day
Vacation pay	none	$100 a year
Lunch time pay	none	81.5¢ a day
Extra night pay	none	4¢ an hour, 2nd shift 6¢ an hour, 3rd shift
Welfare Fund	none	$50 million a year
Tools and equipment	supplied by miners	supplied by companies
Safety rules	state basis	federal rule enforced by joint committee
State compensation for mine accident	not mandatory in some states	applied to all states
Pay differential	5.7¢ an hour lower in South	same rates
Take-home pay	$30 for 35 hours, North $28 for 35 hours, South	$84.82 for 48 hours

Source: Alinsky, 1949, p. 355

pact simultaneously. In place of the customary accusations, Lewis and spokesmen for the industry praised each other's integrity and intelligence and stressed the peaceful nature of the bargaining. This dramatic change in collective bargaining procedure was the first indication of a drastic change in union behavior which was to follow..

On July 22, 1952, Lewis gave the required 60 days' notice of the union's desire to terminate the contract.(3) The negotiations "seemed" to have begun, but nobody was certain. After one puzzling month, the New York Times said,

> Mr. Lewis had been preparing carefully for these negotiations, which he doesn't even admit are going on ...He has given no public inkling of his demands or objectives, and even the operators are not sure of what he is after. (4)

One month later, on September 20, for the first time since the termination notice two months before, Lewis and Moses came back to the public scene with a contract agreement. The new contract, effective until October 1, 1953, raised wages by $1.90 a day and royalty payment to the Welfare Fund by 10¢ a ton.(5)

The new quiet posture of the union in the bargaining process revealed itself again in 1953, 1956 and 1958. During these negotiations, Lewis and the operators agreed to waive the termination notice required in the last contract in order to secure secrecy.(6) This arrangement is good evidence of the constant communication between operators and union officials with or without specific issues. Business Week reported:

> The two men who do the bargaining, Lewis and Fox,(7) also carry on the day-to-day policing of the agreement ...
>
> It is a short walk for the tall, heavy set coal operator from his headquarters to the Sheraton-Carlton Hotel where Lewis lunches almost daily. At both places they can and have talked of conditions in the industry and of contracts.
>
> Not many years ago, this would have been impossible. Lewis was not then in the shadow of other labor leaders; whatever he did was in glaring public light. Now, while he is still recognized on the street, he can, and does, go about his business quietly ...
>
> In such an atmosphere, Lewis and Fox have an opportunity to talk contracts any time they want changes. (8)

In addition to these procedural changes, subtle changes were taking place inside the union in the way it handled collective bargaining. There was a marked decline in the importance attached to collective bargaining as the union put more effort into political and business activities. Table 5-2 indicates this change.

A second change was the decreasing involvement of Lewis in actual negotiations. Although Lewis and Moses (Fox after 1956) constantly met with one another, with or without agenda, in order to exchange information and opinions, actual contract negotiations were increasingly handled by Vice-President Kennedy. By 1956 Kennedy conducted virtually all the negotiations under the "guidance" of John Lewis.[9]

A third characteristic was the union's stress on mechanization and high wages at the cost of employment.

> I think that modernization of coal-gathering techniques is important for humanitarian reasons as well as for economic reasons ... Mechanization in the United States has robbed the industry of some of its elements of slave toil ... If an automatic or semi-automatic machine can be harnessed to use energy and do the work of human hands, I think it's a justifiable enterprise that makes its own contribution to the standards and the culture and the happiness of the population.
>
> If, in addition, the utilization of energy and machines, new formulas, improved techniques, can be made to become an economic advantage in lowering cost of production, in permitting a larger margin between the cost of production and sales realization, in which the investor, the worker and the public as a consumer can participate, then it, indeed, becomes not merely an opportunity but an obligation.
>
> That's been the premise upon which the United Mine Workers of America has stood in the last three or four decades in this country; that, in return for encouraging modernization, the utilization of machinery and power in the mines and modern techniques, the union would insist on a clear participation in the advantage of the machine and the improved techniques. (10)

As a result, unemployment rose very rapidly. But as his following remark shows, this was also a part of Lewis' choice.

> We decided it is better to have half a million men working in the industry at good wages and high standards of living than it is to have a million working in the industry in poverty and degradation. (11)

b. <u>Organizing Campaign</u>

Throughout Kentucky and Tennessee there were numerous small non-union mines which together produced a substantial quantity of coal for the national

Table 5 - 2

Proportions of pages devoted to contract negotiations in the Officers' Joint Reports, 1942-1960

1942	61%
1944	75%
1946	82%
1948	59%
1952	52%
1956	41%
1960	17%

Source: Constructed from the Officers' Reports to the International Convention

market. In the South, the TVA, now in an era of postwar expansion, had a heavy demand for coal which was to be filled by competitive bidding. Non-union mines, which paid substantially lower wages and had no welfare provisions, secured many of these contracts. In addition, many of the small mines in the North, unable to install expensive machinery to compete with large mechanized coal companies in the North or small non-union mines in the South, began to cut union wages illegally.(12) It was apparent that the union could not long tolerate such a threat to its wage scale. Additional pressure came from the Bituminous Coal Operators Association. Moses criticized Lewis:

> Today, the cheap coal fringes are again growing in on the hard core of the industry ... I ask you then, whether or not this indicates that our self-styled partners have been doing a poor job since 1947.
>
> Mr. Lewis, if this be true, and you are skimping your job, it bodes no good for the welfare of your well-disciplined and orderly union, and if continued to its ultimate possibility, can only bring that unwelcome guest, chaos, back to our industry ... (13)

In October of 1950, the International Executive Board set up an international committee to "promote an intensified and integrated organizing campaign in the non-union areas".(14) The new committee started vigorous organizing campaigns in many places: the major ones included Meadow Creek in central Kentucky; Hopkins County, Kentucky; the western tip of Virginia; and Middleboro County in eastern Kentucky. Since all the campaigns followed a very similar pattern, that of Middleboro, the largest one, will be described in detail.

In eastern Kentucky and Tennessee, by March, 1959, there were as many as 176 holdouts against the 1958 industry package.(15) In addition, the rapid expansion of the TVA and easy entry into the coal industry brought in numbers of new entrepreneurs who opened non-union mines.(16)

The UMWA's intensive effort against this massive recalcitrance began as early as 1954. Clifford Osborne, who had recently expanded his mining operation in Kentucky and Tennessee by securing a large contract with the TVA, was chosen as the first target of the union's campaign. Although Osborne successfully obtained an injunction against the union's drive in Kentucky, a large number of union organizers moved to his mines in Tennessee and shut down the production by picketing and threatening the truck drivers. Some mine owners were severely beaten.(17)

A bigger storm came in 1959. The major issue was the 1958 contract amendment. It included a $2.00-a-day wage increase, which was prohibitively high for many southern operators, and a "protective clause" which forbade unionized companies to buy, sell or handle coal produced under non-union conditions.[18] A large number of operators in Kentucky and Tennessee decided not to sign the contract. On March 16, rifles were fired at the operators of a truck coal mine, nearly killing two of them.[19] The next day, four strikebreakers in neighboring Letcher County were thrown to the ground and stoned, thereby suffering neck fractures. Union violence spread to Virginia on March 23, when non-union mines near the Kentucky border were dynamited.[21] On March 31 a twenty-car convoy of UMW members drove up to a small non-union mine on Stinking Creek in Knox County, Kentucky, chased a non-union mine operator up a hill near the mine and shot him to death.[22] A few days later, a truck driver who tried to ship out coal in defiance of the union was also shot and killed. On April 17, after the murder of a coal tipple guard, Governor A. B. Chandler mobilized two National Guard battallions,[23] but the union's motorcades of 100 cars, armed with innumerable shotguns, rifles and dynamite, continued to roam unchallenged.

The violence subsided somewhat in the fall of 1959, and finally came to an end on November 9, when the Joint Industry Contract Committee made up of three international union representatives and three management representatives decided to abandon their efforts to enforce the protective clause of the contract. Both sides agreed that the legality of the ban had been thrown into doubt by a new restriction on secondary boycotts in the new labor reform law (the Landrum-Griffin Act) passed by Congress in the last session of 1959.[24]

As Finley reported,[25] some sympathetic observers interpreted it as a spontaneous revolt of the miners against the operators' suppressive effort to destroy the union. There is plenty of evidence, however, that all the plans, decisions, orders and funds for the campaigns came from the international union. In the first place, a large number of those campaigns at different times and places were conducted in exactly the same well-calculated manner. The use of motor convoys, hired professional gunmen, and street blockades accomplished with practiced precision would require careful planning and direction. UMW representatives on the international payroll were observed to have organized the convoys. Secondly, evidence shows massive financial assistance from the international to the respective districts engaged in the struggle. More than a million dollars were deposited by the international with banks in Harlan County before the fight in 1959.[26] During the turmoil at Middleboro, the Federal Court found that "loans by the International Union to District 19 reached the high monthly total of $425,000 in April of 1959", and "a total for the calendar year 1959 of $2,471,000".[27] More direct evidence is that the mediation meeting of eastern Kentucky coal operators and the United Mine Workers, officials arranged by Governor A. B. Chandler, did not work out. This was because nothing could be decided without the international union's consent; they could only agree to arrange further talks with international officials in Washington.[28] Randolph's testimony at the U. S. Court of Appeals is further direct evidence of the international's involvement:

> ... Prater (a union organizer) had told Randolph that he didn't sign a contract, he couldn't operate - that they would shut him down. Randolph testified: "I asked him, Mr. Prater, what legal right he had to shut us down, and he said he didn't need a legal right, he took his orders from Washington. And I said, 'How will you close me down?' and he said, 'By any means that is required.'" (29)

c. From Labor's Spearhead to Entrepreneur

The third important peculiarity of union behavior in the 1950's was its expansion into business activities. As large sums of money poured into the Welfare and Retirement Fund and the union treasury in 1948, its use became the leaders' concern. The union began making inquiries and, by early 1949,[30] took over the National Bank of Washington.[31] The rank-and-file were completely uninformed of this purchase, as neither the Officers' Reports to the 1948 and 1952 International Conventions nor the United Mine Workers Journal, the union's sole official bi-weekly publication, gave any indication of it. Instead the word went out to local unions not to deposit their money at the bank.[32]

After the takeover, Lewis transferred all the Welfare and Retirement Fund reserves, formally kept in other banks in Washington, to the National Bank, which expanded rapidly. By April of 1950 the UMW had $36 million in deposits in a checking account in the bank, drawing no interest.[33] Using UMWA money, this bank - then thirteenth largest in Washington - began to expand by absorbing the Liberty National Bank, Hamilton National Bank and the Anacostia Bank, finally becoming the second largest bank in the nation's capital.[34]

As the management of this gigantic financial asset required expert advice,

Cyrus S. Eaton, one of the nation's wealthiest men and an old friend of Lewis, began serving the union behind the scenes.[35]

In 1949, when violence failed to organize the West Kentucky Coal Company, one of the largest in the Kentucky-Tennessee area, the union proceeded to purchase it. Indisputable records show that a substantial amount of UMWA funds were loaned to Cyrus Eaton, or to holding companies or investment companies affiliated with him,[36] and to Barum Colton, president of the National Bank of Washington, both of whom then purchased stock in the West Kentucky Coal Company.[37] The loans to Eaton and Colton were made on unusual terms. Eaton's note stated:

> At any time prior to or at the maturity of this note, I shall have the right to tender to the payee the security pledged as collateral for the note in full satisfaction of any amounts due on acount of principal or interest. If such tender is made, I shall have no further interest in the collateral over the amount due under this note, and I shall have no liability for any deficiency in the value of the collateral below the amount due under this note (38)

Thus, if the West Kentucky stock rose in value, the borrower could turn it over to satisfy the note in full, but the union could not gain. If it went down in value, the borrower would not suffer any loss, but the union would. In addition, some of their notes provided that an interest would be one-half the dividends paid under the collateral. In other notes, interest was provided for but with the understanding that no interest would be paid if there were no dividends.[39] In 1952, the UMW acquired 480,400 shares of common stock in West Kentucky Coal Company out of a total of 857,264 by this means.[40] In 1953, Eaton became Chairman of the Board with his associates controlling the Board,[41] and immediately signed the National Bituminous Coal Wage Agreement. In 1955, Nashville Coal Company, one of the largest coal mining and sales firms, became the next target. Although the company was on the verge of collapse at the time of the sale, for a property assessed at $7 million Eaton is estimated to have paid as much as $30 million,[42] without ever reading the books of the company. After this unbelievable business transaction, West Kentucky Coal Company absorbed Nashville Company and became one of the largest in the South.[43] By the end of 1958, loans and investments of the UMW in West Kentucky Coal Company reached as much as $25,456,156.[44]

The purpose of these business operations should be carefully analyzed. The union's official explanation was that they were mere financial investments and were not intended to influence policy decisions of the West Kentucky Coal Company. Lewis testified in 1961:

> The trustees of the United Mine Workers are satisfied with the investment in West Kentucky Coal Company and quite content in the belief that in the end, it will prove to be immensely profitable to the United Mine Workers of America in a financial sense: a wise investment of the fund. (45)

However, this argument conflicts with the union's actual behavior. If its motivation had been that of economic portfolio selection, why did it lend more than $30,000,000, with interest of only one half of the dividends paid on the collateral and any risk being completely covered by the union, when apparently profits would have been almost double if the stock had been purchased directly? The union also paid $30 million to buy a collapsing $7 million company, and $17 million to other operators without even studying risk and profitability. In addition, if the union had been interested only in economic profit and not in influencing company policy, it would be very difficult to explain why the vehemently anti-union West Kentucky Coal Company signed the contract so easily.

The more plausible inference would be that the union's business activities were an extension of its organizing drive. When violence did not bring tangible results, the UMW bought a few of the largest holdouts in the area and made them sign the contract by using the power vested in the stock holders. This motivation is confirmed by Secretary-Treasurer John Owen's address to the 1964 International Convention.

> There had been paid out over $90 million in union wages to those men down there, and there had been paid into the Welfare and Retirement Fund $24,496,483.54. And we sold stock at a loss on my books for $8 million loss ... But we got it back in the $24 million paid into the Welfare and Retirement Fund. We got it back in human freedom that has been established. We got it back in wages paid to the men in that industry down there, and we got it back in the protection of the wages they were destroying in all other mines in America. (46)

Furthermore, the union-owned coal companies began lowering their prices in TVA bids in an effort to eliminate other small non-union mines. Although it is very difficult to establish such an intention behind the pricing policy, Table 5-3 clearly shows that the bidding prices of West Kentucky and Nashville Coal declined drastically relative to other bids after 1956, when Nashville Coal was purchased and merged with West Kentucky.

In summary, union behavior in the 1950's can be characterized as showing:
1) extremely peaceful non-strike policy in collective bargaining;
2) violent organizing campaign in the unorganized South;
3) enormous business operations to counter the threat of non-union mines in the South.

3. Analysis

a. The Declining Industry

The 1950's comprised a decade of general decline and depression for the coal industry, the major threat coming from severe competition by alternative energy sources, most importantly oil. Purchasers preferred oil for its cheaper price and more stable supply.[47] In particular, the heating of private homes, which was highly sensitive to price and to stability of supply, went over almost entirely from anthracite coal to oil.

Coal production, which peaked at 631 million tons in 1947, went as low as 392 million tons in 1954 (Fig. 5-1). The average value of coal per ton, which had been monotonically increasing until the 1940's, stopped growing, even showing a small decline in the 1950's (Fig. 5-2). In 1942, there were 461,991 miners employed; by 1960 this figure had dropped sharply to 169,400 (Fig. 5-3). In addition to this steep decline in employment, the average number of days worked also fell (Fig. 5-4).

It was apparent that militant, prolonged strikes to obtain high wages were suicidal in such a depressed industry. As early as 1948, when a slight decline in coal output was observed, Lewis was already aware of the trend and reportedly said that he was going to "do something about it".[48] What he did was very drastic.

The first important problem was stabilization of labor-management relations. Prolonged strikes could not be tolerated when one of the competitive disadvantages of coal was unreliability of supply. The operators and the union had to meet each other constantly to discuss the state of the industry, and to plan a joint policy of ceaseless production and increasing demand. Union leaders found that disorganization among the operators was the major bottleneck in the arrangement,[49] and

Table 5 - 3

Prices Proposed by West Kentucky and Nashville Coal in TVA Bidding, 1954-1959

Date of Bid	Requisition No.	per Ton	to Other Bids
9-15-54	21-825509	$2.90	13th from lowest
9-15-54	21-825509	$2.67	17th from lowest
5-19-54	16-831970P	$2.32	others lower
9-23-55	364	$2.35	13th from lowest
9-23-55	364	$2.63	13th from lowest
9-23-55	364	$2.31	others lower
9-23-55	364	$2.72	22nd from lowest
9-23-55	364	$2.49	22nd from lowest
7-12-56	11180	$2.80	6th from lowest
7-12-56	11180	$2.71	16th from lowest
11-16-56	16240	$3.21	low bid
10-24-57	23923	$2.68	3rd from lowest
10-24-57	23923	$2.54	4th from lowest
10-24-57	23923	$2.75	3rd from lowest
10-24-57	23923	$2.84	far low
5-20-58	99095	$3.95	5th from lowest
5-5-59	25	$2.66	2nd from lowest

Source: Ramsey vs. United Mine Workers of America, USDC (E.D. Tenn.), Labor Relations Reference Manual, Vol. 64, p. 2523.

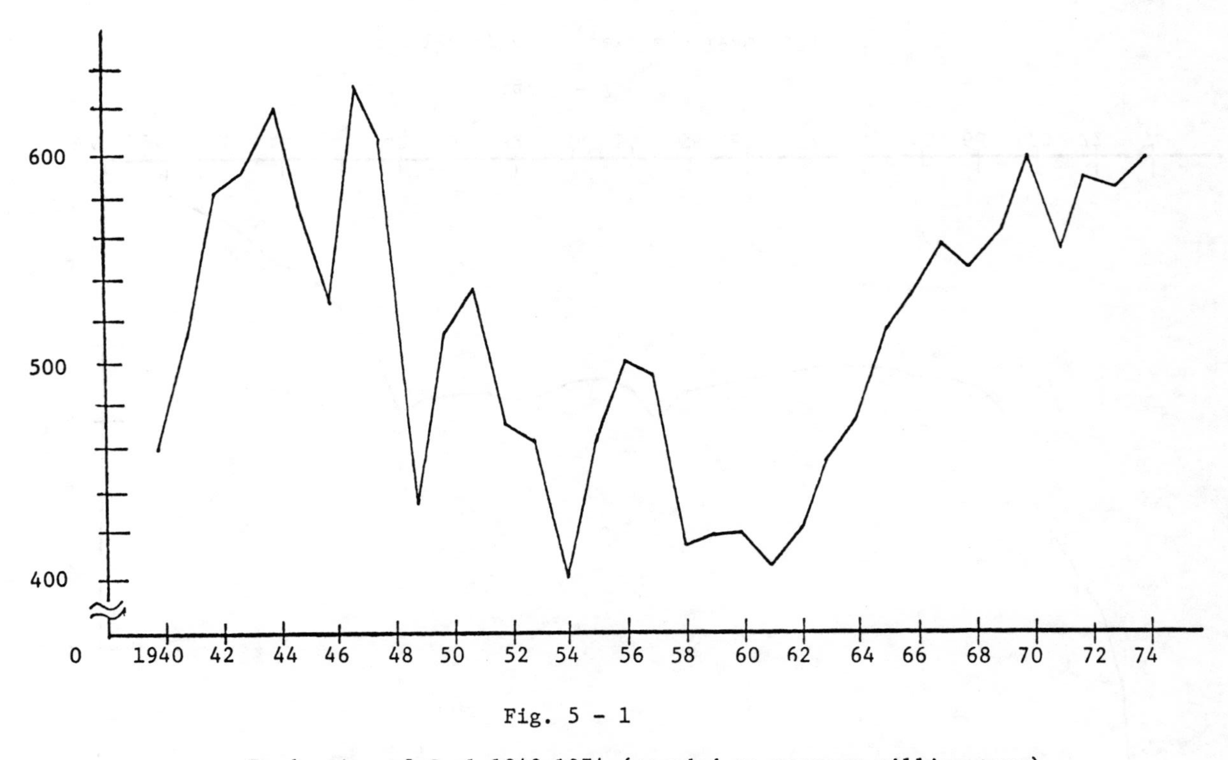

Fig. 5 - 1

Production of Coal 1940-1974 (rounded to nearest million tons)

Source: The National Coal Association, <u>Bituminous Coal Data 1975</u>

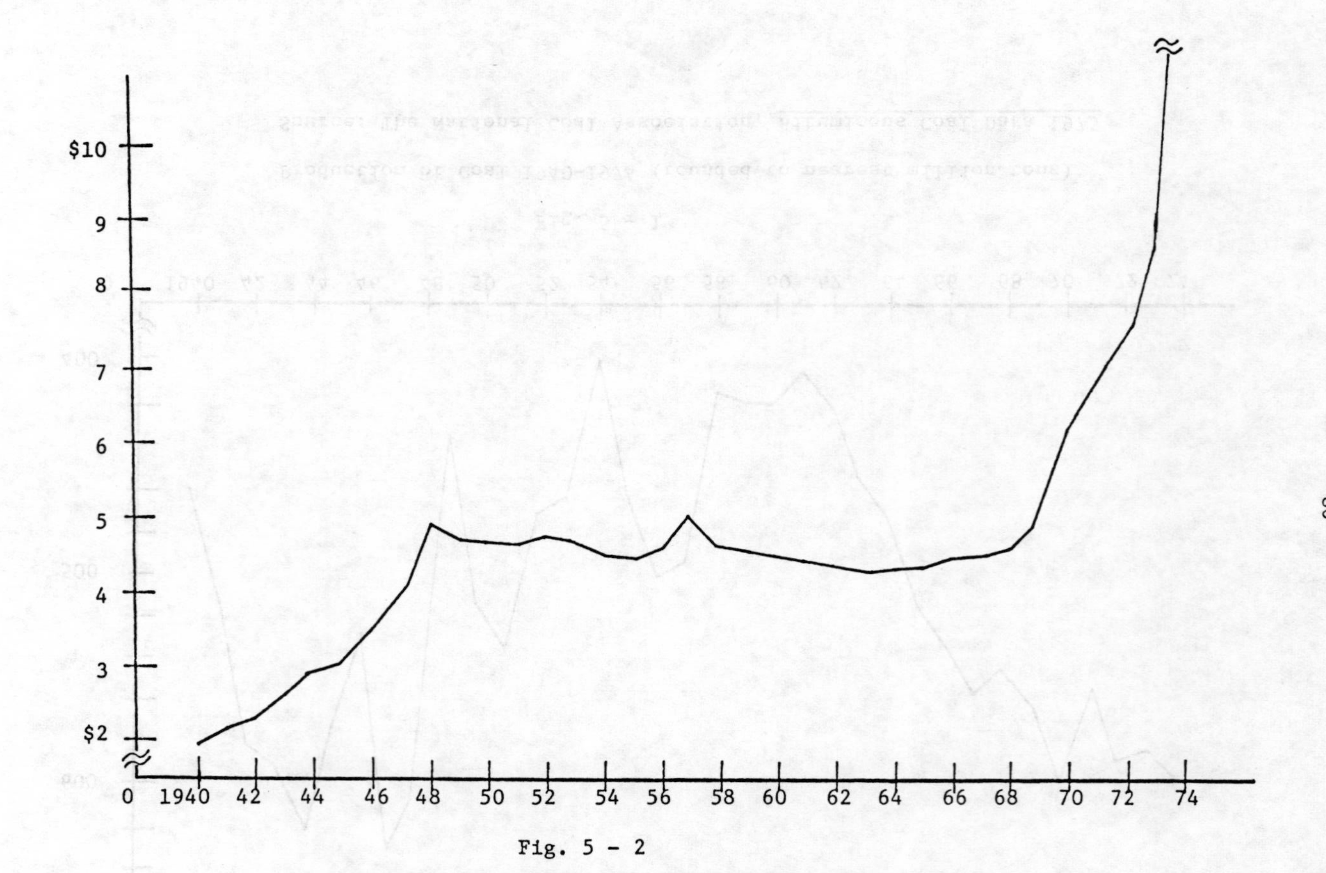

Fig. 5 - 2

Average Value of Coal per Ton 1940-1974

Source: The National Coal Association, Bituminous Coal Data 1975

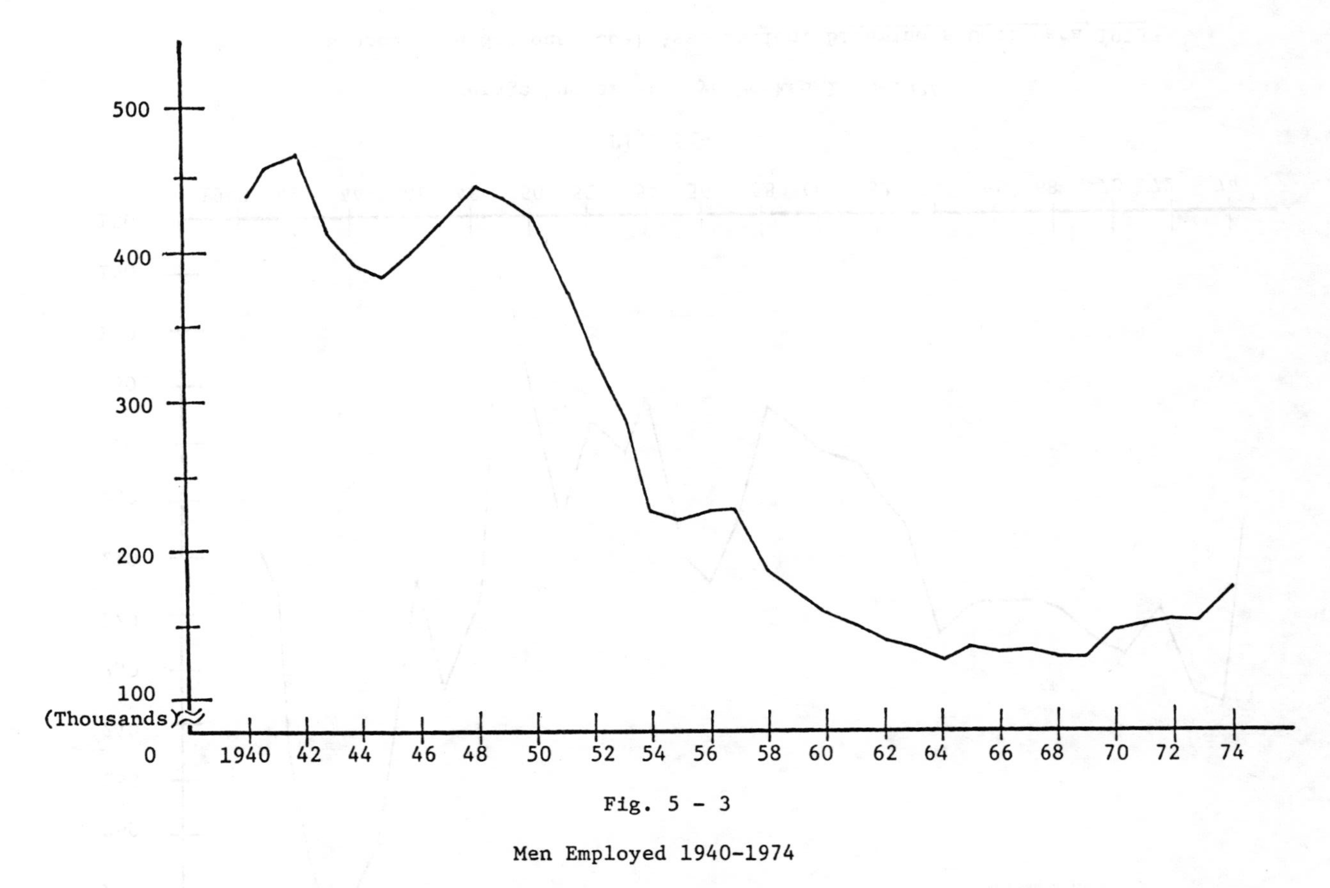

Fig. 5 - 3

Men Employed 1940-1974

Source: Tha National Coal Association, Bituminous Coal Data 1975

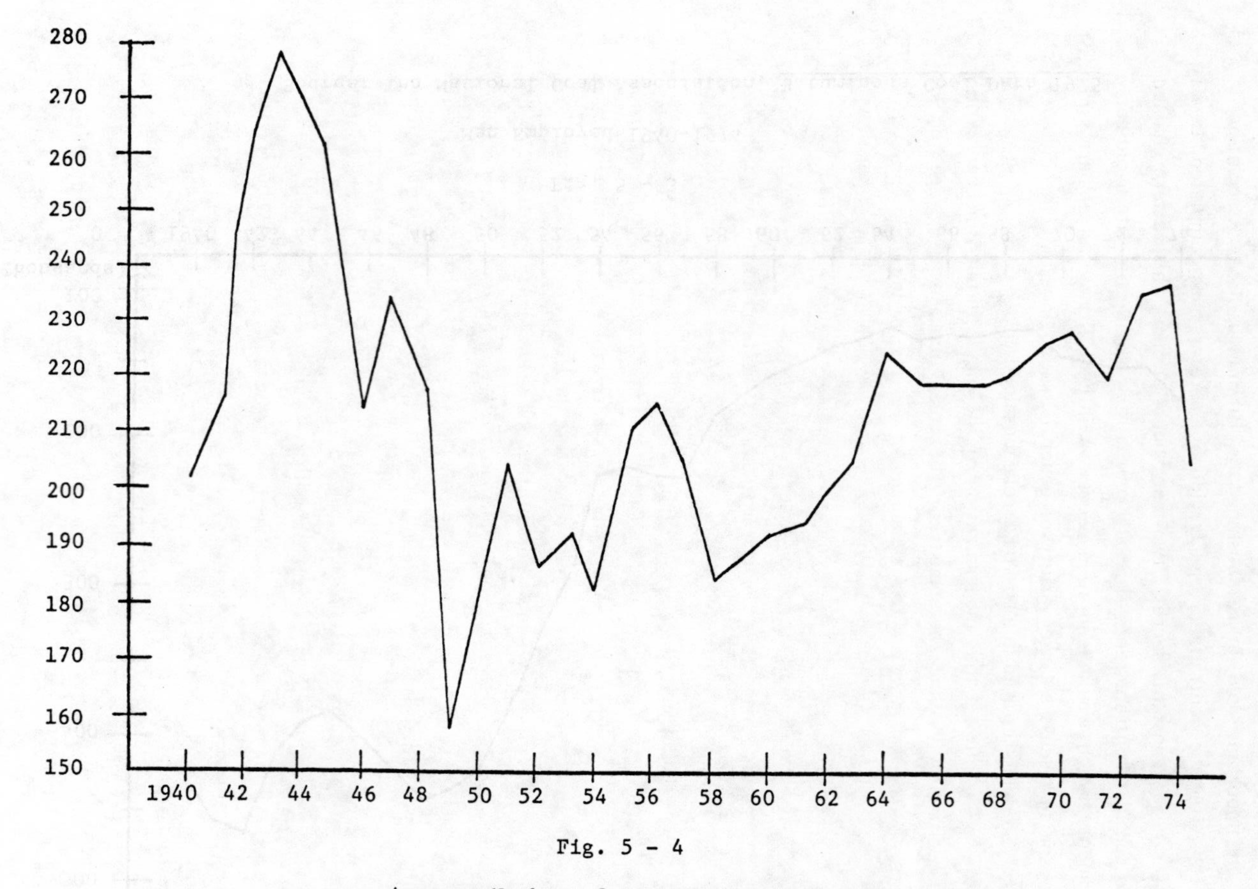

Fig. 5 - 4

Average Number of Days Worked 1940-1974

Source: The National Coal Association, Bituminous Coal Data 1975

played an important role in establishing the Bituminous Coal Association in 1950.[50] After the centralized organization of operators was completed, Lewis and Moses began constant, secret, "two-man" negotiations. This pattern enabled them to consider contract renewal at any mutually agreeable time, to avoid early commitments which would lead to unnecessary inflexibility or an embarrassing retreat, and to discuss a large variety of general issues concerning the industry. Ultimately the plan resulted in a no-strike relationship.

The union believed that modernization of the mines through mechanization would be crucial in saving the industry. The union imposed high wages on all operators, thus pressuring them to mechanize. It was the union's philosophy that a number of mines too small to mechanize should go out of business. In 1950, Fortune labelled Lewis "the best salesman the machinery industry ever had".

The existence of non-union dog-hole mines in the South, however, could seriously threaten the Moses-Lewis program of uniform high wage, heavy mechanization and continuous production. The UMW embarked on a costly, large-scale organizing campaign across the southern coal fields.

The union's great concern for the welfare of the industry and its collusion with the operators were reflected in its business activities. In December of 1951, Lewis suggested that operators join him in boosting the export of coal. He initiated a joint committee to survey export possibilities and made Moody (president of the Southern Coal Producers' Association) chairman of the committee. In June of 1956, as a result of the committee report, coal operators, mostly from the South, the union and some railroad companies announced a plan to form a new $50 million shipping company. The union contributed one-third of the initial financial investment, and Lewis himself sat on the board.[51]

Thus, the peculiarities of UMWA policy in the 1950's resulted from its concern and willingness to take an active role in the declining coal industry, and had very little to do with intra-organizational factors.

Despite this negative conclusion, our organizational perspective can still be rewarding. The first serious question concerns the theory developed in the last chapter. The non-militant behavior of the UMW in the 1950's, with the same leader and members as in the 1940's, seems to serve as a counter-example to the theory. In order to examine the seeming contradiction between the theory and the observation just made, it will be necessary to search for conditional variables which determine the range of validity of the theory. The second and more general organizational question is: How could such a drastic policy change be implemented so smoothly without raising any turmoil within the organization? What characteristics of the UMWA organization enabled top leaders to make substantive decisions without running into organizational constraints?

b. The Previous Theory Reconsidered

(i) Lewis' Charismatic Leadership

Lewis' remarkable achievement of the 1940's undoubtedly enhanced his power and prestige in the organization. Wage increases in the 1940's made miners the highest paid blue-collar workers in the United States. The ground-breaking company-financed Welfare and retirement Fund constituted considerable relief for the miners. They no longer had to worry about starvation after retirement. Disabled miners, once condemned to the life of human wrecks whose only hope was that death would take them quickly, could now look for rehabilitation and a new life. With these remarkable improvements in their welfare, the miners' allegiance to Lewis began to be based not only on their expectation that he would be able to bring greater gains than anyone else could, but also on their grattitude and affection towards him. One unemployed miner praised him in poetry:

We're thankful for the one who gave
His life and wealth to stave
The woes of all the mining slaves
Once burdened down with care.

Who fought but for a righteous cause,
For life with liberty,
For bread and butter without clause
For you, yes, even me.

The pension for dear Mom and Dad,
The welfare for the ill,
To share with others what he had.
"His gavel speaks, though still. (52)

A miner's widow expressed her affection:

Last night I said
A prayer for you,
So brave and true;
Doing things for others
As you always do;
Marching ever onward
Without a sign of fear;

Fighting, ever fighting,
For our welfare,
But all that I can do for you,
I'll do it with a prayer. (53)

This allegiance, based on gratitude and affection toward Lewis, can be found in various other places. For example, it became fashionable among miners to name their sons after John Lewis.

> We named him after one of the greatest men on earth. We have hope for him that he will grow to a man such as the man he was named after. (54)

Every miner had a picture of Lewis in his living room.(55) The words of the first pensioner, "God bless the day when John Lewis was born," spread to every coal field. At every convention tere were resolutions asking to establish John L. Lewis Day, or to make him permanent president until his death.(56)

This subtle change in the source of charismatic legitimacy had an important stabilizing effect. It was argued in the previous chapter that a charismatic leader is inherently unstable because of the necessity constantly to provide remarkable successes in order to sustain belief in his charisma. However, the source of Lewis' legitimacy as leader in the 1950's changed from future expectation to gratitude for past achievement. This reduced the pressure on him to supply constant proof of his charismatic ability, and thus stabilized the leader-member relationship.

One may argue that past successes do not have significant stabilizing effect, because such achievements would soon become an element of everyday life and lose their "supernatural" character.(57) Weber's emphasis on charismatic instability is based on this hypothesis. Although this argument may be generally true, it needs some qualification.

(ii) Stabilized Charismatic Authority

First, the effect of past success needs to be more carefully analyzed. In doing so, economists' differentiation of "flow" and "stock" concepts is useful.(58) "Flows" refer to variables which are consumed or used in a single period without any accumulative effect for the future. "Stocks" refer to those variables whose effect is long-lasting and cumulative once they are purchased. For example, once one purchases a house ("stock"), one can enjoy its benefits for the rest of one's life without repeating the same effort or expense, while if one purchases excellent food ("flow"), one still has to make the same effort and pay the same price to maintain the same standard. Figure 5-5 illustrates these concepts.

Past successes of a leader can also be differentiated as to "flow type" success and "stock type" success. Examples of the flow-type achievements are an accurate prophecy by a prophet, a world championship won by a baseball manager, etc. To secure the same benefit that the followers have once enjoyed, the prophet or the team manager must start their efforts all over again from the beginning. On the other hand, the building of an independent nation by such a leader as Cavour, Tito, Nehru etc. is an example of the stock-type achievement, which gives the benefit of success continuously once it is achieved. With respect to the stability of charismatic leaders, past successes of the stock type are much superior to those of the flow type.

John Lewis' achievement of wage gains and the Welfare Fund in the 1940's are clear examples of "stock" type success. Once the wage was settled at a high level in the contract, the benefit of the successs appeared in each miner's paycheck twice every month for the contract period. The next contract would have to be negotiated with the current wage level as the minimum base. The Welfare Fund, once established, brought benefits every time a miner was in trouble.

One may still argue, however, that even the higher standard of living attained by the "stock" type success will soon be taken for granted and lose its stabilizing effect. Our second observation here concerns the peculiar character of the Welfare Fund. Benefits from the Fund, by definition, were distributed when miners felt it was most needed. Any given amount of aid arouses much more appreciation and enthusiasm in times of hardship. Miners' gratitude can be seen in their words:

> Received the check from the Welfare Fund and only God, my wife and I know how welcome and how much we need that money. Before that we tried to get by on $20 a week with three small children, the two infants. (59)

In addition, unlike benefits which were provided regularly every month, free medical care and hospitalization benefits were offered <u>only irregularly</u> at a time of

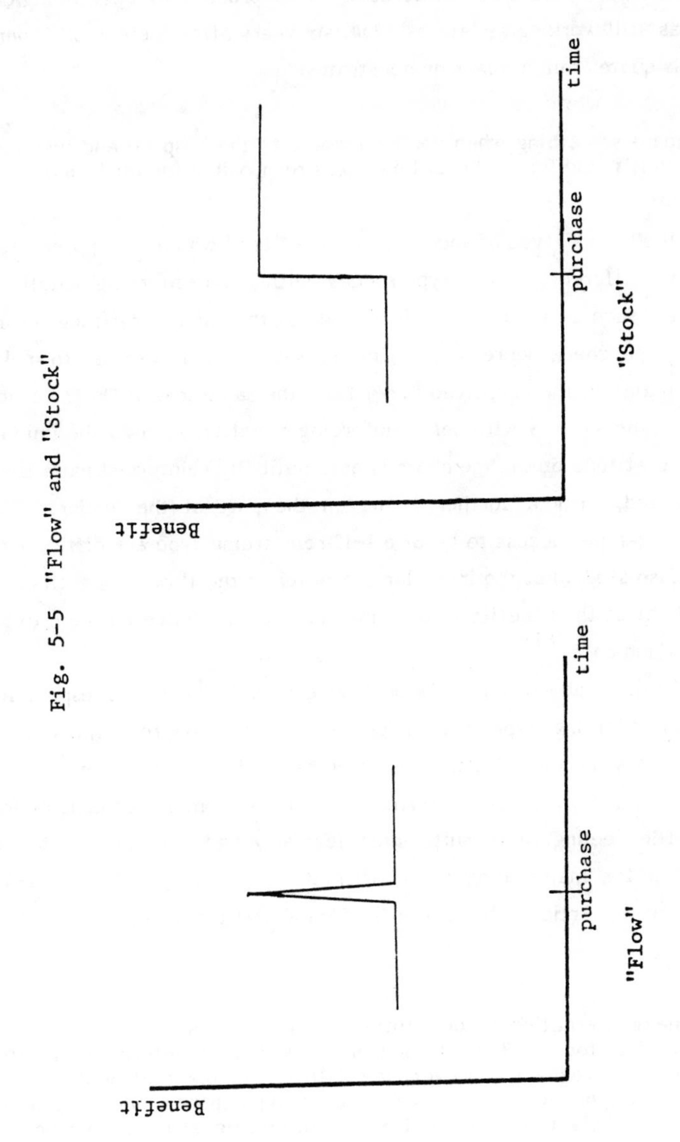

Fig. 5-5 "Flow" and "Stock"

unexpected accident or disease. Such benefits were thus less likely to become an element of everyday life. Every time they received free medical care from a hospital, where a huge picture of John Lewis dominated the entrance lobby, the miners' appreciation of Lewis was reinforced. This process of "psychological reinforcement" was still working as late as 1954, six years after the establishment of the Fund, as this quote from a miner demonstrates:

> It means something when you have to go to the hospital and just sign your name and it's paid for. John L. Lewis was responsible for this! (60)

We can call the "stock" type of success, the benefits of which are appreciated anew every time it is offered, a "stock-type success with self-reinforcing benefits". A stock-type success such as a wage raise is not one of this kind. Gratitude for an increased bimonthly paycheck decreases as time passes, and a leader has to make further efforts to maintain the perceived benefits at the same level. On the other hand, with a stock-type success with self-reinforcing benefits, such as the union's Welfare Fund, the gratitude of the members is automatically reinforced each time the benefit is utilized, without further effort on the part of the leader. The conditions for a stock-type success to be of a self-reinforcing type are difficult to specify from one case study, but the irregular character of the flow of benefits and the unfavorable plight of the benefittee when the benefits are delivered seem to be responsible in this Fund case.(61)

Thus Lewis, with an abundance of "stock" successes in the 1940's, especially those of the self-reinforcing type, was much less pressed to prove himself to maintain his legitimacy in the 1950's. This reduction of pressure is evident in Lewis' decreasing concern with those informal as well as formal mechanisms for gauging rank-and-file feeling, a pursuit which formerly had been so crucial in setting proper goals for maintaining his charismatic legitimacy. At the 1948 International Convention, Article XII, Section 1 of the Constitution was amended to read:

> The next International Constitutional Convention shall be held on the first Tuesday of October, 1952, at such place as may be determined by the 1948 Convention; provided, however, the date and/or place of holding such convention may, upon good cause, be advanced, postponed or changed by resolution to that effect duly adopted by the International Executive Board. (62)

This amendment is significant in two senses: First, the Convention used to be held biennially; henceforth it was to be called quadrennially. Second, the International Officers were entitled to postpone the convention as long as they desired. Since the international conventions were one of the few institutions in the UMWA through which the rank-and-file could influence the international's decisions, this amendment shows a sharp decline of interest on the part of the leaders in listening to members. More evidence is provided by the new bargaining procedure. In the 1940's, demands were formulated through frequent exchange of telegrams, local resolutions to the Scale Committee, and deliberations of the Policy Committee, which consisted of 200 delegates from the districts. In those days Lewis consistently published their demands. The Policy Committee was frequently called upon for analysis of members' resolutions, discussion of the bargaining situation, and final ratification.(63) In the 1950's, however, as secrecy of negotiations became the major concern, information between the locals and the international was exchanged to a much smaller extent, and the Policy and Scale Committees met much less frequently.(64) Lewis stopped publishing demands in order to avoid any kind of commitment.

This finding suggests that Weber's concept of charisma needs to be divided into two categories: unstable charisma, where the leader must constantly prove his extraordinary capacity in order to sustain his legitimacy, and stabilized charisma, where the leader is relatively less pressured to do so, thanks to his past "stock type successes with self-reinforcing benefits". Given this "stock", Lewis could act cooperatively with the organized coal employers to attempt a stabilization of the industry in the face of declining demand.

c. Conditions Under Which Organizational Factors Are Less Constraining: Additional Findings

Although the above analysis may be sufficient for refining the theory in order to reconcile it with seemingly contradictory data, it is not a complete picture of characteristics of the UMW organization which enabled leaders to make decisions with relative freedom from organizational constraints. Additional consideration of this issue will be undertaken here.

(i) Power of the International Leader: Further Centralization

The constitutional provisions which allowed international leaders enormous power to control the rank-and-file in the 1950's remained just as effective in the 1950's. There were no major constitutional amendments during the 1950's. All the districts that had been deprived of autonomy in the 1930's and 1940's were kept provisional throughout the decade. As is shown in Tables A-2 and A-3 (Appendix 1), the powerful offices of district president and representative to the International Executive Board were occupied by the same Lewis men who because of their loyalty had survived Lewis' purges. Therefore, the Executive Committee - the supreme decision-making body between conventions - remained completely powerless to check the conduct of international officers.

The stringent financial condition of local unions remained the same in the 1950's (Table 5-5). Furthermore, administration of the Welfare Fund imposed an added work load on local officers:

> Whereas, Due to the heavy burden the Local Unions have in maintaining and paying a Safety Committee; and
>
> Whereas, There is a great amount of time involved in Welfare Fund work; and
>
> Whereas, Our Districts are continually asking for assessments; therefore be it
>
> Resolved, That the dues to be increased $1.00 per month be divided equally between the District and Local Unions. (65)

In addition to these effective instruments of the previous decade, there were some extra factors in the 1950's which made the psychological as well as the economic cost of an unsuccessful rebellion even higher. For the rank-and-file, the establishment of the Welfare Fund which they welcomed so enthusiastically had ironically robbed them of most of their power against the international leaders. As the Fund offered monthly retirement checks, free medical care, and thus lifetime security, it became increasingly difficult for miners to give up this privilege. Forfeiture of a membership card, a tactic which the international leaders invariably used to curb disobedience, thus became a far more powerful deterrent against rank-and-file rebellion. This deterrent-effect was especially strong for retired or disabled members whose lives depended directly upon the Fund. Although explicit statistics are not available, Officers' Reports in several conventions in the 1950's reveal that the proportion of retired or disabled members who lived on welfare payments increased very rapidly, eventually comprising more than half of the members in some districts. This increased proportion of non-active miners who could hardly take the risk of invalidating their membership further stabilized the leadership power structure.

For local or district union officials, the cost of rebellion was higher yet. With the decline of the coal industry and the resulting high unemployment, it became very difficult for local union officials to go back to the mines. Since alternative employment was scarce, they were all the more eager to hold onto their union jobs.(66) For higher officials, change was more indirect. District presidency or membership on the International Executive Board were highly prestigious and rewarding positions. Salaries and pensions were generous; the jobs themselves were interesting and carried with them both power and finge-benefits. The crucial difference between the career of a UMW-official and those of other equally prestigious executives was that while the ordinary executive can often find another high-status position after losing his current post, district presidents or International Executive Board members in the UMWA had no alternative other than to go back to the mine pits.(67) This contrast between the district post and work in the mine became psychologically greater the longer the leader stayed in office. As Tables A-2 and A-3 of Appendix 1 show, Lewis retained most of the district leaders of the 1930's and 1940's in their offices. As a result, the district leaders in the 1950's had a far longer tenure than those in the 1940's. Having observed the effects of Lewis' purges of their most powerful colleagues, they were more aware than anyone else of the tragedy which Lewis' ruthlessness could create in their personal lives. Having been in the same office for more than nine years, most of them were not only accustomed to, but also content with, being in the second post. By the 1950's, rebellion against Lewis was totally inconceivable for them.

Thus, enhancement of the already enormous power of the international president and the stability of his executives constituted one important reason why the drastic policy changes of the 1950's were initiated surprisingly smoothly.

(ii) Development in Grievance Procedures

While protest through wildcat strikes became more difficult in the 1950's, there were substantial developments in the grievance procedure which gave miners an alternative outlet. The International leaders strongly encouraged local unions to utilize the procedure. The following is one of the many letters sent by the International Union:

May 17, 1956

To the Officers and Members of
the United Mine Workers of America:

Declaration of Policy

Local work stoppages involving a mine, in whole or in part, not officially authorized by the United Mine Workers of America, were prohibited by order of the International Executive Board, dated October 24, 1951...

The International Executive Board, endowed with authority to take such action, reaffirms its previous declaration and again instructs compliance therewith.

1. Local Union will utilize the machinery of the Joint Wage Agreement for the settlement of all disputes arising thereunder.

2. Local Unions failing to do so, and resorting to local stoppages, will be subject to discipline, and penalties will be imposed by the International Executive Board ...

Attest:
John Owens, Secretary-Treasurer(68)

As a result of this emphasis, the grievance procedure began to be used more frequently. Table 5-7, showing the number of arbitration decisions in the northern West Virginia area (under the jurisdiction of District 31) for every three years from 1933 to 1954, indicates that more than 40% of the 500 umpire decisions of these 21 years were filed in the last six years. The number of decisions per 1000 employees gives a much clearer indication of this increasing trend.

Another significant feature of the grievance procedure in the coal industry was its function in filling the gap between the local practice and the national contract. As the contract and union administration became more centralized, grievance settlement, which was supposed to be "judicial" in its function, began to take a "legislative" role. In some cases, the nation-wide contract was not specific enough to apply to a particular dispute; while in other cases, it was in conflict with local customs which had been developed since immigration days in the 18th and 19th centuries. The grievance procedure, which was applied very flexibly in the 1950's, sometimes "legislated" a new rule by citing a precedent case, or often took local practice to be as legitimate as the contract in judging issues. Some of the local practices upheld by arbitration spread widely and later became contract provisions. Somers observed:

> ... Although these local understandings are seldom committed to writing and, even when recorded, are not publicized, the various grievance-settlement agencies, including arbitration, place prior practice on a par with the

contract in reaching their decisions. Occasionally, a practice upheld by arbitration has been in direct conflict with the national agreement. Arbitration decisions have often helped to determine local practice, and in some important issues, such as the interpretation of seniority in recall after layoff, the practice had already become so widespread throughout the district that the umpire had no alternative other than to uphold it in all mines. Some important practices, including seniority in layoffs and recall, finally became part of the national agreement only after they had been customary in a number of areas for many preceding years. At the present time, there is expectation in some quarters that seniority in promotion and choice of shifts and mine seniority units for layoffs, which are now recognized in some districts, will soon be pressed by the union negotiators for incorporation in the national agreement. Other widespread local understandings, such as those concerned with the distribution of temporary work and work sharing are more likely to remain under local discretion. (69)

The third characteristic of the grievance procedure in the coal industry was that settlements were generally in favor of the union. Somer's painstaking survey shows that the union's grievance was granted in one-half of the disputes at the lower level of the settlements and over 60% at the higher level (Table 5-7).

Table 5-8 shows that in grievance settlements of the Bethlehem Steel Company and the United Steelworkers, only 20% of the grievances were granted, while as much as 50% were denied. Table 5-9 indicates that arbitrations of 36 firms in Wisconsin ruled 67% of the disputes in favor of the company and only 27% for the union. Thus, by comparison, the grievance procedure in the coal industry was much more favorable to the union than that in the other industries of those years.

The radical policy change conducted in the 1950's produced a great deal of hardship for miners. Rebellions did not materialize, however, because the grievance procedure worked more satisfactorily for miners and functioned as a "safety valve"[70] which prevented the accumulation of frustration.

Table 5 - 4

Allocation of Dues Revenue, 1956

	Dues	Breakdown	
Regular Member	$ 4.00	International	$2.00
		District	$1.00
		Local	$1.00
Disabled Member	$ 1.00	International	All

Source: Proceedings of the International Convention of the United Mine Workers of America, 1956, Vol. 1.

Table 5 - 5
Average Tenure of District Leaders in the 1940's, 1950's and 1960's

	1940's	1950's	1960's
IEB Member	5.97	9.11	9.99
District President	6.34	9.10	8.53

Source: Table A-2 and A-3

Table 5 - 6

Increasing Utilization of Grievance Procedures in the 1950's

Time Period	Number of Arbitration Decisions	Average Association Employment	Decisions per 1000 Employees
1933-36	45	16,862	2.7
1936-39	79	15,964	4.9
1939-42	54	14,743	3.7
1942-45	66	16,249	4.1
1945-48	47	15,972	2.9
1948-51	95	15,760	6.0
1951-54	114	11,531	9.9
1933-54 Average	71.4	15,298	4.9

Source: Somers, 1956, p. 15.

Table 5 - 7

Disposition of Grievances in the Bituminous Coal Industry in West Virginia, 1933-54

Level of Settlement	Granted	Denied	Compromised	Referred Back	Total
Commissioner	168	87	33	----	288
Joint Board	106	81	30	1	218
Umpire	252	221	73	1	547
TOTAL	526	389	136	2	1056

Source: Somers, 1956, p. 14

Table 5 - 8

Disposition of Grievances in Bethlehem Steel Company, 1942-1952

Total	Granted	Partially Granted	Denied	Dismissed for lack of jurisdiction	Dismissed as untimely	Referred back
1,003	200	121	503	31	57	91

Source: U. S. Department of Labor, Bureau of Labor Statistics, 1954, p. 4

Table 5 - 9

Disposition of Cases by Arbitors, 1950-53, in 15 Wisconsin Firms

Company	Ruled for Company	Ruled for Employee and/or Union	Split Decision
A		Did not specify	
B	6	3	3
C	5	2	0
D	1	1	0
E	24	16	0
F	10	4	0
G	1	1	0
H	1	0	0
I	1	0	0
J	1	0	0
K	1	0	0
L	1	0	0
M	1	1	0
N	20	4	0
O	16	3	6
TOTAL (%)	88 (67%)	35 (26.7%)	8 (6.1%)

Source: Kruger, 1955

CHAPTER VI

THE UMWA IN 1961-1972:

INCREASING MILITANCY AND A CORRUPT LEADER

Lewis' long reign came to an end on December 15, 1959, when he disclosed his decision to retire.[1] The news stunned the miners and anxiety spread in the coal fields.[2] Lewis elevated Vice President Thomas Kennedy, his lifelong follower, to president, and W. A. ("Tony") Boyle, his personal assistant, to vice president. Although Kennedy was a capable and experienced leader, he was seventy-two years old and in ill health. Tony Boyle took over as acting president in 1962, and upon Kennedy's death in 1963 became president. Since most of the significant developments of this period took place after Boyle assumed the office, the following analysis will concentrate heavily on the period after 1963.

1. Union Organization

a. Structure of Organizational Decision-Making

There were very few changes in the structure of organizational decision-making. The formal structure remained the same as that laid out by Lewis in the 1940's, whereby the major decisions were made exclusively at the international level and only relatively minor problems being handled at the district level.

At the international level, Kennedy and Boyle followed the same mode of policy-setting that Lewis had practiced in his forty-year reign. All the decisions of the international union were made privately by the president alone. The other international officers were expected merely to provide information, if requested, and to accept and implement the president's decisions. Since this had worked successfully so far, no one proposed changing it.

At the district level there were some significant changes. A drastic decline in the number of miners in the 1950's[3] left some of the districts virtually without members. The international union merged districts with nearby districts to cut wasteful administrative expense. As a result, the number of districts fell from thirty-one in the early 1940's to twenty-three in the late 1960's.[4] Another cost-cutting effort was to make the district president serve as international executive board member of the district or as president of a nearby district. The proportion of posts within the international executive board served by district presidents rose from 30% in 1948 to as high as 68% in 1996.[5] The result of these changes was the concentration of the district-level decisions in the hands of much fewer people. Table 6-1 compares the number of people responsible for district level decisions in the 1940's and in the late 1960's.

Although the change in structure and mode of decision-making appeared to be insignificant, it had an important and unintended impact on the union's behavior.

b. Leadership Style: Dictatorship and Corruption as a Source of Power

Kennedy and Boyle inherited Lewis' charismatic legitimacy. Since the sole source of their legitimacy was the fact that they had been chosen by the faultless leader, they emphasized their close association with Lewis as his direct heirs. Kennedy, for example, created a President-Emeritus chair for Lewis so that he could symbolically head the union.(6) Boyle constantly repeated that he had been specially picked by Lewis as his personal assistant. However, he failed to sustain the inherited charismatic authority.(7) Compared to Lewis he was far less appealing and effective. While he attempted to imitate Lewis' strong, low voice and brilliant rhetoric, making up for what he lacked in vocabulary and articulation by volume and fury, his speeches were defensive, often incoherent, and incapable of rousing member's emotions.(8) He also disappointed many miners with his repeated failure to secure the gains he promised. As it became clear that he would not be able to rely on inherited legitimacy, he resorted increasingly to self-aggrandizing, dictatorial and corrupt measures as the base of his power.

(i) Self-Aggrandizement

One of the most conspicuous changes in the union's expenditures during the Boyle administration was the outlay for photographs. The amount paid to Chase Studio, Ltd., which was $2,346 in 1963, jumped more than ten times to $26,477 in 1964, and to $66,734 in 1966.(9) Approximately $200,000 was spent solely for pictures of officers, mainly Boyle, during 1964 to 1970.(10)

The United Mine Workers Journal, which had covered Lewis only moderately even at the height of his glory, began to be filled with stories and pictures of Boyle. Especially in 1969, the election year, the front cover page - where even Lewis had seldom appeared - bore Boyle's picture issue after issue.(11) This excessive coverage of Boyle was eventually ruled to be an illegal campaign tactic.(12)

Table 6 - 1

The Numbers of District Presidents and International Executive Board Members

Year	Number	Year	Number
1945	49	1965	35
1946	49	1966	35
1947	49	1967	33
1948	49	1968	31
1949	46	1969	33
1950	45	1970	35

Source: Appendix, Tables A - 2 and A - 3

Even more revealing was Boyle's manipulation of the two International Conventions. The 1964 Convention was filled with paid staff men, all appointees of the object of their adulation, carrying huge placards and banners. Four bands were hired at a cost of $390,000. When Boyle was introduced on the platform, hundreds of well-paid delegates demonstrated enthusiastically, waving placards and pictures, whooping, cheering and stamping their feet to the rousing music for twenty minutes. After they took their seats, the bands continued to play for another half-hour before Boyle finally began speaking. The 1958 Convention also spent $200,000 for three bands.

Another conspicuous example of Boyle's self-aggrandizement at the convention was the distribution of expensive gifts to every delegate. In 1964, $77,000 from the union treasury went for gifts such as portable radios, all prominently embossed with Boyle's name.(13) At the 1968 Convention, an electric clock and a cigarette lighter, both with Boyle's picture and name, as well as a pen with Boyle's name engraved upon it, were given out. This cost the treasury $87,000. Although some souvenirs for the delegates were usual at union conventions, the excessive cost of these gifts and the impression they gave of coming from Boyle personally were clearly exceptional. Incidentally, the 1964 Convention cost more than $1.4 million, approximately three times the cost of the Cincinnati Convention of 1960.(14)

(ii) Dictatorial Repression as a Source of Power

Boyle's dictatorship exceeded even that of Lewis. While Lewis used his power in a well-calculated manner, Boyle used his excessively and arbitrarily. A UMW secretary's statement suggests one reason.

> If anyone ever lived in the old man's shadow, Tony did, almost to the point where it haunted him. He used to watch everyone who went up to see Lewis on the building's sixth floor. Those who counseled with Lewis found themselves on Tony's black list. "You know who I am, don't you?" he would say to me, "I control this organization. I can fire anyone from the basement to the sixth floor." (15)

Several prominent leaders were purged over minor disagreements. For example, when John Mayo, an International Executive Board Member from District 4, opposed the union's investment in 1965, Boyle transferred him to head a temporary office in Iowa.(16) When Vice President R. O. Lewis, a younger brother of John L. Lewis, stated that his transfer was a violation of the constitution, he was forced to resign in January of 1966.(17)

At the Miami Convention of 1964, delegates discovered that their seats and spectators' seats were mixed together.[18] Since the vote was always taken by voice, this arrangement could totally nullify their votes. A troop of helmeted men was stationed on the floor and forcibly prevented protesting miners from reaching the microphone. Some managed to reach the microphone, only to find that it was cut off or that they would be interrupted immediately by the chairman. At this convention, Boyle furthermore extended the term of his presidency from four years to five,[31] and - more importantly - increased the number of local union endorsements required to qualify as a presidential candidate from five to a virtually prohibitive fifty.[22]

Yablonski's challenge in 1969, the most formidable threat that Boyle had ever faced, led him to excessive violence. One week after Yablonski's announcement of his candidacy, Boyle fired him from the acting directorship of the union's political organ, "Labor's Non-Partisan League". In June of 1969, when Yablonski was conferring with hostile local leaders in Springfield, Illinois, he was struck from behind and knocked unconscious. A doctor later found that his injury could easily have killed or paralyzed him.[23] A number of pro-Yablonski meetings were violently disrupted by "Boyle supporters",[24] who were later found to be paid from the union treasury.[25]

The final measure was taken after the election. Yablonski, defeated by a vote of 80,577 to 46,073, demanded that the election results be discussed at the next International Executive Board meeting.[26] In December of 1969, Yablonski was murdered, along with his wife and daugher, by three hired gunmen.[27] Two years later, the FBI investigation showed that Boyle had ordered and financed the execution.

(iii) Corruption as a Source of Power

Illegal use of the abundant union treasury and of the Welfare Fund constituted another important source of power for the Boyle administration. On April 1, 1969, when Boyle's re-election campaign began, he raised the salaries of the administrative officers by $1,000 and of the clerical staff by $600. A later examination of the finances of his campaign organization showed that these union employees systematically donated the same amount as their salary increase, and that the salary increase was a mere device to embezzle union funds for the campaign. On June 11, 1969, when Lewis died at the age of eighty-nine, Boyle became trustee for the Welfare Fund. His new position gave him an excellent chance to win the support of the pensioners in the on-going presidential election.

On June 23, when the neutral trustee Josephine Roche was in the hospital, Boyle deceived the industry trustee George Judy by leading him to believe that he held Roche's proxy,[28] and proposed that the miners' pensions be raised from $115 to $150 per month.[29] Later it was found that Miss Roche had never been consulted about the raise, and that Boyle had never even made an effort to assess the financial implications of his proposal.[30]

Funds from the union treasury were generously poured into all the disctricts for campaign purposes. When pro-Boyle district officials needed money for the campaign, all they had to do was to ask for "loans" for their districts. No justification beyond such ambiguous terms as "organizing expense" or "administration" was required for the loan.[31] In 1969, the international spent more than $2 million in this fashion.[32] In District 5, Yablonski's home district, for example, they spent $360,000 as compared to $180,000 in 1968.[33]

A more straightforward and effective measure was to circumvent the voting process itself. The advance notice and secret ballot requirements of the Landrum-Griffin Act were violated in several instances. At Local 7113, John Aiells, an appointed official of District 17 as well as a financial secretary of the local, suddenly announced that nominations would be held. He then nominated Boyle, swiftly closed the nominations, and ruled a miner who tried to nominate Yablonski out of order. This meeting was held even before the nomination period started. At Local 1687, William Reddington, an Executive Board member from District 25, came to a regular union meeting and opened the election without notice. When he found that a majority of those attending were in favor of Boyle, he tried to close the nomination before Yablonski's name was called. When this attempt failed, he took a voice vote in clear violation of the Landrum-Griffin Act and declared the local's official endorsement of Boyle. At Local 1577, a pro-Boyle international representative set the clock of a union hall forward and completed the nomination before the members appeared.[34]

c. Power Structure of the Organization

As the source of power shifted from charismatic legitimacy to sheer physical force and corruption, the power structure, in the 1940's and 1950's had been characterized by the international's solid control over the district leaders and the rank-and-file, went through a number of changes.

(i) Power Relationship Between the International Leaders and the Rank-and-File

As Boyle failed to maintain the charismatic authority he had inherited, member disobedience against his orders became common. In 1964, after the new contract was signed, many miners refused to return to work, a situation which the Boyle administration found difficult to control. In the Lewis period, wildcat strikes, which were heavily oriented toward facilitating Lewis' negotiations, always stopped immediately after the contract was signed. The post-contract strikes of the 1960's indicated the membership's increasing doubts about the leaders' efforts and capabilities. Many wildcat strikes took place after 1964, but none of them ended immediately upon the international's return-to-work call.

(ii) Power Relationship Between International and District Leaders

The international leaders' power over district leaders remained firm in the 1960's. In contrast to control of the rank-and-file, legitimacy played only a minor role compared to sheer physical power in controlling the district leaders.

The international leaders retained all the power that the constitution had provided for Lewis against insubordination, and invoked the power repeatedly. The resignation of R. O. Lewis, which every district leader knew was forced by Boyle, was highly significant: if the Vice President and a blood brother of John L. Lewis could be expelled over such a minor issue, so could anyone else. Since it was virtually impossible for district leaders to find a job with prestige and reward comparable to the one they had, the cost of losing that job was immense. Huddleston, president of a large local union, summarized their fear:

> If you don't believe your leaders' word, you're in pretty bad shape. You've got to accept your leaders' word. (35)

Additionally, the norm of blind loyalty had been developed and internalized in district leaders during the long reign of Lewis. Disagreement with the president was considered insubordination and treachery against the organization. This blind loyalty, shared by all international and district leaders, was illustrated in a statement by Boyle during a pre-trial cross-examination session held by opposing

opposing lawyer Rauh. When questioned about the dismissal of Yablonski from Labor's Non-Partisan League, Boyle replied:

A. ... Mr. Yablonski was on notice, plenty of notice. He gave his own warning on May 29. (36)
Q. (by Rauh) I didn't understand that. What did you mean by that?
A. You know what I mean by it, Mr. Rauh ... You sat at the press conference and guided him through the press conference as to what to say and when to say it and when not to say it ... And after release of, I don't know, 29 pages or whatever it was of a press release, Mr. Yablonski certainly knew then from that, with all of his experience that he claims he has in this organization, that he was in violation of the constitution.
Q. What was the violation of the constitution on May 29?
A. Because he wasn't carrying out the policies of the international organization or its convention.
Q. In what way?
A. By the statements that are in that 29 pages ... by that statement which in itself - which speaks for itself - is in violation of the principles and policies enunciated by the organization down through the years since 1890. (37)

(iii) Rank-and-File Rebellions

Appalachian life in the early 1960's was characterized by poverty and deterioration of the mining communities. Although recovery of the coal industry had already begun, further mechanization prevented employment from growing accordingly. Due to the psychological and social immobility of the miners, the number of jobless mineworkers had increased since the 1950's. Homer Bigart reported the plight of the Appalachian people:

> The welfare system has eroded the self-respect of the mountain people ... "The present system has encouraged the break-up of families," according to Harry M. Caudill ... "No matter how hungry his wife and children may be, an able bodied man cannot get on the relief rolls," Mr. Caudill explained. In desperation, the man deserts his family so they can qualify for relief checks and get food.
>
> "We are promoting illegitimacy," said Leslie County Judge George Wooten.
>
> "We sure are," added Mayor William C. Dowahare of Hazard. "A widow can get out and have as many illigitimate children as she likes and get paid for it." (38)

Despite the economic plight of the miners, the performance of the union leaders was totally unsatisfactory. The first cause of discontent among the miners was a series of cutbacks in the Welfare Fund benefit.[38] The trustees decided to cut off hospital and medical benefits after one year of unemployment, and to reduce the miners' monthly pensions from $100 to $75. In October of 1962, the fund disposed of the ten hospitals which had been symbols of the union's humanistic achievement, by selling eight to the Presbyterian Church and closing the remaining two. In addition, medical benefits were cut off for miners whose employers had not been meeting their royalty payments. There were angry meetings in some mining towns in Pennsylvania and West Virginia. As one miner put it, suspicion and distrust started "from the day they took my hospital card".[40]

Another source of dissatisfaction was the union's disappointing performance in collective bargaining. As will be described in the next section, in all contract negotiations the Boyle administration consistently failed to satisfy the members' needs. Rebellion grew along with the accumulation of discontent. The number of men involved in unauthorized strikes after the contract agreements in 1964, 1966 and 1968 were 8,000, 40,000 and 100,000 respectively.

The problem facing the rebellion was lack of organization and coordination. Establishing an organization to promote the movement would immediately give the Boyle administration a chance to name it a "dual movement", which was punishable by expulsion. Loss of union membership meant loss of job, pension and the hospital benefits, which even the angriest miner could hardly afford.

The opportunity to organize came in 1969 as a result of Yablonski's tireless campaign for the presidency and his tragic death. Despite the corrupt and dictatorial measures taken by the Boyle camp, the eight-month campaign with high publicity and outside aid[41] successfully penetrated almost all the districts, enabling rebellious local leaders who had been acting independently to unite with each other. Right after the announcement of his candidacy, Yablonski successfully obtained endorsements from two other candidates, Steve Kochias and Elijah Wolford. Kochias was a local leader who had been working to organize the insurgent movement in Pennsylvania ever since his unsuccessful bid for the presidency in 1964. Wolford was a rebellious local activist in northern West Virginia. Both of them withdrew from the campaign and began working for Yablonski. By August of 1969, Yablonski succeeded in securing strong support from many rank-and-file rebel leaders like Bill Savitsky, Mike Trbovich, Arnold Miller, Ed Monborne, Bert Cross, Ray Jutchison and Karl Kaften.[42] Establishing a link among these independent local leaders was no small achievement.

Although the defeat of Yablonski in December was a big step backwards for the movement, Yablonski's murder pulled the forces together. The rebels were well aware of the cause of the murder, and were fully determined to fight until they could expel Boyle. On June 15, 1970, the rebels organized themselves as "Miners for Democracy",[43] and began pushing for enforcement of the improved mine safety law. They promoted the more militant settlement of local disputes by staging wildcat strikes, which the rank-and-file, in effect, saw as sharply contrasting with the inactivity of the Boyle administration.[44] The dissidents also filed a number of law suits against the Boyle administration;[45] and Secretary of Labor George Shultz, who had refused to invoke the Landrum-Griffin Act during the crucial stage of the campaign, finally decided to investigate the union. In June of 1971, the U. S. District Court in Washington ordered that Boyle should be removed from the Board of Trustees of the Welfare Fund. In May, 1972, the same court ruled the 1969 election void and ordered a new election in late 1972 under the supervision of the Department of Labor. The growing momentum of the dissident movement finally removed Boyle from office in 1973.

2. Union Behavior

In this period, four contract negotiations were conducted. Union behavior during each set of negotiations will be described briefly, and common characteristics will be identified.

a. The 1963-64 Contract Negotiations

When the new administration took office in 1960, mining communities were suffering from severe unemployment and poverty. Despite the miners' plight and the recovery of the industry, the new leaders were totally inactive. Contract talks had not been opened since 1958. Although miners' wages were still among the highest, other unions were rapidly catching up. With respect to fringe benefits, which Lewis had neglected, the miners were far behind the auto- and steelworkers.

On December 18, 1963, Boyle opened negotiations with the Bituminous Coal Operators Association. The rank-and-file's concern was clearly for job security, safety and fringe benefits. Content analysis of local resolutions shows that 1) the miners' concern with the wage issue, and particularly with wage increase, declined drastically, and that 2) their interest in fringe benefits, job security and the health/safety issues became very important in the early 1960's (Table 6-2).

However, when the contract was signed on March 23, it was found that although the wage was to go up by $2 a day, very few gains had been obtained in job

Table 6 - 2

The Rank-and-File's Concerns in the Early 1960's

Item	Average of the Six Conventions Prior to 1960	Average of the 1960 and 1964 Conventions	Rate of Increase(+) or Decrease(-)
Wages	29.8%	13.7%	- 54%
(Wage Increase)	(8.0%)	(0.7%)	(- 91%)
Work Hours	5.7%	6.2%	+ 8%
Fringe Benefits	38.3%	52.4%	+37%
Job Security	9.8%	13.8%	+41%
(Seniority)	(3.5%)	(6.0%)	(+ 71%)
Health and Safety	7.6%	8.0%	+ 5%
Contract Agreement	4.9%	4.3%	- 12%
Working Conditions	2.7%	1.3%	- 52%
Miscellaneous	1.8%	1.4%	- 22%
TOTAL	100 %	100 %	

Source: Appendix, Table A - 1

security and fringe benefits. For example, demands regarding seniority rights included (1) company-wide seniority rather than the existing mine-wide seniority within each classification, and (ii) the strict seniority rule in hiring order. The agreement contained abolition of the classification provision, but not company-wide rule or hiring privilege. Even this abolition of classification-wide rule had a loophole and was not expected to improve job security particularly.(46) Boyle further failed to obtain full pay for vacations and holidays, though this had already been put into practice in other industries. There was a $25 increase in vacation pay, which still fell far short of full payment level, and holidays were without any pay.

b. The 1966 Contract Negotiations

On February 14, 1966, Boyle called the National Policy Committee to form the final contract demands. On February 17, in a press interview, he declared that he would seek substantial improvements in job security and fringe benefits, and that he would not be bound by the government's non-inflationary guideposts. Despite Boyle's strong statement, progress in the negotiations was very slow. On April 8, the union signed a new pact, not with its traditional partner, the Bituminous Coal Operators' Association, but with Peabody Coal Company of St. Louis. Although the Peabody pact called for a $2.32 wage increase for skilled workers and a $1 increase for the unskilled over the two year period, skilled workers accounted for only a small part of the mining work-force, and the $1 increase for the unskilled would be effective only after one year. The seniority right was enhanced to include first claim on jobs at nearby mines owned by the same company, but the controversial qualification clause was retained. Full pay for vacations and holidays was attained.(47)

Union officials boasted about the gains and announced that they would seek a similar contract from the Bituminous Coal Operators' Association, which immediately opposed it on the grounds that Peabody Coal was mainly a strip-mining company and that the same conditions could not apply. A wave of large-scale unauthorized strikes spread through the eastern segment of the industry, opposing not only the BCOA but also the union's intention to extend the Peabody agreement. After long negotiations, accord was finally reached on April 24. The terms of the settlement were broadly similar to the Peabody pact, but with some changes which are difficult to evaluate. It provided an immediate wage increase of $1.32 a day for skilled workers and $1.00 a day for the unskilled, in an attempt to pacify the striking miners;(48) but a second pay increase for the skilled workers was eliminated. The union also had to give up sole jurisdiction and maintenance work at the mine site. More importantly, the provision in the Peabody pact giving all laid-off miners seniority-based job claims in the same company within their geographical districts was modified to include only miners displaced by mine shutdown.(49) Despite acclaim by the international union, April 29 found sixteen thousand protesting miners in Kentucky, West Virginia, Pennsylvania and Ohio on a strike(50) which the nternational leaders had a hard time quieting down.

c. The 1968 Contract Negotiations

1967 was a relatively quiet year for the union leaders. The 1966 contract was also open-ended, allowing either party to terminate the contract with the required 60-day notice after August 1, 1968. On July 17, 1978, Boyle called a National Policy Committee meeting "to find out what the fellows want"(51) for the next contract negotiations. The demands formulated at the meeting went back to those of the 1940's, emphasizing a sizeable wage gain. Boyle broke with tradition by filing the termination notice on August 9.

The operators reportedly made a relatively large offer, but the union leaders rejected it, arguing that the union needed to make up for the "lost time" of the 1958-1964 period, when it did not re-open the contract.(52) By October 8, the negotiators had failed to reach an agreement and the nations 100,000 miners walked out of the pits - the first legal nation-wide strike since 1950.

The strike lasted for six days, until October 14, when the union gained a sizeable three-year pact. It provided a wage increase of $3 a day for the first year and $2 a day for each of the next two years. It also had a graduated vacation schedule based on seniority, which would provide up to a four-week paid vacation for men with 19 years- continuous service.(53) Other important gains were a highly unusual $120 Christmas bonus for miners who had not taken part in any wildcat strikes in the previous year, and an expansion of the seniority clause to make length of service the basis for shift preference.(54)

d. The 1971 Contract Negotiations

On June 8, 1971, Boyle called the National Scale and Policy Committees and proposed extremely militant demands which included $50 a day wage instead of the present $33.37, and an 80¢ a-ton royalty payment instead of the present 40¢. On July 28, the union formally filed the termination notice, by which the current contract would expire on September 30. The negotiations began immediately, but made hardly any progress. The September 30 deadline passed without the wage issue even being discussed.[55] The nation's 80,000 soft-coal miners working in mines belonging to the Bituminous Coal Operators Association, walked out of the pits.

On October 20, negotiations reached an impasse and were recessed indefinitely. Boyle accused the operators of "seeking to turn the United Mine Workers of America into a slave-herder and strikebreaker for the companies".[56] However, pressure to settle the dispute was mounting for both parties. The American Public Power Association, representing 1,400 small public utilities, warned that the coal stockpiles were being used up.[57] In the rail industry at least 20,000 workers were laid off due to lack of coal.[58] On the other hand, the decline of coal production drastically reduced the revenues of the Welfare and Retirement Fund.

The final agreement came on November 14 after 44 days of a nation-wide strike. The package itself included a 39% wage increase to about $46 a day, with an immediate basic daily wage increase of $3 to $5 a day.[59] The royalty payment of 40¢ per ton was doubled to 80¢, with 20¢ added immediately and the rest to be added in installments of 5¢ every six months in the last two years of the contract. The Welfare Fund's priority was shifted to include sick leave benefits of $50 a week for 52 weeks to seek and injured miners after they had been off the job for 14 days. Long-term disability payments to injured and retired miners were made the second priority of the find. Pensions, third on the fund priority list, were expanded to invlude the option that workers,at the age of 55, could retire after only 10 years on the job with half benefits, or they could continue to work and qualify for as much as $225 a month if they retired at age 65 with 30 years of employment. These were undoubtedly sizeable gains by the Boyle administration.

e. Union Militancy in the 1960's: a Summary

The above historical account shows that the union's behavior in collective bargaining situations in the 1960's can be characterized as follows:

a) Official militancy gradually increased from very low at the beginning of the 1960's to very high at the end.

b) Despite its growth, the official militancy was not responding sensitively enough to the changing needs of the membership, and was far too low to satisfy the members.

As was very clear from local resolutions and interviews, the miners' interests no longer lay in wages, but had shifted to job security, fringe benefits and safety. The 1964 pact, however, contained virtually nothing but a $2 wage raise; the 1966 contract failed to eliminate the controversial qualification clause, one of the most serious concerns of the miners; even the sizeable 1968 pact traded more important paid sick leave, royalty increase and coal-dust precaution for the substantial wage gain which Boyle had promised to get. With the exception of the 1971 contract negotiations, insufficient militancy and insensitivity to the members' needs characterized the union's bargaining behavior in this period.

3. Analysis

a. Growing Militancy during this Period

(i) Economic Recovery of the Coal Industry

The coal industry was recovering rapidly in the 1960's. Figures 6-1 and 6-2 show increasing production and increasing total sales respectively. Union leaders quickly grasped this trend, as was evident in Boyle's reappraisal of the industry's situation at the 1964 Convention.

> It may interest the bituminous miners to know that the anthracite industry is a sick industry. I don't think that it is true in the bituminous any more. I think they used to say it was sick. It looks pretty good to me from the profit some of them are making. (60)

In 1968, his appraisal became stronger and more explicit.

> The coal industry in 1968 is enjoying a better position than it has for many years. Production has increased each year since 1964. Long-term contracts with electric utilities and others insure continued operation. New and large mines are being opened at a rate not seen for many years. The demand for coal miners has become acute and the opportunity for employment in the coal industry has greatly improved. (61)

As the leaders regained confidence in the state of the industry, they could afford to demand sizeable contracts. For example, in 1968, when the leaders were fully convinced of the recovery of the industry, they rejected the operators' reportedly generous offer by arguing that since the industry had recovered, it should make up for the time lost during 1958-64, when the union restrained itself from seeking any improvement because of the recession.

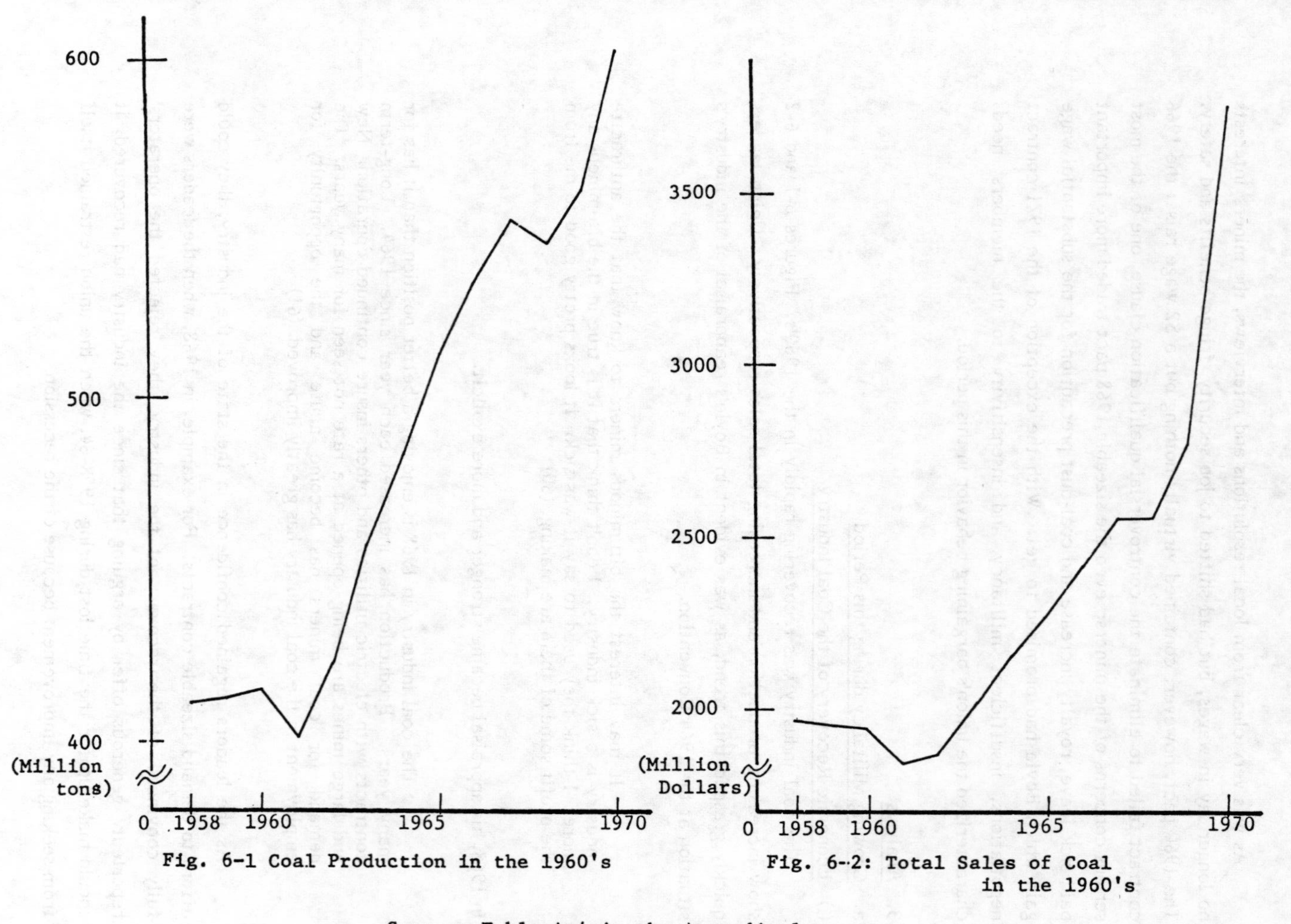

Fig. 6-1 Coal Production in the 1960's

Fig. 6-2: Total Sales of Coal in the 1960's

Source: Table A-4 in the Appendix 1.

b. Growing Rebelliousness of the Membership

Although the economic explanation of union militancy is most popular, it is not by itself very persuasive because it leaves out a motivational aspect of the actor. Its essential point is to identify the existence or non-existence of "opportunities" to be militant. "Opportunities" to do something, however, are merely the necesssary condition but do not elicit actual behavior by themselves. This additionally requires the actor's motivation. The economic explanation therefore may explain a decrease of militancy by showing a lack of "opportunities", but does not suffice to explain an increase in militancy.

In the example of the UMWA in this period, constantly growing pressure from rank and file insurgency appears to have provided the motivation for the union's increasing official militancy. For example, close observers linked Boyle's decision to break a six-year silence and open contract talks in 1963, with rank-and-file uprisings early that year.

The insurgent members were not yet powerful enough to keep up their pressure during negotiations. But in 1966, when the union could legally open the next contract talks, they came back in greater force. On February 17, Boyle re-opened the talks with inflated demands. When he reached an agreement with Peabody Coal and declared his intention to seek a similar contract with the BCOA, spontaneous unauthorized strikes spread across the nation.(62) The rebellious nature of the strikes became clear when Boyle's back-to-work order was totally ignored by 30,000 striking miners. This mounting pressure from the rank and file could not but have an impact on Boyle's behavior. For example, when on April 13 the news leaked out that an accord was near, the Boyle administration suddenly took a firm stand and walked out of the negotiations.(63) Informed sources speculated that this was his attempt to demonstrate militancy by holding out a little longer.(64)

The effect of the insurgent movement on the leaders' behavior was clearer in the 1968 and 1971 negotiations. In 1968, 40,000 miners left the pits before the contract expiration in defiance of Boyle's order. In 1971, the movement passed totally out of Boyle's control and put him into a maze of political attacks and lawsuits. Under such tremendous pressure, Boyle could not easily concede without at least giving the impression that he was fighting hard. The operators, on the other hand, knowing that the negotiations were bound to last a long time, were unwilling to give ground in the early stages. They were also aware that no contract would be accepted easily by the rank and file, and were ready to let Boyle call a short strike in order to make acceptance easier.(65) Under these conditions the negotiations would naturally proceed very slowly and strikes were bound to take place. A sizeable contract gain with a 44-day strike were the results.

c. Insufficient Militancy and Insensitive Response

Although the rather common-sense explanation above seems to account adequately for the growth of militancy over time, it is incapable of explaining the union's insensitive response to the growing and changing needs of the rank-and-file at each decision period. This section is devoted to this question.

The decision of a top leader of an organization is a result of a variety of processes. In examining these processes, the cybernetic or information-processing view of organization seems useful. First, the cybernetic model of organization will be briefly summarized, and then it will be used in presenting the explanation for the above question.

(i) Cybernetic Model of an Organization: A Short Digression

The cybernetic persective of an organization, which was originally developed by Norbert Wiener[(66)] amd Ross Ashby[(67)] and applied to human organizations by Beer,[(68)] Boulding,[(69)] Deutch[(70)] and Williamson[(71)] can be summarized as follows.

An organization has to cope with a set of constraints in order to maintain its viability in an environment ("Goal" in Fig. 6-3).[(72)] Information about a disturbance is perceived by the "receptor",[(73)] and transmitted to the "controller" where an evaluation of the disturbance is made. If the disturbance goes beyond the viable constraints, the controller issues an order to the "effector",[(74)] who implements the order to restore equilibrium. The receptor receives information about the effect of the action, and the same process is repeated until equilibrium is actually regained. In addition to this simple feedback control model, Ashby showed a model of an ultra-stable system with a double feedback mechanism.[(75)] He argues that adaptation to environmental change is twofold: one being the adaptation to relatively minor disturbances, which requires only a change in degree or restoration of the equilibrium; the other being adaptation to infrequent large disturbances, which requires a change in kind or the movement to a new equilibrium.[(76)] Ashby then shows that the latter large-scale qualitative adaptation demands another feedback loop. In Figure 6-3 this is illustrated as a "policy decision" which may change the goal and operate on the environment to attain a new equilibrium.

The UMWA organization can also be described within this framework. For

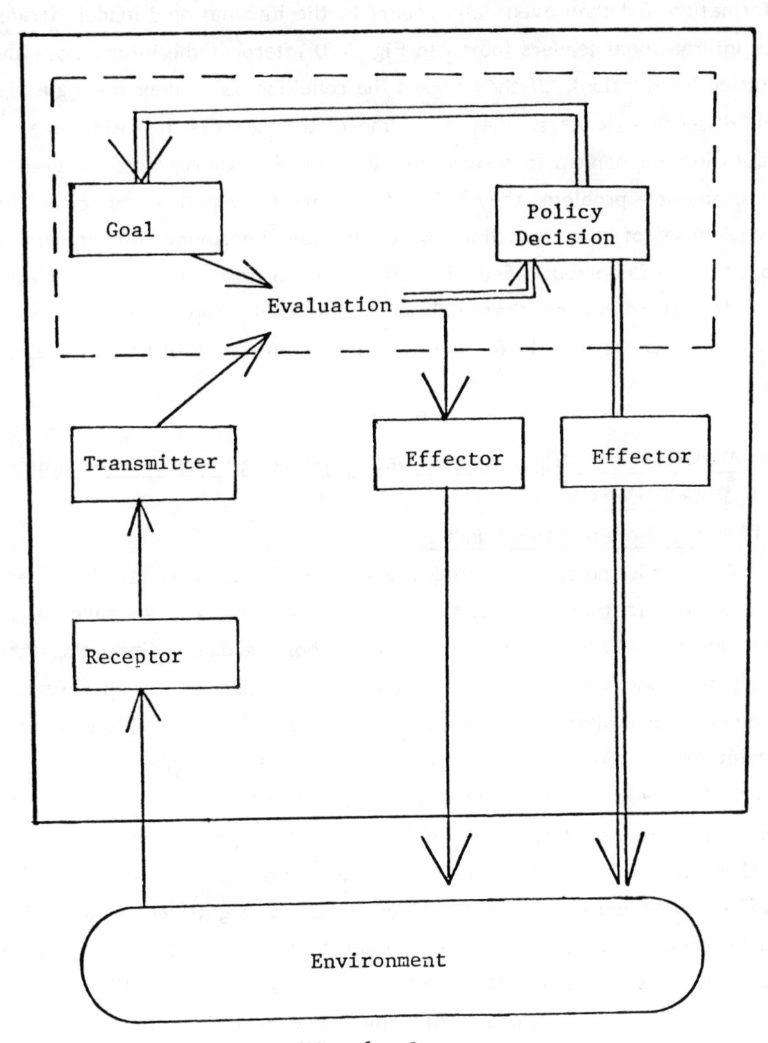

Fig. 6 - 3

A Cybernetic Model of an Organization

Note: ═══ :the Second Feedback

purposes of this section, the following conceptualization will be adopted. If a rank-and-file rebellion emerges, the local and district leaders (receptor)[77] receive the information and then eventually report to the international leaders (transmission). The international leaders (box a in Fig. 6-3) interpret the information and make a decision (evaluation). If they regard the rebellion as a minor one caused by only a few dissenting leaders, they may move to suppress it (using the routinized adaptation mechanism to restore equilibrium). If they regard it as an indication of a fundamental problem, they will reformulate their policy and try to remove the basic cause of the rebellion by drastically improving the miners' condition (application of non-routinized adaptation mechanism to move to a new equilibrium).

It will be argued that malfunction at each step of these decision-making processes was responsible for the insufficient militancy of union leadership in this period.

(ii) Analysis of the Organizational Decision-Making Process of the United Mine Workers

(aa) Defect in Perception Function

The rank-and-file's attitudes and movements were at first detected by district organization and international representatives. We have already found that, due to mergers and to the custom of holding dual offices, the district-level decision-making was performed by far fewer people than in the previous period. Mergers forced district leaders to cover large geographical areas far from the district office. Without having a strong control mechanism in the newly-added areas, their information collecting capability deteriorated. Some of those who were appointed as international officers naturally spent more time in Washington, travelled less in their districts, and began losing contact with the rank-and-file. Local customs and regional differences, which had significant meaning in the work and in union activities, were not familiar to them. Furthermore, all the leaders that had survived the reduction had been in office since the 1940's and 1950's. In this period most of them had not campaigned in any election, which could have forced them to organize the information-gathering activity more effectively and to be constantly alert to the needs of the rank-and-file. Their poor capacity to grasp the local situation can be seen clearly in the district leaders' failure to effectively handle local grievances. For example, on August 17, 1965, a small-scale wildcat strike took place at the Freeman Mine in Farmersville, Illinois, to protest the discharge of one miner. This ordinary local dispute, which could have been settled routinely, spread to involve 2,700 miners and went beyond the district's control simply because the district officer did not present this grievance to the industry's joint board. As one miner put it, "Hell! If the district does not help us, we do it ourselves."[78] A similar failure of the district officers caused a more serious work stoppage in District 6. The walkout initially began in early September, 1965, over a minor question of job placement[79] at the Ireland Mine of Hanna Coal Corporation in West Virginia. It rapidly flared, however, shutting down the whole production of District 6, when district leaders failed to support the local's position and permitted the company to discharge six miners, including the local president and four local officers.[80] When District President T. A. Williams began trying to settle the dispute, the strike spread further into Western Pennsylvania, idling 11,000 men and affecting 15% of the nation's coal output.[81]

These wildcat strikes were caused by relatively minor issues which could have been settled promptly. There was nothing technically difficult to solve, nothing outrageous in the miners' demands. The major factor in the trouble lay in the district leaders' lack of understanding of the situation or slow and unenthusiastic response to it.

(bb) Defects in Information Processing and Transmission

Poorly-gathered information was poorly transmitted to international leaders. As extensive communication research in social psychology has shown,[82] distortions tend to be introduced into vertical communication within organizations in proportion to the positive or negative motivation of the communicator. Simon summed up the phenomenon:

> Information does not automatically transmit itself from its point of origin to the rest of the organization; the individual who first obtains it must transmit it. In transmitting it, he will naturally be aware of the consequences its transmission will have for him. When he knows that the boss is going to be "burned up" by the news, the news is likely to be suppressed.(83)

The dominant theory of this distortion phenomenon is the instrumentality theory proposed by Cohen[84] and supported by many studies.[85] It argues that upward communication is "instrumental" to the need-satisfaction of subordinates, and that they manipulate the content of the communication so as to maximize its utility in creating good relations in their interaction with their superiors. It was inferred from this theory that the more influence the superior has on the welfare of the subordinates, the closer the content of the upward communication will be to what the superior wants to hear a priori.[86]

In Lewis' period, the international leaders were always very alert and willing to get the true picture of the rank-and-file. Lewis himself made a great effort to get accurate information. Boyle, on the other hand, was far less tolerant of criticisms; he lost his temper easily and shouted at the person who mentioned something unpleasant to him. As a result, when a wildcat strike took place, the district leaders rarely reported the cause of the mineworkers' dissatisfaction. Instead, they would present the rebellion as the act of a few anti-union agitators. For example, at the first meeting of the International Executive Board after Yablonski's announcement of his candidacy, no rational discussion of the challenger's influence in each district or of the effective strategy was heard. A typical statement was made by Albert Pass, a board member from District 19:

> President Boyle, we are not going to leave you and the other officers sitting out in that field and these damn fellows behind the bushes shooting at you, you out there by yourself. By God, we will run them out from behind those bushes. (87)

Thus, in the process of upward communication, the real cause and effect of dissatisfaction among the miners was suppressed, with undue emphasis on the "evil" character of the agitators. This unidirectional distortion of information made it very difficult for international leaders to realize the necessity of more fundamental adaptive measures (the second feedback loop called "policy decision" in Fig. 6-3).

(cc) Defects in the Decision-Making Function

It has been pointed out that decisions at the international level were made in exactly the same way as in Lewis' days. Just like any other formal or informal feature of organizational structure, the effectiveness of such a mode of decision-making varies with the person practicing it. One-man rule of a huge organization in a highly complex environment requires tremendous cognitive and mental capability from the leader. It might have worked very well for an outstanding man like Lewis, but not for Boyle, who soon found himself overwhelmed by a tremendous amount of complicated work. His job as President of the National Coal Policy Committee, the joint political lobbying organization of the union and the operators for the protection of the industry, occupied most of his time and energy,[88] leaving him very little time to closely review the materials in other areas.

Although the pressure was mounting, he refused to delegate authority to others. Harrison Combs, the UMW's assistant general counsel, describes Boyle's style of making decisions.

> Although Tony had never done any wide, general reading that I know of, he was articulate. He had a quick, sharp mind. The trouble was that Tony wanted to do all the talking regardless of the subject. If you wanted to give him information, you couldn't do it. He wouldn't listen. As an administrator he wouldn't delegate authority to anyone and it didn't matter how professional the person was. He had a habit of quarterbacking the legal department and he didn't know what he was talking about. (89)

This overburdening contributed to the malfunctioning of the decision mechanism in three ways. First, it made it very difficult for the international leaders to assess reports and correct any bias carefully. As Miller[90] and Baker, et al. found,[91] one of the most common ways top organization leaders use to assess information is to adopt several information channels in addition to the orthodox hierarchial source, and to evaluate carefully the differences among the reports. The problem with this method, however, is that it demands time, resources, and long, painstaking analysis.[92] Boyle, who was already buried under a flood of information, could not process or carefully analyze further information.

Secondly, the overloaded decision-maker is apt to make omissions or mistakes in the act of receiving information. After a thorough review of communications literature, Guetzkow concluded:

> The deletion of aspects of messages is a common phenomenon within social communication. Sometimes omissions take place at the point of message reception, in that the two or three levels of the communication simply are not grasped. Or, more grossly, the message may be neglected because of sheer overload in message-processing capability ... response to overload is made by reducing the inflow, either by sporadic avoidance of processing ("omission") or by leaving the situation entirely ("escape"). (93)

Because of this process, it was apparent that the overloaded international leader failed to grasp many important messages.

Thirdly, as Gaus and Warcott observed,[94] the work overload tended to favor the short-run, day-to-day decisions. This phenomenon is what March and Simon have called the "Gresham's Law" of planning. They argued that, other things being equal, organization members tend to engage in already-programmed activities rather than in those that are non-routine and unprogrammed, and that this tendency is larger when time pressure is greater.[(95)] In the UMWA in the 1960's, where the decision-making capacity was extremely limited, the attention of decision-makers was naturally directed to more urgent, short-term issues rather than to the long-term problems with no apparent immediate relevance. Boyle's decisions were thus increasingly incremental,[(96)] short-sighted, opportunistic and spontaneous.

(dd) The Career and the Character of the Leadership

The second relevant factor determining the quality of the international's decisions was the character of the international leaders formed through long careers.

All international officers followed the same career pattern. They were first elected as local union officers. If they served several terms, district leaders might assign them particular tasks. Those who continually performed these tasks well would be elevated to district offices. If they looked promising, they might be assigned tasks by the international. Those who could repeatedly show their brilliance in these jobs might be picked for an international office or a top district post.[(97)]

This promotion scheme imposed an unintended bias on the selection process of the leadership. First, this process unjustly emphasized trouble-shooting ability as opposed to objective or policy-formation capability. As the United Mine Workers was a very centralized organization in which all major decisions and instructions came from the top level, the tasks to which local or district leaders were assigned were invariably minor and technical. In addition, many of the tasks were assigned temporarily only when some trouble arose. Because trouble-shooting required neither the ability to detect the trouble at an early stage nor the ability to take a long-term perspective, this selection process suppressed planning ability within the UMW hierarchy. Many of the leaders would implement whatever order given to them, oblivious to long-term goals.[(98)]

Secondly, as a result of long careers as trouble-shooters, leaders tended to regard wildcat strikes as temporary phenomena which required suppression rather than as indicators of the insufficiency of union service. For them, Lewis' policy was faultless and could not be the underlying cause of the wildcat strikes. The framework formed in the lower career stages greatly distorted their perception of the UMWA's situation in the 1960's.

In previous decades the union operated successfully despite the same selection procedure because Lewis knew how to detect the defects in his policies through wildcat strikes, as well as how to reformulate his policies accordingly. Other leaders simply carried out his directives. The tragedy for the union was that this successful practice of the 1940's and 1950's made it impossible for a second Lewis to mature within the system.

Another important phenomenon in this regard was the emergence of Boyle's two personal assistants, General Counsel Edward L. Carey and Executive Assistant Suzanne V. Richard, whose power increased directly proportional to the increase in Boyle's work-overload. Suzanne Richard had an office next to Boyle's and helped to guide almost all the union's day-to-day operations. She interviewed executives of coal companies, interpreted the wording of contracts, and issued instructions to local and district officers. She not only handled all the routine chores which Boyle found too tedious, but also "cleared" everyone who wanted to see Boyle, read every paper that was directed to Boyle, and knew all of Boyle's incoming telephone calls.[99] Even in contract negotiations she exercised immense influence. As former BCOA President George Judy recalled,

> Suzanne was always there. Whenever there was anything important to discuss, Tony would have her with him. I could always tell how I was doing by counting the number of times Suzanne would have to butt in. "Miss Richard," he would ask - he never called her Suzanne - "is that right or isn't it?" With Suzanne at his side, he was a tough negotiator. (100)

Although there was no doubt about their competence, the trouble was that neither Richard nor Carey had any experience in actual mining at any time during their careers. Carey was a former assistant U. S. Attorney for the District of Columbia; Richard was hired as secretary to John Owens when she was a student at George Washington University, and had served the UMWA headquarters in Washington as a secretary ever since. Both assistants had spent their lives in Washington and had no idea whatsoever about the miners' life and problems. As Downs argues,[101] a general understanding of the miners' life is absolutely necessary to correctly assess the distorted information transmitted from below, and lack of such understanding left the international leaders totally vulnerable to the distortion.

4. Discussion: Orientation of the Middle-Level Leaders

The above analysis has shown a number of factors responsible for the union's lack of militancy. In this section, some effot will be made to formulate generally applicable propositions.

Many studies in business and public administration point out that middle managers often face insoluble dilemmas caused by two often incompatible pressures: one from their superiors, which demands that they emphasize the welfare of the organization or the top leaders; and the other from their subordinates, which requires them to be concerned about the welfare of the individual employees or the work group. The same holds true in national labor unions. District and local leaders are responsible not only for representing the rights and will of their constituencies, but also for controlling and disciplining them so that the top leaders' policies can be implemented best.

When there is a conflict of interest between the upper and lower levels, each leader in the middle has to make a choice as to how much the forces from above should be emphasized as opposed to the forces from below and vice versa. In this sense, a middle-level leader can be characterized by a particular combination, consisting of his orientation toward his superior plus his orientation toward his subordinate. Figure 6-4 illustrates the measuring scale of this orientation (a superior-subordinate orientation continuum), with one pole representing the leaders who always push their constituency's need at the cost of their superiors' interests, the other pole representing leaders of the opposite orientation, and a variety of compromising cases in between.

Many arguments presented in this chapter may be neatly put by using this concept of the superior-subordinate orientation pattern of middle leaders. The factors enumerated above (such as the reduction in the number of district leaders, longer time spent in Washington, Boyle's dictatorial power over their caree-s and their extremely high stakes in their posts) changed the orientation of the middle leaders toward more a greater on the international's will to the detriment of that of the rank-and-file.

The UMWA under Tony Boyle may thus be described in terms of the cybernetic model:

(i) information about the rank-and-file was only poorly collected;

(ii) the upward transmission of that information was very much distorted in order to please the top leader.

The pattern would be qualified by a case in which the top leader is charismatic and very sensitive to the mood of the rank-and-file: the distortion in the course of

Fig. 6-4

A Superior-Subordinate

Orientation Continuum of the Middle Leaders

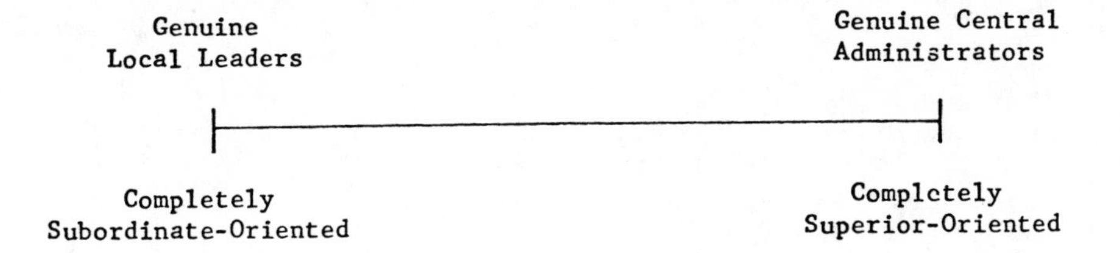

transmission may not then occur to the same extent.

From these considerations, one may form the following hypothesis:

Proposition 6-1

In labor unions where leaders are not charismatic, the more the district leaders are oriented toward the international in the superior-subordinate orientation continuum, the less sensitively will the union policy respond to pressures toward militancy.

Figures 6-5a and 6-5b represent an organization with centrally-oriented district leaders and one with locally-oriented district leaders respectively. The above proposition can be illustrated by Figure 6-6.

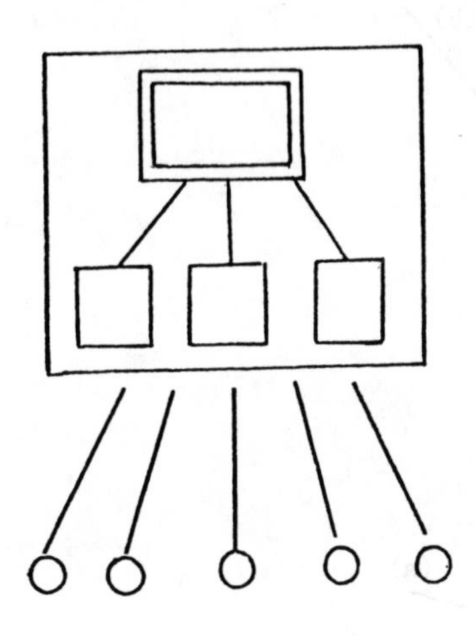

Figure 6 - 5a
An Organization with
Centrally-Oriented
Middle-Level Leaders

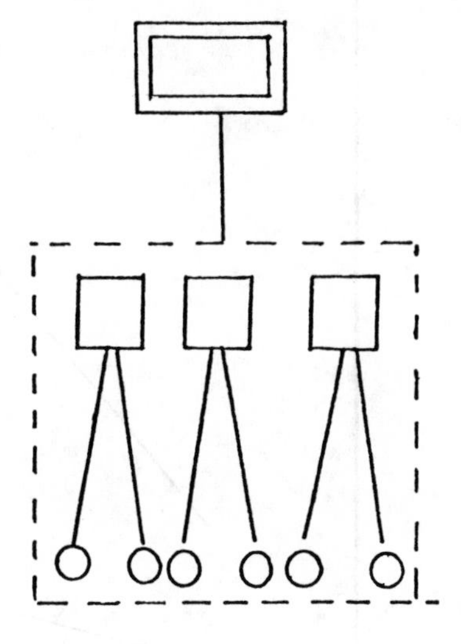

Figure 6 - 5b
An Organization with
Locally Oriented
Middle-Level Leaders

Fig. 6-6

Hypothesis 6-1

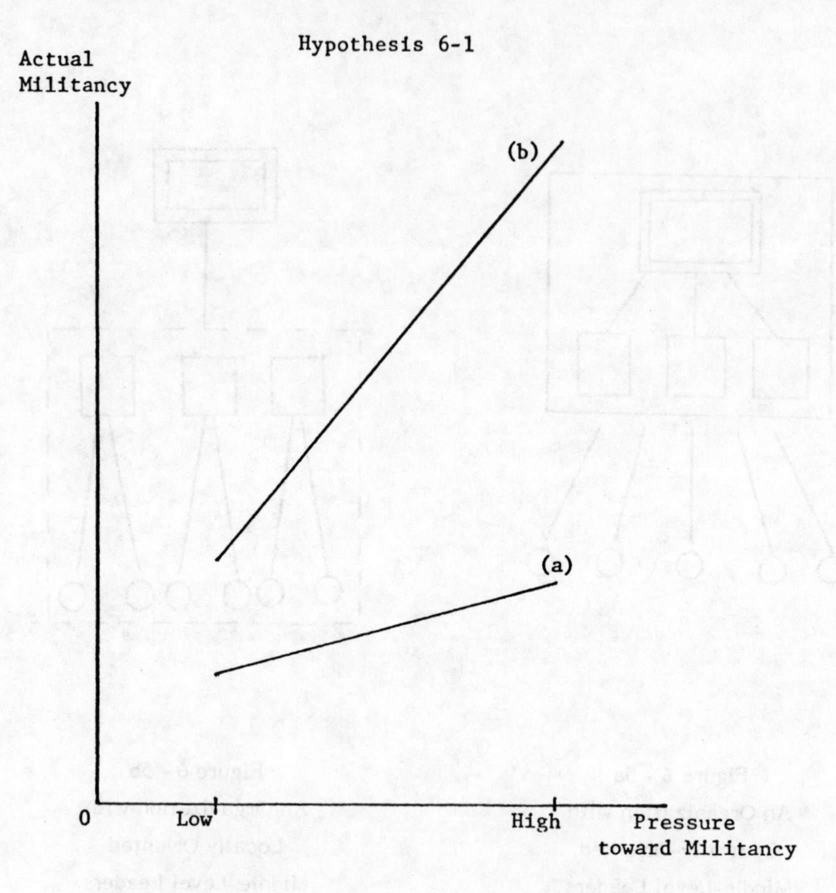

(a): an organization with centrally oriented middle-level leaders

(b): an organization with locally oriented middle-level leaders

CHAPTER VII

THE UMWA IN 1972-1974:

HIGH MILITANCY, A WEAK LEADER AND DEMOCRACY

On May 1, 1972, Federal District Judge Bryant ruled the problematic 1969 election void and ordered new elections under the supervision of the Secretary of Labor. A month later, on May 28, the Miners for Democracy, the rank-and-file reform group within the union, held a convention[1] and nominated Arnold Miller, president of the West Virginia Black Lung Association, as presidential candidate, with Mike Trbovich and Harry Patrick as candidates for vice president and secretary-treasurer.[2]

These reform candidates went into pro-Boyle regions, which Yablonski had not dared to enter. Instead of physical threats, they were welcomed warmly. On December 22, 1972, the Miller forces defeated Boyle by a tally of 70,373 to 56,334.[3]

1. Union Organization

The Miller administration immediately began large-scale reconstruction of the organization. On December 22, it swiftly purged twenty pro-Boyle International Executive Board Members,[4] and temporarily appointed thirteen Miller supporters. Miller dismissed general counsel Edward Carey as well as Boyle's executive assistant Suzanne Richard, naming Joseph A. Yablonski, a son of the slain challenger, as general counsel and Richard M. Bank, a 28-year-old Charleston lawyer, as his executive assistant. Many inactive department-heads were fired. The director of the safety division, Kenneth Wells, was replaced by a working miner, Steve Liming, on an acting basis; the director of the organizing department, Jess M. Vicini, was replaced by Laverne Lawrence; the director of research, Joseph Brennan, was also removed.[5] A former high official of the Steelworkers' Union, Meyer Berstern, was appointed director of public and international affairs. UAW President Leonard Woodcock also visited UMW headquarters and offered to train the three new international auditors at the UAW office in Detroit.[6]

a. Decision-Making Structure: Decentralization of the Line Organization and Centralization of the Staff Organization

One of the most important campaign promises of the MFD was the abolition of one-man control. Probably the most significant reform in this regard was substantial decentralization of the union's internal procedure for decision-making in the collective bargaining process. The new constitution required that local unions begin discussing the demands in coming negotiations about one year before the expiration of the current contract. Representatives of locals were then to be sent to district conferences, where they would put forward local demands and act upon the district's recommendations.[7] District were should to then take these recommendations to the Bargaining Council, which would then decide on final demands.[8] The Bargaining Council, composed of the International Executive Board members and district presidents,[9] was the union's ultimate decision-making body in contract talks. The actual negotiations were to be conducted by the Negotiation Committee appointed and headed by the president, under the instructions and supervision of the Bargaining Council.[10] Any agreement reached by the Negotiation Committee was to be evaluated by the Bargaining Council.[11] If the council approved the agreement, the district presidents would reconvene the district conferences to explain it.[12] A referendum would then be held for ratification by the membership.[13] Any agreement would be tentative until it was ratified by both the council and the membership. In the case that one of the ratifications failed, the council would instruct the president to renegotiate. The above procedure is illustrated in Fig. 7-1.

In addition to formal changes toward decentralization, Miller's mode of decision-making further contributed to this trend. Unlike Lewis and Boyle, Miller rarely made a decision by himself, and was very reluctant to exercise any political influence on anyone. He would present the issue to the IEB meetings or to the conventions, let people discuss it without pressure from him, and accept their decision as a mandate for his future actions. His handling of the International Convention illustrates this very clearly. Whereas Lewis and Boyle had controlled all the recommendations made by various committees to the convention and had used all available measures from persuasion to violence to manipulate the delegates, Miller played the role of chairman without stating his opinion even on crucial issues. For example, in the 1976 Convention, the Constitutional Committee recommended an amendment to increase the number of IEB members required to repeal the president's interpretation from a simple majority to a two-thirds majority. This amendment was very crucial for Miller because the anti-Miller majority of the IEB had been blocking every possible proposal of the Miller administration.[14] Although the general mood of the delegates was unfavorable to this recommendation, Miller did not make any effort to persuade them, or even to discourage the opponents' early effort to close the debate.[15] Consequently, many union decisions were very decentralized and can be characterized as the decisions of uncontrolled aggregates of semi-independent individuals.

While decentralizing the union's decision-making procedure, the new leaders substantially strengthened the staff function of the international union. The Safety Department, for example, had only one full-time staff member in Boyle's period and had done virtually nothing for decades,[16] Miller dismissed Director Kenneth Wells, and appointed William Craft, a manager of the Bureau of Mines sub-district office in Madisonville, Kentucky.[17] The new director was very active in searching for trained safety experts, and by the end of 1973 the staff had expanded to forty-two, making the UMW Safety Division the largest among American unions. Immediately thereafter, this division embarked on the long neglected task of safety-training and education across the nation.[18] Emergency plans were established, with a 24-hour emergency toll-free hot-line and an airplane always standing by so that safety officials could reach a mine disaster site quickly.

The Research Department was also substantially reorganized. In the Lewis and Boyle periods, the department had merely prepared reports or statistics for the National Coal Policy Conference, and had done very little research for the union itself.[19] Tom Bethel, whom many observers termed one of the brightest researchers in the American labor unions, was named director, and five highly qualified professionals were appointed as researchers.

Their first task was to prepare for the 1974 contract negotiations. They restructured the department's chaotic files for systematic use, undertook a comprehensive review of collective agreements in other industries, embarked on a survey of miners' interests, studied the effects of various agreements in the contract, and compiled information on manpower availability and productivity. They also participated actively in forming final demands for negotiation, and conducted extensive educational meetings in the coal fields concerning the state of the industry and contract demands.[20]

These new, competent and professional departmental staffs not only carried out democratically-reached decisions more effectively, but also began to have a decisive influence on the decision-making process itself. They prepared elaborate and professional policy proposals for the IEB meetings. Often Miller could not fully explain the details of the proposals and began asking the staff to attend the IEB meetings. Their detailed, sophisticated and professional explanations in IEB meetings had a strong impact on the final decisions of the Board.

b. Leadership Power Structure

To fulfill a major campaign promise, the reform administration began relinquishing the arbitrary powers granted to the International President. One of the very first decisions of the reform leaders was to purge all district leaders "appointed improperly by the predecessor", and to hold fresh elections. By the end of 1973, the autonomy which the rank-and-file had sought for decades was well established in all districts.

More important in this respect was the abolition of, or substantial moderation of, three instruments of presidential power described in Chapter IV (i.e. limitation of inter-local communication, creation of provisional government in district and local unions, and suspension of membership). The new constitution not only lifted the ban on inter-local communication but also went so far as to encourage it. Sections 5 and 14 of Article VI instructed the International Union to provide a candidate for an international office with information, technical assistance and equal accessibility to space in the Journal. Furthermore, the members' rights to free assembly and free speech were guaranteed explicitly for the first time (Article XII, Section 2).

Arbitrary abuse of presidential power to revoke local and district charters was made difficult by a variety of measures, First, while the old constitution allowed the President to exercise this power whenever he found it necessary, the new constitution specifically stated the conditions under which the exercise of power was legitimate. He now had to prove clearly that these conditions actually existed, which would deter him from applying his power too freely in borderline cases. (Article XVIII, Section 1). Secondly, sophisticated procedures for public hearings were spelled out in detail. When the trouble specified by Article XVIII, Section 1 took place in a district union, the president was to appoint a three-man panel, approved by the International Executive Board, to investigate the charge. The district leaders would be given ample opportunity to defend themselves before the panel, including the right to call witnesses and to cross-examine adverse witnesses. The panel would then make a written report to the Executive Board. All members involved in the charge would receive a copy of the report and submit their response in writing to the Executive Board.(21) The Executive Board, on the basis of the hearing, the report and the responses, would make the final decision.

This new procedure had two significant deterrent effects on presidential power. One was the larger number of people participating in the decision with specific rights, power and obligations. The greater the number of people involved in the process, the harder it is to control the final decision. This is particularly true when every individual involved is quasi-independent with specific constitutional powers.

The second deterrent effect stemmed from the requirement that every step of the process should be formally recorded in a written document. Since these documents, once recorded, could be used in future legal or political fights, it would be very difficult for a leader to unduly ignore any position explicitly stated and recorded in the investigatory process

Another significant restriction on the presidential power to command district suspension was provided by Article XVIII, Section 5, which limited the duration of trusteeship government to 180 days.

The power of the president to suspend membership was also substantially reduced. The new constitution provided specific reasons for which a suspension could be valid. Furthermore, detailed trial procedures were designed to give the accused enough opportunities to defend themselves, and every decision was required to be recorded formally in a written document. Table 7-1 summarizes the changes in trial procedures.

The new constitution also modified election procedures so that corruption, irregularities and excessive influence of the incumbent would be effectively checked. A variety of rights and obligations for the candidates were carefully delineated; the number of local endorsements required for candidacy was reduced from fifty to twenty-five; and election procedures were spelled out in great detail, which would allow very little of the corrupt irregularities observed in the 1969 election. A detailed comparison between the old and the new election rules is illustrated in Table 7-2.

As presidential power declined, certain district leaders began to emerge as powerful figures, whom Miller could not ignore in his policy decisions. Karl Karton, Lou Antal and Mike Trbovich were at least as strong and as prominent as Miller. After Miller's victory, Kafton and Antal remained powerful, Kafton as the IEB member from District 6, and Antal as the President of District 5. They also chaired many permanent and ad hoc committees, and maintained a strong influence over top union decisions. Whereas the functions and powers of vice president had been nebulous or insignificant in the previous administrations, Trbovich took over formal responsibility in a variety of important areas, such as organizing and safety programs, which kept him influential and visible.

Table 7 - 1

Differences in Trial Procedures, Before and After 1973

	Before 1972	The 1973 Constitution
Reasons for charges	Not specifically stated.	Five specific conditions given.
Procedure for charging	No specific procedure given.	Written and signed statement under oath, attested by notary public
Trial committee	Executive Board of the Local, District or International	Right of the charged to complain about a biased trial committee
Trial procedure	No specific procedure given.	1) A variety of time limits for decisions. 2) Written notice of time, place and reasons of hearing to all concerned. 3) Right of the party to call Witnesses, present all evidence, hear all evidence presented, confront and cross-examine all witnesses and to present oral or written briefs.
Judgment	Majority	1) Majority to find a member or local official guilty. 2) 2/3 majority for district and international officers. 3) Unanimous vote to suspend or remove from office.
Appeals	Provided.	Provided

Source: The UMWA Constitution, 1932 and 1973

Table 7 - 2

Differences in the Election Procedure

	Before 1972	After 1973
Freedom of speech and support.	Not stated	1) Explicitly stated. 2) Sanction explicitly stated for members who have intervened in others' freedom.
Right of a candidate for nomination	Not stated.	Equal rights as to: 1) attendance at local meetings; 2) access to services of the international union (official publication, list of local addresses, mailing of campaign literature, etc.); 3) sending an observer to any local nomination.
Local nomination procedure	Not stated.	1) Choice of time and place which permits maximum voter participation. 2) Notification of time and place to international union all members of the local. 3) Nomination meeting to be a closed session. 4) Equal right of members to speak. 5) Procedure for absentee balloting.
Number of local endorsements required	Fifty.	Twenty-five
Right of official candidate	Not stated.	1) Access to a list of the local union addresses, members and local union officials. 2) Entitled to three mailings of campaign literature using the international's services. 3) Equal space in the Journal. 4) Right to challenge time and place of any local election. 5) Two observers at any voting site.
Obligation of candidate	Not stated.	Disclosure of a financial statement.

(Continued next page)

(Table 7 - 2 cont.)

	Before 1972	After 1973
Election procedure	Not specifically stated	1) Notification of the list of candidates from the international to the local. 2) Time and place to allow voter participation. 3) Notification of time andplace to the international. 4) Detailed procedure for challenging the ballot.

Source: The UMWA Constitution, 1932 and 1973

In the first round of district elections, pro-Boyle candidates defeated reformist leaders in at least six districts and immediately became vocal in criticizing Miller.(22) Lee Roy Patterson, IEB member from District 23, emerged as leader of the pro-Boyle elements at the top level. Particularly after 1974, many pro-Miller IEB members either changed their position or were defeated by anti-Miller candidates in the district elections.(23) Patterson's influence on union decisions grew substantially.(24)

c. Leadership Style: a Symbol of the Democratic Movement

When the reformists' campaign began in 1972, many miners thought it impossible to topple Boyle. However, their campaign generated unexpected enthusiasm among the miners and grew to a massive movement. As a result of his success, Miller became a hero and a symbol of reform. Unlike the charismatic leader of a mass movement, who actually initiates the mission and commands total loyalty from his followers, Miller was selected from a movement already in process, not because he had extraordinary personal capacities but because the movement had to elect someone. He was legitimate only in so far as he could represent the essence of the movement. His style had to reflect honesty and democracy in contrast to his predecessor's corruption and dictatorship.(25)

The degree to which democracy had taken over union procedures is nowhere better illustrated than by the marked difference in time and opportunities allowed to the rank-and-file for speaking at the conventions (Table 7-3). Miller's idea of democracy seemed to be that all decisions of the union should be made solely by the rank-and-file, and that these decisions should be implemented no matter how unreasonable they might be. He was extremely reluctant to exercise any control over the rank-and-file's deliberations. For example, at the 1976 Convention where many resolutions against the Miller administration were discussed, he played only a neutral role as chairman, strictly following parliamentary rules and rarely trying to influence the delegates in his favor. The only exception was an occasion when the anti-Miller group attempted to shorten his tenure by holding the presidential election half a year earlier. Even against such an apparent political challenge, Miller merely asked Secretary-Treasurer Patrick to take over the chair temporarily, came down from the stage to the floor, waited until he was recognized, and made a short speech within the five minute restriction imposed on every delegate. His speech, just one among many, failed to impress the delegates, who ultimately voted against his plea.(27)

Table 7 - 3

Rank-and-File Participation in International Conventions

1942-1976

Year	Average number of rank-and-file delegates who spoke per day	Proportion of space in the proceedings devoted to rank-and-file
1944	17.2	13.4%
1948	13.7	12.2%
1952	15.2	10.4%
1956	12.2	10.4%
1960	13.5	11.5%
1964	17.7	12.3%
1968	13.3	10.9%
1973	93.4	33.4%
1976	104.0	36.6%

Scource: Proceedings of the International Convention of the United Mine Workers of America, for the above-listed years.

When seeking ratification of a tentative agreement, without which, he believed, the industry would become totally chaotic, Miller made the following statement which would have been inconceivable from his predecessor:

> I will be guided by the membership. If it's their mandate, I will go back to the bargaining table. But I think you should know the risk. I don't think we can get any more and we could bankrupt the union. (27)

One newspaper report fittingly summarized Miller's style as sincere, honest, democratic and apolitical.[28]

d. Internal Strife

While strong enthusiasm for reform prevailed in the coal fields, International Headquarters were plagued by serious internal conflict. Although Miller's open, candid, sincere and democratic style of leadership might have been the only style acceptable to the rank-and-file, it proved to be a liability in the highly political world of the international union. When a series of district elections was held in 1973, Miller chose reformist candidates against the remaining Boyle supporters but did not actively campaign for them. This resulted in their defeat in at least six districts, and created a sense of insecurity and distrust among pro-Miller IEB members. As Miller failed to take the necessary steps against politically motivated attacks by opposing members of the IEB, the latter became more powerful.[29]

Another source of internal strife was the role of the newly-expanded staff. As pointed out above, staff functions were strongly centralized and professionalzed at the international level. Although many decisions were delegated to district leaders as a result of the democratic reform, most policy proposals came from the staff departments. The professionally-educated staff members tended to produce voluminous and sophisticated recommendations which were difficult for most of the district leaders to read through.

> These staff people were so dedicated and competent that in every single damn issue they couldn't but produce volumes and volumes of fat policy recommendations full of sophisticated arguments. Some guys were so brilliant and were prepared to give a brilliant answer to any question (at the IEB meetings). In 1973 and '74, at least, there is no doubt they were very influential. I even suspect that those IEB members did not read those damn fat materials and needless to say did not understand them. (30)

These staff professionals were not miners. Many district leaders came to feel that the union was being operated by the non-mining elements in the international headquarters. Trbovich, in his open attack on Miller in the 1976 Convention, criticized the role of the staff members in the administration.[31]

> ... out of VISTA came a group of people who were going to save the coal miners from the free enterprise system and the democratic government. They came to Appalachia. They worked up until 1972, and lo and behold, they got into the reform movement of the United Mine Workers, and when we won the election they moved into the United Mine Workers.
>
> There are some recent articles out of New York and other areas which have pointed out the fact that the United Mine Workers is not under the control of the line officers, but the staff of this union. These elements, these people, who do not believe in the philosophy of a democratic government, have disrupted and have undermined the leadership of this organization. (32)

e. The Membership

As the coal industry began recovering, the number of miners grew rapidly. Figure 7-1 shows the increase in the number of working miners in the 1970's. The membership grew more than 50% from 92,000 in 1964 to more than 137,000 in 1974,[33] which made the UMW one of the fastest growing unions in the nation.[34] The growth rate was accelerated in the 1970's, with the membership expanding more than 30% in the two years after 1974.[35]

The most significant consequence of this increase was the entry of a large number of young miners into the union. Although complete data on the average age of the UMW membership is not available, Table 7-3a, constructed from census data and UMW data, clearly shows this change.

The entry of young miners resulted in a generation gap between aged old-timers and the young, inexperienced miners. Figure 7-2 illustrates this phenomenon. Since one-third of the UMW members were retired and were not included in Figure 7-2, the age distribution of the whole membership would be far more prominently M-shaped.

2. Union Militancy in the 1974 Collective Bargaining Negotiations

a. Prologue to the Negotiations

After his election in 1972, two years before the expiration of the current contract, Miller frequently delared that he would fight hard to obtain a sizeable gain in 1974.[36] In the International Convention of 1973 a variety of highly militant demands were adopted:

(1) Six-hour day including a one-hour lunch break to replace the current eight-hour day with a half-hour break.[37]

(2) Strict health-safety plans including full-time safety commitment at every mine, full pay during mine closure due to unsafe conditions, establishment of a first-aid station with a doctor and a nurse at every mine, etc.[38]

(3) An immediate increase in the industry-paid royalty from 80¢ to $1.40 a ton and a further 20¢ raise every six months up to $2.40 a ton by May 12, 1977.[39]

(4) Strict seniority without qualification clause.

(5) Sick pay of thirty days a year, with unused days to accumulate without any limit into successive years.

(6) Establishment of a cost-of-living escalator.

(7) A substantial wage increase, a decrease of the gap between top and bottom pay, and an increase in differentials for the second and third shifts.

(8) Doubling of the vacation period from two to four weeks and an unspecified graduated increase in accordance with seniority.

(9) Four new holidays in addition to the current nine.

(10) Supplementary unemployment benefit at least equal to the top level achieved in other industries, and severance pay, neither of which was included in the current contract.

(11) Lowering the retirement age from 55 to 50.

On August 19, Miller called a five-day memorial-period shutdown.[40] Although the union's public statement issued a week earlier referred only to the commemoration of the "thousands of coal miners killed while working in the nation's mines",[41] union officials privately acknowledged that building up bargaining power by reducing the above-ground coal stockpiles was the main strategic objective of the shutdown.[42]

On August 28, the UMW's newly established Bargaining Council gave the final approval to more than 200 demands based on the resolutions adopted at the Convention.[43]

b. The Actual Negotiations

The talks finally started in September of 1974, two months before the contract expiration. It had been mutually understood that although the current contract expired on November 12, the tedious and time-consuming ratification process would take a minimum of eight days and more likely ten, making November 4 the latest

Table 7 - 3a

Median Age of Working Miners and Members

	1940	1950	1960	1964	1970	1973	1974	1975	1976
Census data (miners)	46.8	38.1	43.6		43.6				
UMWA data (members)				48-49		38.2	36.7	34.8	34

Sources:

1940: U. S. Department of Commerce, Bureau of the Census, 16th Census of the United States, Vol. III, Part 1.

1950: Ibid., 1950 United States Census of Population, Special Report, Vol. IV, Part 1, Chapter B.

1964: Ibid., 1960...Census..., Vol. II, Part 7, Chapter A.

1970: Ibid., 1970 Census, Vol. II, Part 7, Chapter A.

1976: UMWA Research Department (unpublished).

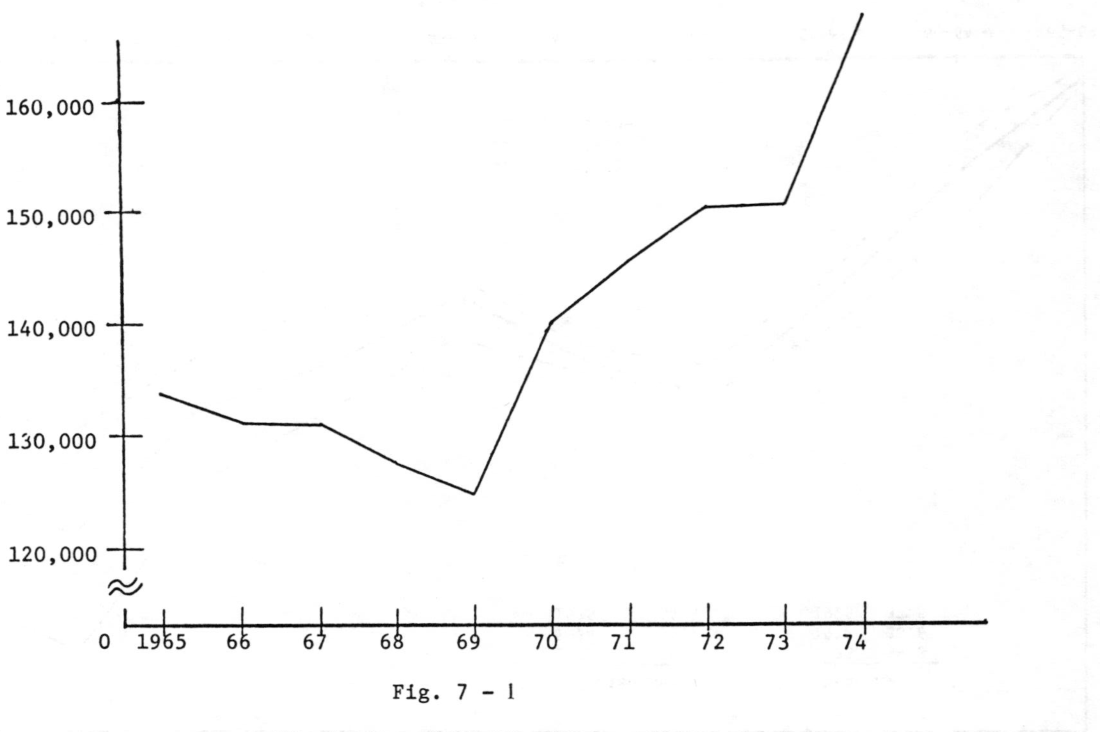

Fig. 7 - 1

The Number of Working Miners 1965 - 1974

Source: The National Coal Association, Bituminous Coal Data 1975

Fig. 7 - 2

UMWA Active Miners by 5-Year Age Group

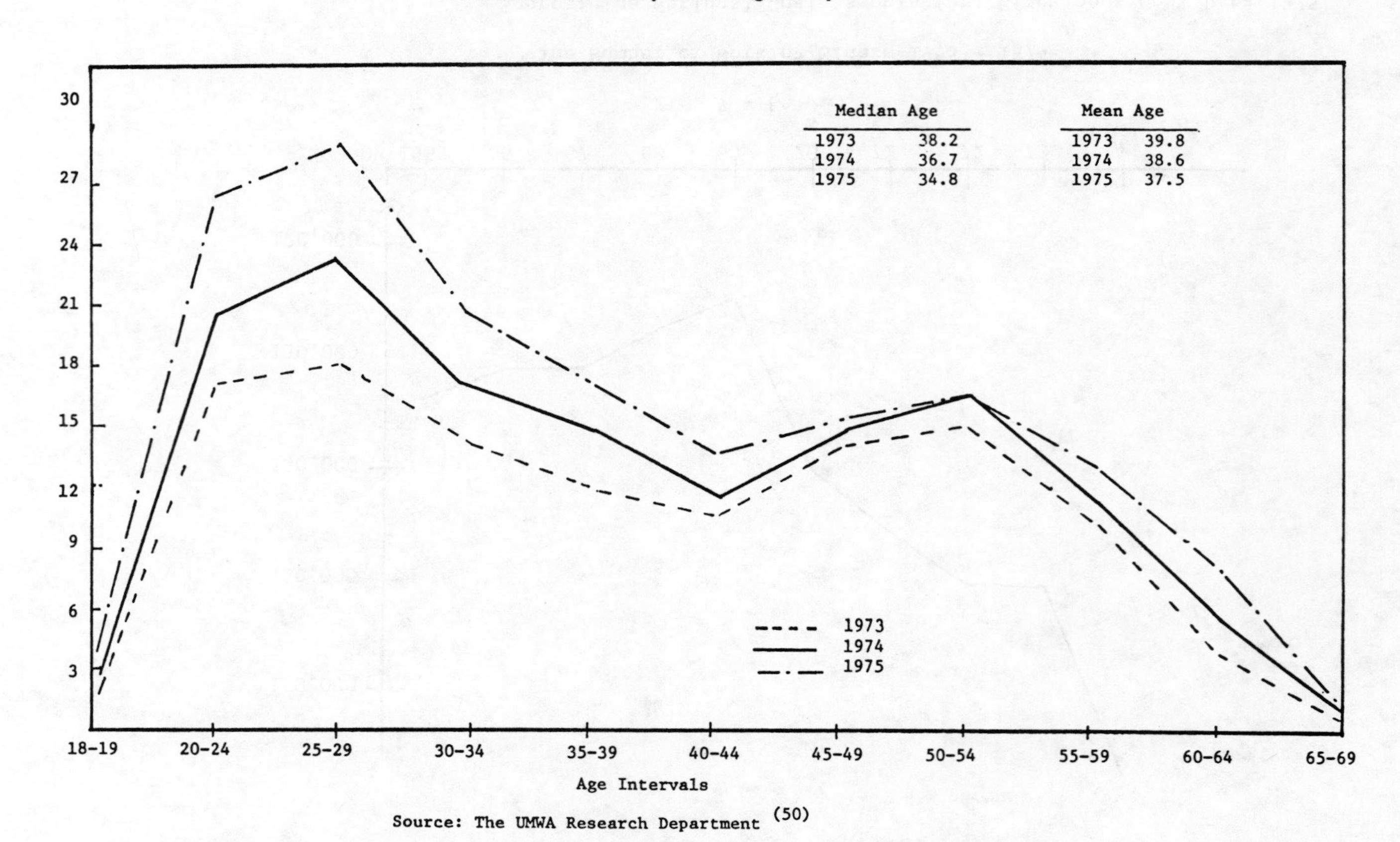

Source: The UMWA Research Department (50)

actual deadline. Due to the novelty of the union demands, the first several days were devoted to procedural questions only. A variety of subcommittees were established for substantive negotiations on specific issues, on the assumption that the involvement of a large number of bargaining council members in the negotiations would make ratification easier.

On September 18, company negotiators submitted their position-paper. The industry's major concern was to raise productivity, which had been declining for the last few years, and the owners seemed prepared to yield on a wide range of economic benefits with the condition that higher productivity be guaranteed. For example, their counter-proposal reportedly left the door open for accepting - at least in principle - the union's non-wage demands such as cost-of-living wage escalator, sick pay, higher pensions, more holidays and graduated vacations. However, it characterized many of the union's non-wage demands as "totally unacceptable".(44)

The negotiations reached the first impasse on October 8, when industry bargainers responded to the union's proposals on five major non-economic areas. Miller angrily walked away from the bargaining table and promptly called a press conference in which he accused the operators of adopting an "inflexible position", making "garbage proposals which were so close to the current contract that they were essentially asking for a three-year renewal of their license to kill".(45) On their part, the operators seemed genuinely surprised at the union's sharp reaction. Their negotiator, Guy Farmer, called it "a highly charged emotional response to something that wasn't that emotional".(46)

The stalemate, which lasted several days, came to an end on October 14 when the operators agreed to negotiate further on non-wage issues.(47) The negotiations began to show slow but steady progress. On October 22, the industry had made significant concessions on safety and manpower training, two important union priorities, and both sides had allegedly reached "understandings" on key points of the five major non-economic issues. In addition, the health and retirement subcommittee, which was discussing increases in miners' pensions and increased benefits for disabled workers and widows, were agreed on most aspects of the welfare structure. On the negative side of the picture was the industry's insistence on seven-days-a-week operation, which could jeopardize the general non-wage "understanding". The subcommittee on classification had also reached a standoff, with operators resisting further changes in the current wage structure. The subcommittee on surface mining had proven ineffectual, and most of the issues which it was supposed to discuss were sent back to the main bargaining table without any agreement.(48)

As the operational deadline, November 4, approached, a tense and confused atmosphere prevailed at the negotiation table with some sources firmly expressing optimism and others pessimism. October 30 saw considerable "horse-trading" on economic issues. Non-economic issues, however, particularly the union's demand for the right to strike at local mines, were not making any progress.

On the night of November 1, the talks again broke down over the wage issue. Failure to agree on economic issues, which had been considered comparatively close to agreement, produced increasing pessimism. The next morning, W. J. Usery moved to arrange further meetings. Due to Usery's effort, the negotiators met late that afternoon but parted in only one hour without any progress. Usery said, "They are at a critical stage. The issue gets harder and harder as you get down near the end. You have your ups and downs, and they just got to a point last night where they either wouldn't or couldn't make progress."(49)

On November 3, the two sides were still so far apart that a strike could not possibly be avoided. The UMW had given its third set of economic demands at the meeting the day before, and had understood that the industry would make counter-proposals in the morning meeting of November 3. Instead, the industry negotiators brought forth proposals on the right to strike locally and the grievance procedure.(50) Miller charged the industry with refusal to negotiate economic issues, and ordered the members of the Bargaining Council, who had spent a week in Washington waiting for the expected agreement, to disperse.(51)

Usery began energetic behind-the-scene activities, shuttling between the deadlocked parties in at attempt to mend the situation.(52) Both sides began to draft proposals, and met briefly at 9 P.M. on November 4. The union retired to a separate caucus to study the company proposal. At 1:30 the next morning, looking tired and drawn, Miller came out to announce their decision: "The operators' offer was totally unacceptable."(53)

Two days later, the talks were resumed. To the surprise of both sides, the eight-hour negotiations made tremendous progress. Both sides stated that the session had been "excellent all day long" and that they were within a few days of agreement.(54) The bargaining continued to make progress, but on November 9, a nation-wide strike went into effect.(55)

At this point, even with an immediate agreement, the strike would last at least two weeks because of the ratification process. High government officials had been warning that serious economic consequences would appear if the strike went into a third week. Both sides began to feel the pressure, but the talks slowed down. Meetings were sporadic, and progress was made only on minor issues. Such important issues as wages, a cost-of-living wage escalator, medical and retirement coverage, company-paid sick leave, and the right to strike locally were left unresolved.(56)

When the official deadline of November 11 passed without any agreement, Miller formally called the nation-wide strike: "The 120,000 working members of our union will mine no coal until they have a contract they can work under safely and live under with decency."(57) Pressure was mounting from the government, from other industries, from the press(58) and the public. Late on November 12, the United States Steel Corporation, itself one of the most influential members of the BCOA, announced that it would lay off 13,700 workers by the end of the week due to the coal shortage.(59) At 1 A.M. on the morning of November 13, just after U.S. Steel's announcement, the coal companies made a new proposal at the bargaining table.(60) The meeting was recessed immediately for a detailed study of the proposal. Secretary Treasurer Patrick said when he came away from the table, "At this point I am very, very optimistic."(61)

The meeting was reconvened at 10 A.M. and continued until late that night. The negotiators came out in a cautiously happy mood. Miller stated, "We have reached an agreement. It's a very good contract. It's one I think we can sell to the membership."(62) Guy Farmer, the industry's chief negotiator, commented that it was a "very expensive, costly agreement but would improve labor relations and productivity".(63) It was indeed a very generous agreement, which included:

(1) Wage raise of 9% in the first year and 3% in each of the last two years; an $80 one-time inflation catch-up bonus, and the first cost-of-living wage escalator of one-cent-per-hour for every 0.4-point rise in the Consumer Price Index, all of which would amount to a 49.7% (64) increase in the miners' income.

(2) An increase in royalty payment from 80¢ a ton to $1.55 a ton.

(3) Paid sick leave benefit of five days a year.

(4) A substantial increase of benefits for the disabled and widows.

(5) An improvement in the grievance procedure to shorten adjudication-time.

(6) A variety of increases in safety standards, including the right of miners to refuse to work at an unsafe place and of the union safety man to have access to any part of the mines for inspection.

(7) Change in work rules to create more jobs and to secure more safety.

(8) Enhancement of seniority protection.

(9) A sickness and accident benefit program providing $100 a week for up to 52 weeks.

(10) Improvements in the training program.(65)

c. The Ratification Process

The Miller administration immediately summoned the Bargaining Council the next day, but found the Bargaining Council in an unexpectedly hostile mood. The decision of the council, which had been expected to take only one day, was postponed until the next. Miller continued actively persuading the members, but again failed to obtain approval.(66) According to sporadically leaked information, many council members were disenchanted by the wage raise, the lack of a right-to-strike clause, and the split vacation.(67) Upon the proposal of Harry Patrick, the union's three top officials decided to embark on a drive to build direct support from the rank-and-file and thus create grass root pressures on council members.(68)

Despite all these efforts, the Bargaining Council decided to send the negotiators back to the table on November 20 to seek further "adjustments".(69) On the following day the coal industry stiffened its position against any further bargaining with the union.(70) Economic pressure was also mounting: Bethlehem Steel Corporation announced that 2600 workers would be laid off, and U.S. Steel predicted that it would have to shut down all its plants if the strike lasted until December 1.

On November 22, Guy Farmer met with Miller briefly, "not to negotiate", but to "listen to their problems".(71) In the meeting, however, Miller's "minor adjustments" were found to be major demands. They included an 18% pay increase instead of 15%,(72) a further reduction of wage differentials between job classifications, additional vacation time with no split, improved medical care for disabled miners and reduction of working hours in strip mines.

The two sides met early on November 23, but failed to make any progress. With the increasing fear of disastrous economic consequences, Usery, who had been very active behind the scenes throughout the negotiations, took the first formal

Step to intervene in the deadlocked dispute. He sent a telegram to both parties, ordering them to appear in his office next day and to assemble their ratifying committees in Washington.[73] On November 24 the Federal Government made an extraordary arrangement for settlement. Secretary of the Treasury William Simon held a meeting with coal operators at his office, with Usery present, before the bargaining started. At 3 P.M., the requested time, Simon and Usery shuttled back and forth between the two parties, seeking an area of agreement.[74] It was apparent that the operators' concession would be an absolute necessity for the settlement. The impasse stemmed from strong political pressure against Guy Farmer from the BCOA's board, which had felt all along that Farmer had been giving in too much. Although the government had been active informally throughout the negotiations, this particular intervention was effective in two ways: the formal order to renegotiate gave Farmer a powerful excuse to engage in bargaining, and the active participation of William Simon - exceptional in labor disputes - gave at least an implicit assurance to the BCOA board that the government would not oppose a wage increase and the industry's subsequent price increase as being inflationary.

A new agreement was finally reached late that night, with the union's demands being met completely.

d. The Second Attempt at Ratification

On November 25, union officials were busy preparing for the crucial council meeting which would be held next day.[75] In the mid-afternoon of November 26 the Bargaining Council, in a surprise move, rejected the revised pact. Miller recessed the council for a few hours. He issued his first public charge that the "council unsincerely breached the promise by rejecting the pact which they had advised me to seek". Usery was in the union's headquarters, ready to use his persuasiveness at any time.

In the reconvened meeting, with everybody waiting apprehensively, the council reversed its position and voted 22-15 for the pact.[76] From November 27 to 30, Miller administration officials conducted an intensive campaign to sell the new pact to the rank-and-file. Copies of the contract along with its explanation were sent out. Radio and television times were booked for Miller's speech, and the officials of each district held meetings with local delegates who were to go back and explain the pact to the members.

On December 1, final votes were cast across the nation. On the next day, it was announced finally that the majority of the members voted favorably for the pact.

3. Analysis of the Union's Militant Behavior

a. Economic Prosperity of the Industry

The economic recovery of the industry, which had started in the mid-1960's, was steadily accelerating in the 1970's. As the energy crisis was more commonly discussed in the nation, coal began to be considered as the major industrial fuel for the future. President Nixon's energy proposal urged tripling the coal production by 1985. The Arab oil embargo of 1973 dramatically increased the significance of coal as the nation's energy source. Figure 7-4 shows that the steady increase in the price of coal since 1966 accelerated in the 1970's. The increase in the profits of coal companies in 1974 was astonishing, at least quadrupling in most companies and increasing more than ten times in some (Table 7-5).[77-80] The Miller administration, fully aware of the prosperous conditions in the industry, was ready to take advantage of them. In his opening speech at the 1973 International Convention, Miller addressed the delegates:

> Coal that was selling for $15.75 a ton in January is selling for $20 a ton today, and the energy crisis ensures that it will be a seller's market for years to come ... The pick and shovel days are over (for the coal miners), and we intend to let the coal company know it in our next contract. (81)

This explanation, however, requires some qualifications. First, as was asserted in the previous chapter, the economic prosperity of the industry merely provides "opportunities" for the union to make militant demands. Second, the company operators considered the rapid rise in profits during 1974 largely a temporary phenomenon resulting from the oil embargo, and they were not ready to commit themselves for the next three years solely on the basis of this idiosyncratic profit rise. Third, although demand and profits showed an excellent rising trend, production figures did not look so rosy. Table 7-5 shows that production increased only at a moderate rate, while the value of coal was skyrocketing. The productivity of the industry actually dropped 15% between 1972 and 1973, and that of underground mines, for which most of the UMW members were working, declined as much as 30% (Table 7-6). Since the operators regarded the new safety law and wildcat strikes as causes for the decline, the union's major demands - stricter safety rules and the right to strike locally - were not necessarily so easy to obtain as pecuniary demands.

Thus, the economic prosperity of the industry alone cannot adequately explain the union behavior of the 1970's.

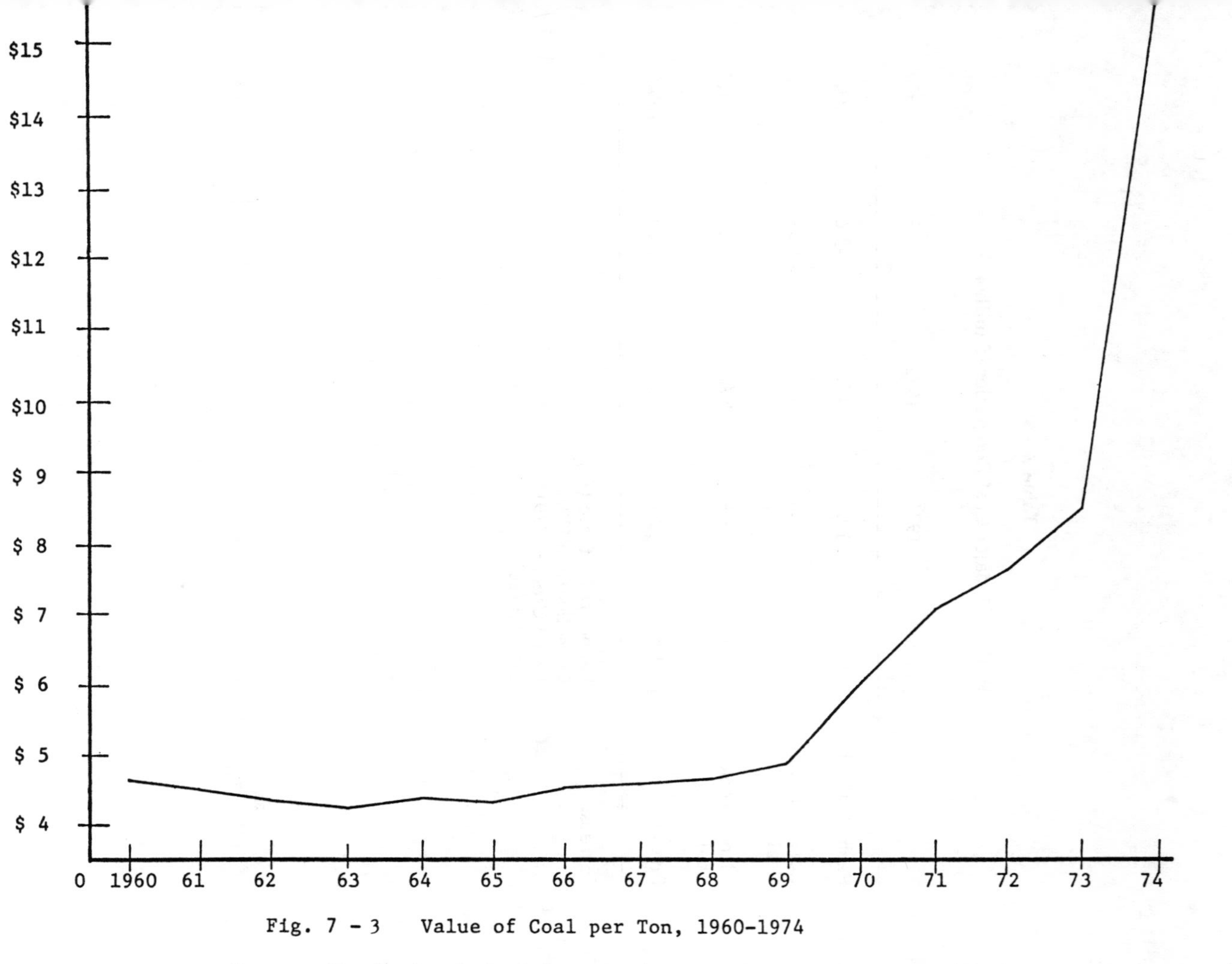

Fig. 7 - 3 Value of Coal per Ton, 1960-1974

Source: The National Coal Association, Bituminous Coal Data 1975

Table 7 - 4

Profits of Major Coal Companies ($ millions)

	1970	1971	1972	1973	1974
Peabody Coal	20.9	10.1	10.1	-3.6	23.5
Consolidation Coal	21.3	7.6	16.6	-12.8	43.8
Island Creek Coal	2.4	2.6	NA	10.6	101.5
Pittson	23.5	19.8	12.8	16.0	100.0

Sources: Peabody: footnote (77)
Consolidation: (78)
Island Creek: (79)
Pittson: (80)

b. Organizational Process of Accelerating Militancy.

The union's decision-making process in the 1974 negotiations will be analyzed in detail to determine whether there was a built-in mechanism in the process which made the union policy more militant. As explained in Section 2, the new decision-making process for collective bargaining was composed of eight stage. For clarity of explanation, these eight stages will be grouped into three categories: the demand-formation process at the local, district and Bargaining Council levels (processes 1, 2, 3 in Figure 7-4); the actual negotiation process by the Negotiation Committee (process 4); and the ratification process (processes 5, 6, 7, 8).

(i) The Demand-Formation Process: Process of Acceleration

The differences between pre- and post-reform demand formation procedures are summarized in Table 7-7. As will be shown, these differences had various consequences for the quality of decisions.

(aa) Characteristics of the Decision-Maker in the Demand-Formation Process

The first significant difference to be noted in Table 7-7 is the nature of the actual decision-maker. While in the previous period final demands were directly controlled by the president, who would actually conduct the negotiations, in the Miller period they were mainly formulated by the rank-and-file and by local and district leaders, who were not at all involved in actual collective bargaining. Generally any demand formation process involves two different considerations: the desire aspect and the feasibility aspect of the demands. Because of the lack of involvement in actual negotiations, the decision-makers in the Miller period were less motivated and less informed as to the feasibility of demands. Consequently they tended to solve conflicts of priority among different demand items by pushing demand levels upward for all items.

(bb) High Heterogeneity of Interests Expressed in the Process

The second difference is the greater number of people who were actively involved in the demand-formation process after 1973. The increase in number of people represented in the process increased the heterogeneity of interests, which was accentuated even more by the split of membership between young and old miners. A survey of the UMWA research department shows that young miners had substantially different interests from those of their older co-workers, the former being more interested in higher wages, longer vacation and safety, the latter in

Table 7 - 5

Production of Coal, 1965-1974

	Production (ton)	Annual Value per Ton
1965	512,088,236	$ 4.44
1966	533,881,210	$ 4.54
1967	552,626,000	$ 4.62
1968	545,245,000	$ 4.67
1969	560,505,000	$ 4.99
1970	609,932,000	$ 6.26
1971	552,192,000	$ 7.07
1972	595,386,000	$ 7.66
1973	591,738,000	$ 8.53
1974	603,406,000	$ 15.75

Source: The National Coal Association, Bituminous Coal Data, 1975

Table 7 - 6

Productivity of the Coal Industry, 1965-1973

	1965	1969	1972	1973
Underground	14.0	15.6	11.9	11.2
Surface	32.8	36.0	36.4	34.9
All Types	17.5	19.9	17.7	16.8

Source: Federal Energy Administration, Interagency Task Force on Coal, Final Task Force Report, Project Independence, Coal, 1974

Table 7 - 7

Differences in the Demand Formation Processes

	Before 1973	After 1973
Local Level	Low participation and involvement	High participation and involvement (meetings, resulutions, delecations).
District Level		High participation and involvement (Conferences, recommendations)
International-Level Committee	Classification of resolutions; rubber-stamp president's decisions	Classification of resolutions; (*) Formulation and approval of final demand
President	(*) High involvement, strong influence	Little involvement, little influence

(*): The place where the final decision-making power actually lay.

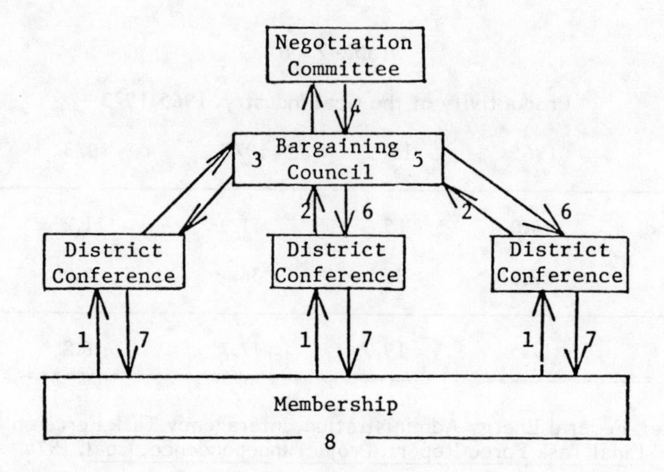

1. electing representatives, expressing the desires for the new contract.
2. Recommendations for the contract demands.
3. Formation of the contract demands.
4. Discussion and guidance of the course of the negotiations.
5. Approval of the tentative agreement. If not approved, instruct the Negotiation Committee to renegotiate.
6. Explanation of the tentative agreement to local representatives.
7. Explanation of the tentative agreement to the membership.
8. Membership ratification. If not ratified, further effort to improve the pact.

Fig. 7 - 4

The New Bargaining Procedure, 1973

Source: the UMWA Consitution, 1973

welfare and retirement benefit.[82] Since trade-offs among the different demands were not taken seriously, almost all the demands once expressed in the process tended to survive until the final formation stage. Therefore, high heterogeneity of interests resulted in militant final demands.

(cc) Personal Involvement of District Leaders in the Process

The third difference lies in the degree of personal and political involvement of the local and district leaders in the demand-formation process. In the previous era, all the local demands were expressed in the form of resolutions, with no leader personally or politically involved in any particular demand. In the Miller period, however, Bargaining Council members were supposed to represent the recommendations of their own district conferences. Each councilman had a stake in the degree to which the recommendations of his district were reflected in the final demands. Every minor demand had to be taken seriously and included in the final list. Since there was no pressure to consider the feasibility of the demands, placing the demand at the highest level on each issue was the easiest and quickest method of reaching an agreement in council. Consequently the disagreements frequently observed in IEB meetings did not take place during discussions of the final demands. As one Bargaining Council member suggested:

> Everyone is united on demands. But when it comes to a contract, that's something else. (83)

(dd) Specificity of the Publicized Demand

While in the pre-reform period demands were formulated by a few individuals behind closed doors, demands adopted at every step in the new procedure were printed and reported back to the rank-and-file members. Some of the printed demands were so specific (such as cost-of-living escalator with a rate of 1¢ per hour for every 0.35 percentage-point rise in the consumer index, thirty days paid sick leave, vacation period increase from two to four weeks, royalty payment increase from 80¢ to $2.40, etc.)[84] as to make flexible negotiations very difficult. One district president voiced this concern:

> When you put it on paper, a coal miner thinks he's going to get it.[85]

Since all the demands were highly "inflated" by the process described above, this publicity and specificity of the final demands inevitably made the negotiators very militant.

(ii) The Negotiation Stage

At the negotiation stage, there were several forces preventing negotiators from being compromising and flexible.

(aa) Negotiations as a Test of New Leadership

In the first place, Miller and his aides regarded the contract negotiations as his testing ground. Miller, who had become president only two years before, had not yet received full endorsement from the members. In the corridors outside the convention hall in 1974, for example, news reporters found that rank-and-file members generally witheld judgment on Miller's performance, preferring instead to wait until they saw what he could do at the bargaining table.(86) In addition, Miller not only failed to cut down the influence of the pro-Boyle faction, but allowed it to grow. The contract negotiations would be a watershed: success would increase his prestige and power over the insurgents, but failure might lead to uncontrollable rebellion. Miller's address in the 1973 Convention shows his keen awareness of this point.

> These negotiations will be as tough as any the UMW has ever faced before, and what comes out of them will determine the future of the union for a long time to come. If we are on an equal footing with industry, we will be entitled to feel some confidence that the rights of our members will be protected. If, however, we emerge from negotiations with anything less than equal footing, then it may well be that the skeptics will have been proven right, after all. (87)

(bb) Cost of the Council's Rejection for the Administration

The second obvious deterrent to compromise was the new constitutional requirement of approval by the Bargaining Council and ratification by the membership. A rejection of the proposed agreement would be very embarrassing to the new administration. At a time when members were evaluating the quality of the Miller administration, such a rejection would serve as evidence of Miller's incapacity to comprehend and deliver what the miners needed, which might result in severe political recriminations from the already uncontrollable insurgents. It would be politically far safer for Miller to prove his militancy by staging a strike and to lessen the chances of rejection than to face the higher probability of rejection by obtaining a settlement too quickly.[88] In the course of the negotiations, one of his aides assessed the mood in the coal fields as ranging from "militant" to "venomous",[89] and termed the ratification anything but automatic. Miller himself showed his concern when he was asked to settle.

> I am not going to ask them (the rank-and-file) because if I would ask them right now I know what their answer would be. It's "no". (90)

The administration was well aware of the mood of the Bargaining Council from frequent hints by council members that approval would be far from sure unless Miller brought back a fat contract. Being aware of the unfavorable mood of the council and the membership, the Miller administration was strongly tempted to stage at least a short strike to decrease the risk of rejection.

(cc) Self-Fulfilling Prophecy of Strike

Given the chaotic militancy of the membership and the weakness of the leadership, the operators had sufficient reason to suspect that any generous offer could be rejected either by the Bargaining Council or by the membership, and that they would be forced to give more in the second round of negotiations. Under such circumstances they would be extremely reluctant to offer their best at any stage of the negotiations. If union negotiators accepted their second best offer and the membership ratified it, it would be an excellent windfall victory. If it was rejected by the membership, they could slowly give out what they had originally been willing to offer only after the probability of membership rejection was considerably reduced. If union negotiators did not accept and then staged a strike, they could gradually improve their offer as the continuing strike decreased the likelihood of rejection by the membership.

Since such a strategy of inviting the union to strike would arouse severe criticism from the public if news of the plan were leaked, it is very difficult to find direct evidence that the operators actually adopted it. The important question, however, is not whether the operators consciously behaved this way, but the fact that the union negotiators believed that they did. The author's interviews with union aides revealed that the union negotiators were apparently going by "if-I-were-they-this-is-what-I-would-do" reasoning,[91] and firmly believed that the operators were taking the strategy elucidated above.[92]

If the union negotiators chose their strategy based on this reasoning, they would inevitably regard any generous offer as the operators' second or third best offer, and would be reluctant to accept it any any point in time. Thus, if there were a high expectation of strike on both sides, no matter how unrealistic, the process of interaction of the expectations would tend to bring about the strike by making both negotiators unconciliatory.

(iii) Rejection at the Bargaining Council

The union under the new administration had already shown itself to be extremely militant, but was forced to become even more so when the Bargaining Council instructed the president to renegotiate. In order to understand the union's high militancy, therefore, the process of rejection by the council should be analyzed.

(aa) Political Calculations of District Leaders

The first explanation of the rejection is provided by the Miller administration itself. Secretary-Treasurer Harry Patrick explained the cause of the rejection:

> It's the result of anti-leadership union politics. Some of the members are playing politics - there is some nit-picking there. (93)

At least six districts were strongly and consistently anti-Miller and had been trying to block all his policy proposals. As one union staff member speculated,(94) an ambitious anti-Miller leader, Lee Roy Patterson, had already decided to run for the presidency in 1977 and had concluded that getting his opposition on the record at this time would be beneficial later in his campaign. The election of 1977 would coincide with the next contract renewal, when everyone would be complaining about the 1974 contract no matter how generous it had appeared in 1974. The fact that he had attempted to block the contract in 1974 would be a strong political asset in his 1977 campaign.

A close scrutiny shows, however, that many strong Miller supporters, who would be politically weakened by wrecking Miller's prestige, also moved to oppose the contract.(95) In fact, the 38-member council's final decision was made by a 37-1 margin, which was too large to be explained merely by factional fights.(96)

(bb) Lack of Involvement and Unrealistic Concept of Feasibility

It is an important point that no council member was closely involved in the negotiation process and that many of them were not kept informed of developments. The seven subcommittees, established primarily in order to involve bargaining council members, had not been functioning properly, three of them having met only sporadically at the beginning stages of the negotiations.[97] One member described his anger:

> I had never been informed of what had been going on there in the hotel (the Hay-Adams Hotel, where negotiations took place). I was in one of the subcommittees but never called upon. When we were asked to wait in Washington in early November for the possible agreement, Miller didn't give us any information of the process. Then, he asked us to go home, and we had absolutely no idea what happened since then. (98)

As a result, most of them developed a basic distrust in the secretly-conducted negotiations. More importantly, because they were not involved, the members of the Bargaining Council failed to develop a realistic concept of demand feasibility One union aide commented when he faced the opposition from the council:

> The trouble is that there is a tremendously overblown conception of what can be taken from the industry simply because they are right now having these enormous profits ... Our guys read about a 100% or 200% increase in the profit of a coal company in their territory and they want a 100% increase in contract. (99)

(cc) Vulnerability of Bargaining Council Members

The council was composed of International Executive Board members and district presidents elected less than one year before. Since the MFD organization had dissolved and the former pro-Boyle organizations had broken down in most of the districts, none of them had any substantial political base. Consequently the miners' voting behavior in district elections was totally uncontrolled and unpredictable. Many incumbents were defeated in subsequent elections. The instability of their position is clearly seen in Tables 7-8 and 7-9.

The questions and criticisms about the tentative agreement raised by council members were based on their concern as to what their constituency in the coal field would accept. One council member explained,

> We know the questions the miners are going to bring up (when we go down there do sell the contract) and we just want answers (before we go down there). (100)

When a reporter asked whether they should stop arguing and ask the rank-and-file, another member said:

Table 7 - 8

Average Tenure and Turnover Rate of the District Leaders

Districts	Average Tenure (Year)	Turnover Rate/Year	Average Tenure (Year)	Turnover Rate/Year
2	1.92	0.52	3.83	0.26
4	1.92	0.52	3.83	0.26
5	1.92	0.52	1.92	0.52
6	3.83	0.26	3.83	0.26
11	1.92	0.52	1.83	0.55
12	3.83	0.26	3.83	0.26
14	1.88	0.53	1.92	0.52
15	1.23	0.78	1.92	0.52
17	1.92	0.52	1.92	0.52
18	1.92	0.52	1.88	0.53
19	1.25	0.80	1.92	0.52
20	1.23	0.78	3.83	0.26
21	1.92	0.52	1.92	0.52
22	1.92	0.52	1.23	0.78
23	1.92	0.52	3.83	0.26
25	1.92	0.52	3.83	0.26
26	3.83	0.26	1.92	0.52
28	1.92	0.52	1.25	0.80
29	1.92	0.52	1.92	0.52
30	1.92	0.52	1.22	0.82
31	1.92	0.52	2.45	0.48

Source: The United Mine Workers Journal, 1972-1975

Tables A - 2 and A - 3 in Appendix 1

Table 7 - 9

Comparison of Turnover Rates of District Leaders

Periods	IEB Members	District President
1940's	0.16	0.16
1950's	0.17	0.16
1960's (-'70)	0.19	0.19
1970's ('73-'76)	0.48	0.52

Source: Tables A - 2 and A - 3, Appendix I

> We can either get the tough spots out now, or we can take it to the field and get it shot down. It's we who have to live with those people back home. (101)

(dd) Lack of Understanding and Distrust towards Staff Members

Another difficulty with the agreement was its complexity. Many highly professional staff members were involved in the netotiations. The new agreement, which rewrote virtually every sentence of the old contract, became voluminous and extremely complicated. During the sessions of the Bargaining Council, a union aide said,

> I am scared to death that we are vulnerable to misconceptions, because this is a tough contract to explain. (102)

His worry turned out to be quite valid. One of the strongest objections of the council, insufficient wage increases, was found to have resulted partially from a lack of understanding of the new cost-of-living clause, which was a totally new concept for them. One staff member who was working closely with the council stated:

> I guess many council members didn't read the contract. Some of their questions show it. I even have some doubt that even Miller himself understood it well. (103)

The trouble was that the council members had a deep distrust of the staff members, who apparently had a strong influence on the final agreement. If the council members had only a vague idea about the actual contents of the agreement, but clearly believed that it was written by "questionable" people, it was natural for them to take a negative position.

CHAPTER VIII
SUMMARY AND CONCLUSIONS

Union strike activities have attract substantial interest from a large number of academicians and practitioners. Social scientists have succeeded in identifying five sets of variables (economic, institutional, intraorganizational, community character-and plant character-variables) as major determinants of strike activities. From the standpoint of practicality, however, the present state of academic literature is highly unsatisfactory. It provides little information about the effects of intraorganizational variables, which negotiators find crucial in their real experiences. There has also been little investigation of the interaction effects of the five independent variables, which is again critical in real collective bargaining situations. The aim of this study has been to contribute new knowledge which can bridge these gaps. From the events and structures analyzed herein, certain relevant hypotheses may be posited.

1. Official Militancy as an Organizational Decision: an Interaction Effect

Throughout the four periods studied, the degree of militancy of union policy is seen to be a conscious decision of the top governing level. It may be a one-man decision, as in the John L. Lewis period, or a joint decision by many semi-autonomous leaders, as in the Arnold Miller period. Whatever form the decision-making may take, it decides its policy under a variety of influences. These influences may be categorized as perceived pressures toward militancy and perceived pressures toward non-militancy. The top decision-makers are subject to both pressures, compare them, calculate the consequences, and choose the appropriate degree of militancy. Figure 8-1 illustrates this process.

Throughout the four periods, many factors appeared to influence these two perceived pressures. For example, in the first decade (1940-1950), economic impoverishment of the members during wartime wage-price regulations, combined with the leader's obvious commitment and the competition with other labor unions, constituted pressure toward militancy. In the second decade (1950-1960), the economic recession in the industry as a result of severe competition from oil posed a strong pressure toward non-militancy. Impoverishment of the members also functioned as a pressure toward militancy in the Boyle period (1963-1972). Commitment of top leaders and economic prosperity of the industry constituted pressure toward militancy in Miller's period (1972-1974). Figure 8-2 summarizes these findings.

It should be noted that the independent variables listed in the left column of Figure 8-2 are external and objective as opposed to perceived. Since it is only the

Table 8 - 1

Cabinet Model and Parliamentary Model

	Cabinet Model	Parliamentary Model
Middle level leaders' post and career	Appointment by or strong influence from the president	Election from the constituents, little influence from the president
Middle level leaders' job description	No involvement in policy making; responsible for executing president's policy	High involvement in policy making representing constituents' will
Middle-level leaders' responsibility	Responsible to the president	Responsible to the constituency

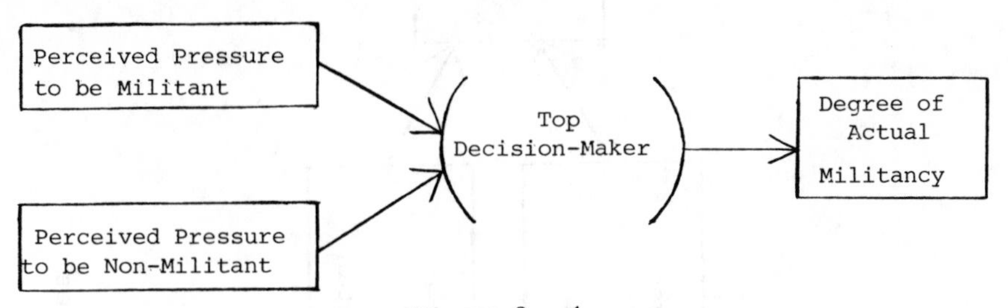

Figure 8 - 1
Actual Militancy as a Conscious Decision of the Top Decision-Makers Under Pressure

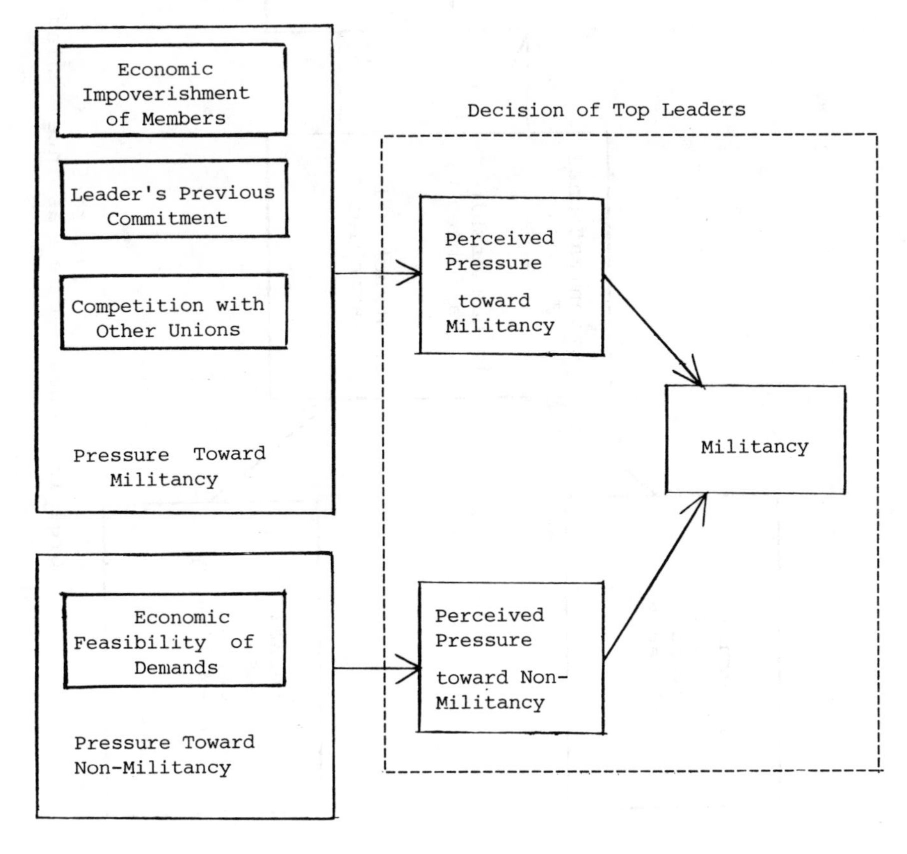

Figure 8 - 2
Factors Affecting Perceived Pressures

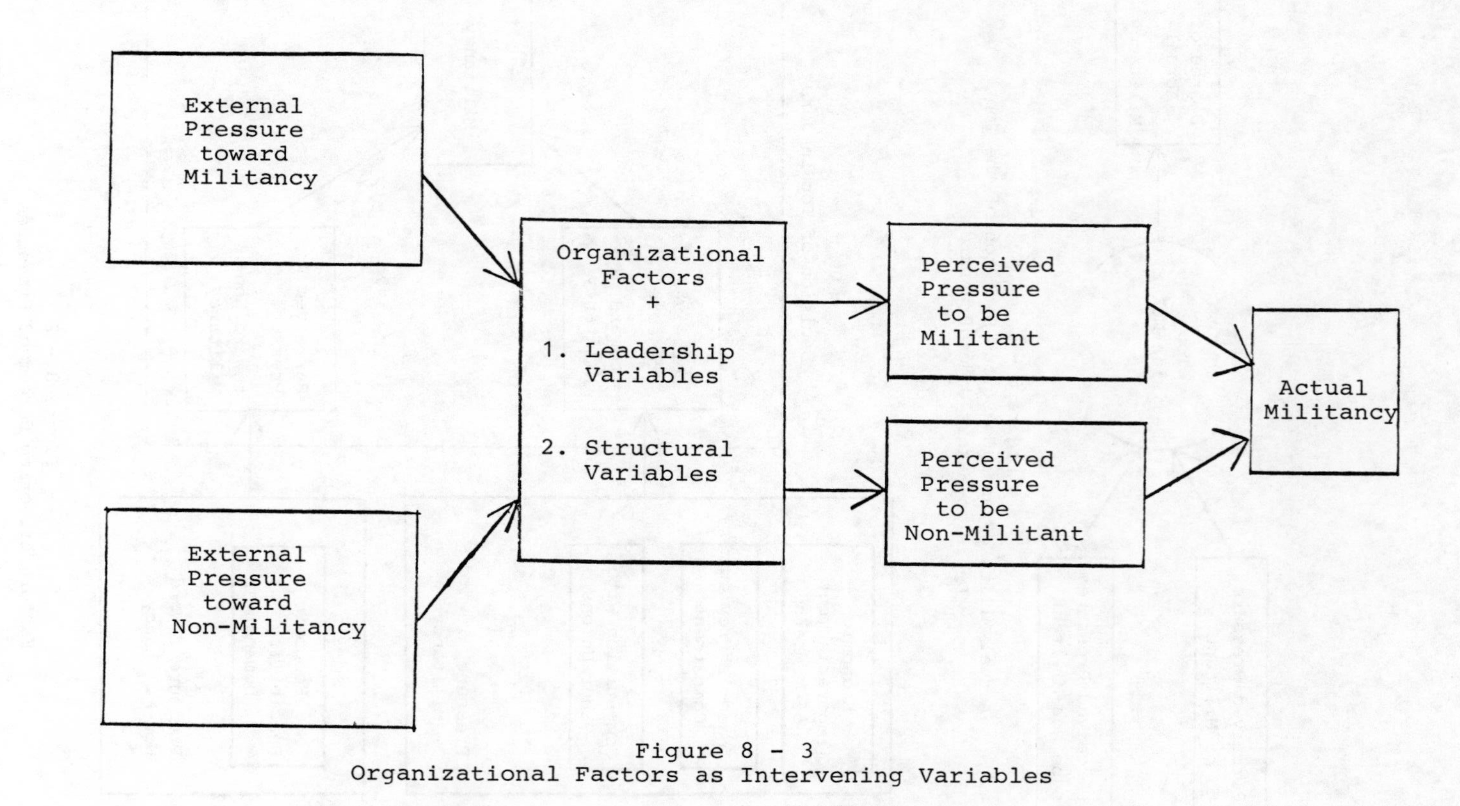

Figure 8 - 3
Organizational Factors as Intervening Variables

pressure perceived by decision makers that is relevant to union militancy, the transformation process from objective pressure to perceived pressure needs to be studied.

This study indicates that two sets of organizational factors are important in this process: One set concerns the characteristics of the "perceiver", viz. the top decision-maker. It is argued that Lewis perceived the "external" pressure toward militancy far more sensitively in the 1940's than in the 1950's because his charismatic authority had stabilized in the latter decade. It was also observed that Lewis in the 1940's and Miller in the 1970's seemed to respond to such pressures far more seriously than did Boyle. The second set of organizational variables which influence the transformation from "external" to "perceived" governs the quality of information-flow to the top decision-maker(s). In collective decision-making, the first recipient of external pressure is not usually the top decision-making group. For example, economic impoverishment of the members will be perceived first by the members themselves; their complaints may or may not reach the district leaders, who in turn may or may not inform the president. The research department may conduct an economic survey of the coal fields, but the union president may not have the time or motivation to read the report. In this process, information is eliminated, amplified or distorted. The degree and nature of such filtering is determined by a variety of organizational, structural variables (e.g. who receives the information first, who communicates what to whom, what power relationship the former has to the latter, etc.). These arguments can be summarized in the framework shown in Figure 8-3.

The above observations suggest that intra-organizational variables are not really independent but are intervening variables, making top leaders' decisions sensitive or insensitive to the external pressure. Our answer to the question of interaction effect is therefore:

> Hypothesis 8-1
>
> Organizational variables function as a set of modulating variables, which intervene between external pressures (independent variables) and actual militant union policy (the dependent variable) to determine the magnitude of the effect of the former upon the latter.

What organizational form, then, makes the union policy respond more sensitively to external presure? Our study provides insights into this question.

2. <u>The Impact of Organizational Factors on Union Militancy: a Proposed Theory</u>

The case analysis presented in this study identified the charisma-noncharisma classification as the most relevant dimension of the leadership variable.

Weber argues that charismatic authority is unstable in two ways: one stemming from the danger of adopting the wrong "mission" (because a charismatic leader should not appear to be influenced by concrete pressure from the members), the other coming from the constant pressure to prove his extraordinary capacity. A careful examination of Lewis' leadership in the 1940's has shown that (1) Lewis not only was personally very sensitive to the miners' needs, but also had a well-constructed institutional mechanism for remaining so; and that (2) he faced particularly strong pressure to prove his charisma in 1943 because of a series of previous failures. This instability made him respond sensitively to the external pressures toward militancy.

In the 1950's, however, Lewis did not show this sensitivity. The members allegiance to Lewis changed from expectation of future gains to gratitude and respect for his past success. Although such gratitude generally fades away unless the leader continues to bring further benefits, there was a special condition in the 1950's which helped to sustain gratitude. Any success brings about either "flow-type" benefits (a one-shot benefit only at the time of success), or "stock-type" benefits (a continuous flow of benefits after the time of success). All of Lewis' successes in the 1940's rendered stock-type benefits. These are more stabilizing than the flow-type. One may still argue that even the stock-type benefit loses its initial extraordinary character sooner or later, just as a $2 a day wage increase gradually becomes a part of everyday life. However, free medical service, which Lewis secured in the late 1940's, had a much more far-reaching impact. Its benefits came irregularly at such times when the miners needed them very badly, and reinforced miners' grattitude every time they received the benefits. Such successes were called stock-type successes with <u>self-reinforcing benefits</u> and were observed to have acted as a substantial stabilizer on Lewis' charismatic authority. To summarize the above observations:

<u>Hypothesis 8-2</u>

A union with a charismatic leader tends to respond to the external pressure toward militancy more sensitively than a union with a non-charismatic leader.

Hypothesis 8-3

Charismatic authority can be stabilized by past "stock-type" successes with "self-reinforcing" benefits. When stability is achieved by the leader, he will be less sensitive to pressure toward militancy.

As shown in Chapters IV and V, in the case of a union with a charismatic leader, it was sufficient to examine only the direct relationship between the top leaders and the rank-and-file. The discussion in Chapters VI and VII suggests, however, that in the case of a union without a charismatic leader, the characteristics of the middle-level leaders also need to be analyzed.

In the Boyle period, it was noted that the local and district leaders were centrally oriented to a high degree, because of the selectivity of the promotion process and the unchallengeable power of the president. Their upward orientation resulted in distortions in the flow of communications, which ultimately made the report to the top decision-maker less reflective of members' demands. In the Miller period, on the other hand, local and district leaders were extremely vulnerable to the will of the members, which caused inflation of members' demands in the course of the communication process.

These differences in orientation resulted partially from the different organizational roles played by the middle level under the various administrations. The middle-level leader of the Boyle period was appointed by the president and was responsible for executing the presidential decisions; the same level leader in the Miller was elected by the constituency and was responsible for representing the wishes of his constituency in policy-making. The former resembles a cabinet member, the latter a member of parliament. Table 8 - 1 summarizes the ideal type-characteristics of the "cabinet" and "parliament" models. Our observations can be stated as follows:

Hypothesis 8-4

The closer the union organization to the parliamentary model vis-a-vis the cabinet-model, the more sensitive the union official militancy tends to be in response to pressure toward militancy.

In the Boyle period, the increasing internal conflict within the UMWA was found to be responsible for its growing official militancy. In the Miller period, high internal conflict was observed to have contributed to militant policy by (1) inflating the demands in the demand-formation process, (2) making it difficult for the negotiators to compromise, and (3) resulting in the Bargaining Council's rejection of preliminary agreements. The literature also provides a similar observation in more general terms.[1]

Hypothesis 8-5

The higher the internal conflict, the more sensitive the top-level leadership tends to be to external pressure toward militancy.

However, the pre-reform UMW, which was also ridden with intensive internal conflict, was found to be relatively unresponsive. The most important difference between pre- and post-reform periods in this regard lies in the leadership power-structures. Boyle faced no rival leaders with power comparable to his, while Miller allowed a few equally influential rival leaders to grow within the international union.

The power structure with one overwhelmingly powerful leader dominating the rest may be called the "Gulliver type", while the power-structure with several equally strong leaders may be termed the "federation type". Comparison of the pre- and post-reform periods shows that if the organization has a Gulliver-type power structure, high intensity of internal conflict may not have any effect on the union's official militancy.

Hypothesis 8-6

The closer the leadership power-structure is to the Gulliver type as opposed to the Federation type, the less the effect of internal conflict upon the union's official militancy. (Cf. Hypothesis 8-3)

Figure 8-4 proposes a model for the set of hypotheses advanced in this summary.

The impact of organizational variables on the policy of organization has been a relatively neglected area for both industrial relations and organization studies. Particularly in the case of union and management, this lack of knowledge is critical because intra-organizational factors often cause a serious impasse in the collective bargaining process. The present study provides some insights in the form of hypotheses. Similar exploratory studies as well as validation studies are clearly needed to further enrich the little knowledge we have in this area.

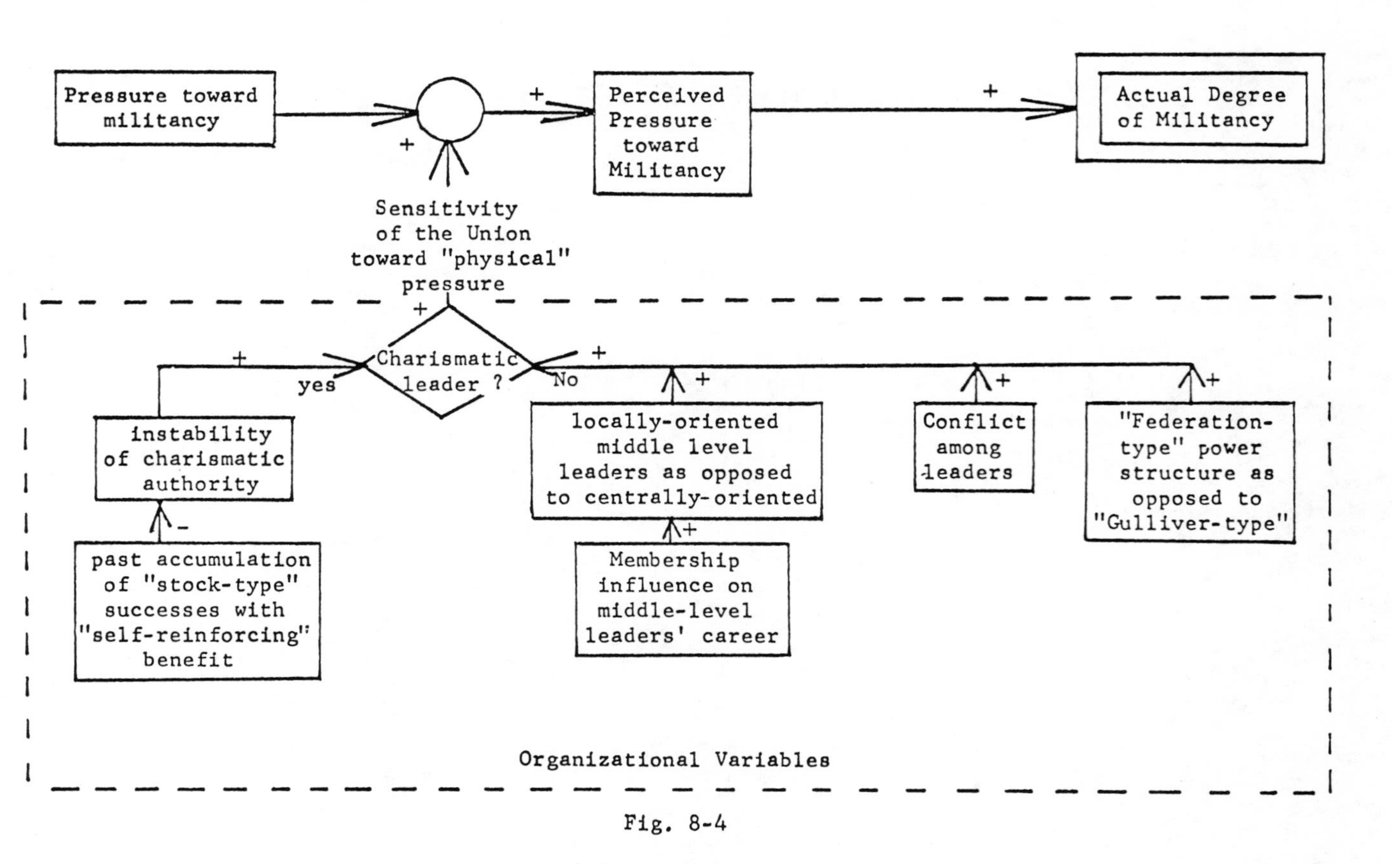

Fig. 8-4

A Proposed Model

APPENDIX 1
TABLES

Table A - 1

Content Analysis of Local Resolutions Presented at Conventions

1. External Direct Demands

Number of resolutions submitted in each year

	1942	1944	1946	1948	1952	1956	1960	1964	1968
Wage Issue	174	202	186	97	97	71	63	35	85
Wage Raise	67	86	49	17	13	1	3	2	20
Others	107	116	137	80	84	71	60	33	65
Work Hours	6	43	42	25	22	22	19	24	16
Shortening	0	2	36	18	18	18	13	24	13
Multiple Shift	6	41	6	7	4	4	6	0	3
Fringe Benefit	100	197	122	174	251	184	177	190	315
Vacation	20	23	9	13	36	22	20	32	71
Holidays	10	7	22	18	41	28	20	40	44
Overtime	7	4	3	7	2	1	1	2	3
Lunch	1	35	6	7	7	1	4	5	4
Housing	9	13	18	23	12	4	5	0	5
Welfare	24	88	36	72	133	113	105	92	97
Hospital	11	14	3	27	10	14	15	7	26
Free Blasting	18	13	24	8	10	3	2	1	8
Sick Leave	0	0	1	0	0	0	5	7	43
Severance Pay and bonus	0	0	0	0	0	0	0	4	14
Job Security	45	50	47	25	60	40	60	38	105
Seniority	5	11	22	11	30	15	28	15	26
Guaranteed work	28	17	12	8	7	9	5	7	15
Unemployment	0	7	1	0	1	2	3	5	0
Hiring and placement	12	15	12	7	22	14	24	11	64
Health and Safety	26	34	45	46	28	24	33	24	31
Contract agreement	35	41	38	9	18	22	25	14	35
Work Conditions	15	10	20	17	1	8	0	2	7
Others	0	25	5	0	4	1	7	3	10
TOTAL, 1.	401	602	505	393	481	375	384	330	604

(Table A - 1 cont.)

2. External Indirect Demands

	1942	1944	1946	1948	1952	1956	1960	1964	1968
Racial Discrimination	4	5	4	6	7	1	1	0	0
Political Activities	10	32	0	5	2	1	0	1	0
Against Leaders	1	8	0	0	0	0	0	0	0
Neutral	7	12	0	0	0	1	0	0	0
Pro-leaders	2	12	0	5	2	0	0	1	0
District 50	1	1	0	1	0	0	0	2	3
Support	0	1	0	1	0	0	0	0	0
Against	1	0	0	0	0	0	0	2	3
Labor Movement	20	2	2	0	3	1	0	0	0
More Aid to the Industry	0	2	1	1	3	2	1	1	6
Inflation Control	0	0	12	0	0	0	0	0	0
Tax	0	0	2	1	0	0	1	0	0
Prohibition of Strip Mining	0	0	1	0	0	0	0	0	0
War Support	18	4	0	0	0	0	0	0	0
Against Taft-Hartley Act	----	----	----	8	3	3	3	0	0
Against Imports	0	0	0	0	0	0	1	0	0
Declaration of Support of Leader	3	18	5	19	7	3	3	14	25
Others	1	1	2	0	4	0	2	1	0
TOTAL, 2	57	64	29	41	29	11	12	19	34

(Table A - 1 cont.)

3. Internal Demands

	1942	1944	1946	1952	1956	1960	1964	1968	
Autonomy	64	76	1	10	13	8	16	6	3
Perfect autonomy	31	17	0	4	8	7	14	5	2
Conditional	25	28	1	4	5	0	1	0	0
Against autonomy	8	31	0	2	0	1	1	1	1
Internal Strife	5	5	0	0	0	0	0	7	0
High	4	4	0	0	0	0	0	5	0
Low	1	1	0	0	0	0	0	2	0
Administrative Service	7	7	2	9	5	5	3	3	1
From international	3	2	2	6	2	3	2	1	1
From district	4	5	0	3	3	2	1	2	0
Organizing	6	1	5	0	8	1	3	2	2
Dues	31	7	3	93	26	21	1	56	11
Reduction	10	2	0	1	1	1	1	1	0
Increase	1	2	0	45	4	2	0	24	5
More to Locals	19	3	3	27	21	18	0	24	6
Less to Locals	1	0	0	0	0	0	0	7	0
(De)centralization	35	67	2	29	15	18	16	26	19
More referendum	12	0	1	3	4	2	3	2	4
Longer tenure	9	1	0	0	0	0	0	7	0
More power to locals	1	31	0	3	2	10	6	12	8
Less power to locals	13	35	1	23	9	6	7	5	7
Qualification of officers	0	1	0	1	2	5	0	23	1
Relax	0	1	0	1	1	2	0	0	0
More rigid	0	0	0	0	1	3	0	23	1
Fair Election	17	4	0	0	4	1	0	0	5
Benefits to leaders	0	0	16	20	0	0	0	0	0
Membership Qualification	0	2	0	22	16	2	0	1	0
Privilege to miner's relatives	0	0	0	0	8	1	2	3	1
Fewer Jobs to locals	0	0	0	8	9	0	0	0	0
Welfare Fund operation	0	0	1	4	1	2	9	0	0

(Table A - 1 cont.)

	1942	1944	1946	1948	1952	1956	1960	1964	1968
Declaration of Support	0	25	2	2	8	5	4	2	1
Others	12	13	2	3	13	2	14	17	4
TOTAL, 3.	177	208	34	201	128	71	68	146	48
GRAND TOTAL	635	874	568	635	638	457	468	495	686

Note:
1942, 1944, 1946, 1948: Randomly sampled 1/3 of the local resolutions.
1952, 1956, 1960, 1964, 1968: Randomly sampled 1/4 of the local resolutions.

Table A - 2

International Executive Board Members

Districts	1940 41 42 43 44 45 46 47 48 49 50
1	John Kmetz (1939-)
2	John Ghizzani(1932-)
3	Frank Highs
4	William Hynes
5	J. O'Leary (1932-) | Joseph Yablonski
6	McCormick (1932-) | Peter Phillipi
7	David J. Stevens(1932-)
8	O.E.Gasaway (1932-)
9	John J. Mates(1932-)
10	Sam Nichollis
11	H.Kelly (1934-) | Charles Funcannon |
12	Curtis Mundel
13	| Frank D. Wilson
14	Henry Allai (1930-)
15	O.E.Negro(1923-) |
16	John T. Jones
17	
18	Robert Livett(1930-)
19	James W. Riding
20	James H. Terry
21	David Fowler
22	Tony Radalj(1932-) | Vlakovich | Malcolm Condie
23	W. D. Duncan(1932-) |
24	Fleming (1939-) | Spink |
26	S.Barret | Massini | Barret | John McDonald
27	J.Massini | Wagner | Joseph Massini
28	
29	| Ray Thompson
30	| Tom Raney
31	| Joseph Angelo

Table A - 2 (Con'd)

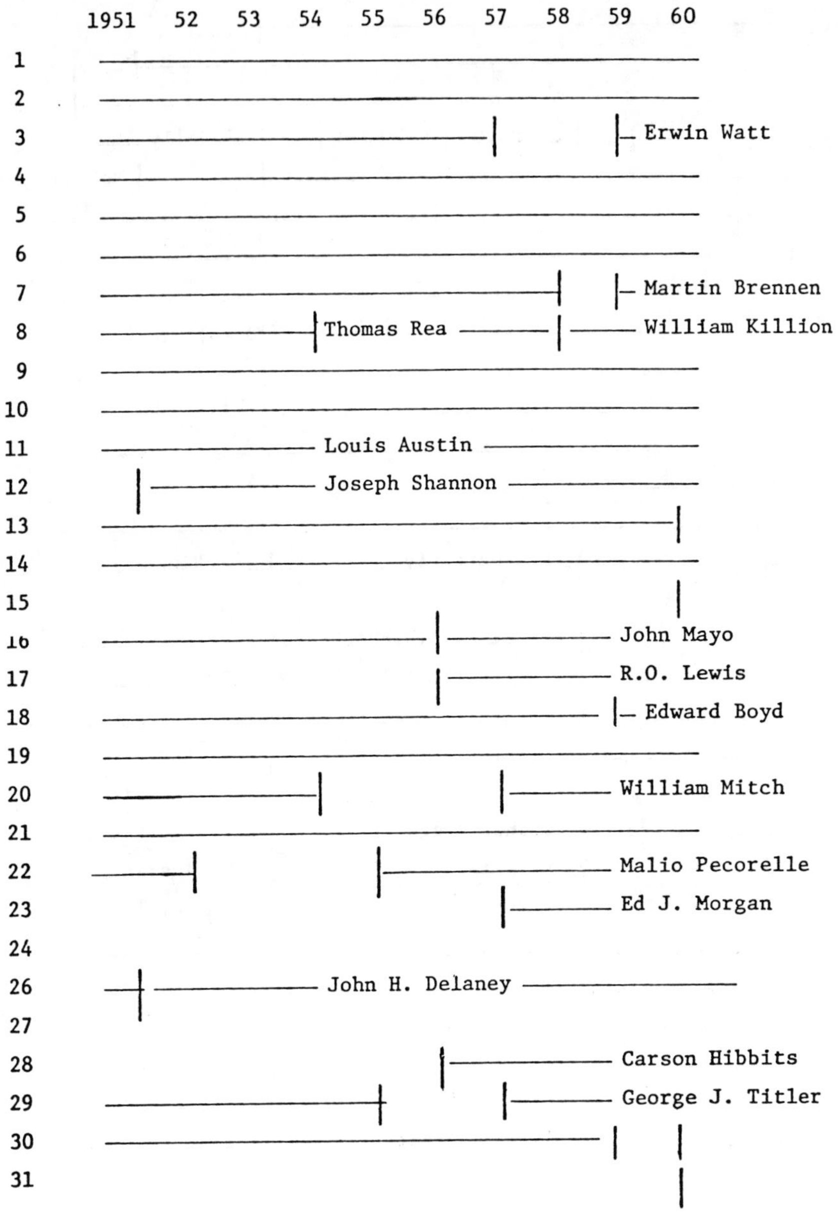

	1951	52	53	54	55	56	57	58	59	60
1										
2										
3									Erwin Watt	
4										
5										
6										
7									Martin Brennen	
8				Thomas Rea				William Killion		
9										
10										
11				Louis Austin						
12		Joseph Shannon								
13										
14										
15										
16						John Mayo				
17						R.O. Lewis				
18									Edward Boyd	
19										
20							William Mitch			
21										
22					Malio Pecorelle					
23							Ed J. Morgan			
24										
26		John H. Delaney								
27										
28						Carson Hibbits				
29							George J. Titler			
30										
31										

Table A - 2 (Con'd)

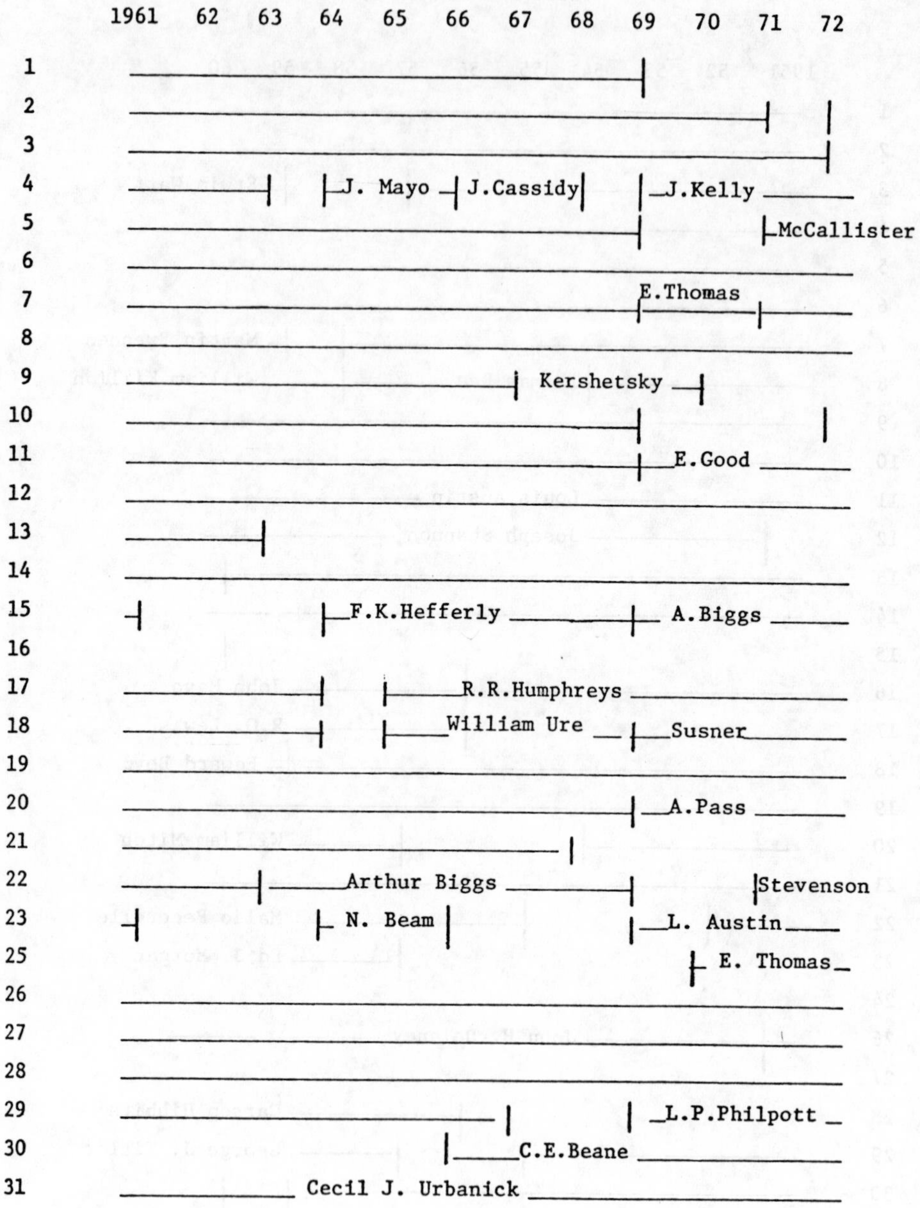

1961 62 63 64 65 66 67 68 69 70 71 72

Row	Entries
1	
2	
3	
4	J. Mayo; J.Cassidy; J.Kelly
5	McCallister
6	
7	E.Thomas
8	
9	Kershetsky
10	
11	E.Good
12	
13	
14	
15	F.K.Hefferly; A.Biggs
16	
17	R.R.Humphreys
18	William Ure; Susner
19	
20	A.Pass
21	
22	Arthur Biggs; Stevenson
23	N. Beam; L. Austin
25	E. Thomas
26	
27	
28	
29	L.P.Philpott
30	C.E.Beane
31	Cecil J. Urbanick

Table A - 2 (Con'd)

1972 2/1/73 3/15 6/15 7/15 8/15 9/1 10/1 11/1

2 De Gretto —| —— Edward F. Monborne ——

3

4 ————————————————

5 ———————————| —— Nick DeVince ——

6 ————| —— Karl Kafton ——

10 S.Nicholls ————————

11 ——————————————| —— R.Edney

12 ————| —— Gene Mitchel ——

14 ————| —— Elmer Clark ——————| — Robert Long —

15 ————| —— David Oxford ——

17 ————| G.Ballard ——| —— Ivan White ——

18 ————| | —— Stanley Grocutt ——

19 ————| —— Hugh Jones ——

20 ————| —— F. Clements ——

21

22 ————| —— Louis Kosec ——

23 ————| C.Schmidt ——| —— Lee Roy Patterson ——

25 ————| —— William Savitsky ——

26 ————|————————

27

28 ————| Ray Hutchison ————| —— Tom Owens —

29 ————| —— Joe Malay ——

30 ————| B.Roberts ——| T. Raney | | — J.B.Trout —

31 ————| D.Weaver ——| —— Andy Morris ——

Table A - 2 (Con'd)

2/15/74 3/1 10/1 1/15/75 7/1 1/15/76 4/1 9/15

2	
3	
4	
5	
6	
11	
12	
14	
15	Nick Halamandaris
17	
18	S.Johnson
19	Lonnie Brown
20	
21	D.E.Lawley
22	Frank Stevenson; F.Roybal
23	
25	
26	Allan Foley
28	Elmer Church Jr.; A. Sykes
29	Francis Martin
30	
31	

End of Table A - 2

Table A - 3

District Presidents

Districts	1940 41 42 43 44 45 46 47 48 49 50
1	Michael J. Kosik(1936-)
2	James Mark(1936-)
3	Frank Hughes(1936-)
4	William Hynes(1934-)
5	P.Fagen (1932-) | John Busarello
6	John Owens(1936-) | A. Pacifico
7	H.Brown (1936-) | Martin F. Brennen
8	L.Lambert (1938-) | Thomas Rea
9	M.Brennen (1932-) | Josheph Kershetsky
10	Sam Nicholls
11	Foncannon (1932-) | Louis Austin
12	Ray Edmundson(1936-) | Jugh White
13	L. Bodlrive | Montgomery | Aggenssen | F.D.Wilson
14	Henry Allai(1931-)
15	Frank Hefferly(1934-)
16	John T. Jones(1934-)
17	Van Bittner (1934-) | P.Titler | William Blizzard
18	Robert Livett(1926-)
19	W.Turnblazer(1932-) | Abe Vales
20	William Mitch(1934-)
21	David Fowler(1932-)
22	J.Ross (1935-) | A.Carey | H.Martin
23	Ed. J. Morgan
24	John Hatton(1937-)
25	
26	D.Morrison(1932-) | Freeman Jenkins
27	J.Hunter (1932-) | W.A.Boyle
28	John Sexton(1935-) | William Minton
29	George Tetler
30	Samuel Caddy(1934-)
31	C.F.Davis | C.J.Urbanick

(Con'd)

Table A - 3 (Con'd)

Districts	1951 – 60 (52, 53, 54, 55, 56, 57, 58, 59, 60)
1	August Lippi
2	John Ghizzni
3	
4	William Hynes
5	J. Yablonski
6	
7	
8	James Miller – Elias Dayhuff
9	
10	
11	R.McKinney – R. Anderson – Ernes Goad
12	
13	J.A.Hupton
14	
15	
16	
17	R.O.Lewis
18	E.Boyd
19	Hicks – Ray Thompson
20	
21	
22	Brinley – Henry Mangus
23	
25	
26	T.McLachlan – W.Marsh
27	R.J.Boyle
28	Allen Condra – Carson Hibbits
29	
30	Carson Hibbits
31	

(Con'd)

Table A - 3 (Con'd)

Districts	1961 – 72
1	Lester Thomas
2	Henry Younker; O.Slagle
3	
4	J.Mayo; J.Cassidy; J.Kelly
5	Michael Budzanoski
6	Thomas Williams
7	
8	
9	John Eegan
10	
11	
12	Joseph Shannon; K.F.Wells
13	J.Mayo
14	
15	H.Allai; Fred Hefferly; Authur Biggs
16	John Mayo
17	R.R.Humpheys; J.Ellis
18	William Ure; M.Susnar; J.Delaney
19	James Ridings; William J. Turnblazar
20	T.Crawford; Hollyfield; C.E.Beane
21	H.Allai; D.Laoley
22	Frank M. Stevenson
23	Neil Beam; Louis Austin; Lee Paterson
25	J. Eagan
26	
27	
28	
29	L.S.Philipot; J.Leever
30	C.E. Beane; Carson Hibbits
31	L.Pnokovich

(Con'd)

Table A - 3 (Con'd)

Districts	1972	2/1/73	3/15	4/15	6/1	7/15	9/1	10/1	11/1
2			Bruno Telk						F.Kulish
3		B.Olmizze		L.Yablonski					
4							J. Diviase		
5			R.Nuccetelli				Lou Antal		
6				John Guzek					
10									
11				Robert Edney					
12				Kenneth Dawes					
14						Elmer Clark			
15	Lorenzo				Arthur Biggs				
17							Jack Perry		
18					Donald McDonald				
19								Hugh Jones	B.J.Floyd
20									S.Littlefield
21									
22									
23							B. Nofsinger		
25								W. Kranska	
26									
27					R.J. Boyle				
28				Tom Owens					
29					Levi Daniel				
30			Farley Gilly				Squire Feltner		
31			Joseph Lerdich				Lawrence Floyd		

(Con'd)

Table A - 3 (Con'd)

Districts	2/15/74	3/1	10/1	1/15/75	7/1	4/1/76	12/1/76
2							
3							
4							
5							
6							
11				Donald Gibson			Larry Reynolds
12							
14							
15				Bill Hurtado			
17							
18						Michael Tomtom	
19							
20					Loyd Baker		
21					Hubert Nicholas		
22					H.A. Brownfield		
23							
25							
26							
28						Ray Marshall	
29				Richard Carter			
30							
31							

The End of Table A - 3

APPENDIX 2

METHODOLOGY AND THE NATURAL HISTORY OF THE RESEARCH

The rich and complex history of the UMW always refused to be framed into my initially naive view of the world, and continually threw me into confusion, but in the end helped me to reach a more sophisticated view. Having a rather obstinate skepticism about the fashionable one-shot hypothesis-testing approach, I enjoyed every minute of the constant surprise, confusion, and enrichment of my view that this study brought forth.

Although it is difficult to fully describe the history of this study and the series of my methodological decisions in a short section, it is probably meaningful to end with a brief description of them.

Emergence of the Topic

Two years ago, when this study began, I persistently confined my efforts to non-empirical mathematical modeling with an amateurish, self-complacent contempt for any non-mathematical studies in the social sciences as being non-scientific. I was particularly interested in mathematical organization theories such as n-person game theory, the theory of teams and economic theories of central planning, and mathematical conflict theories such as two-person non-zero-sum game theory, bargaining theories, and Richardson's theory of international conflict. In time I found myself very frustrated by the latter theories. They uniformly assume some kind of "individual" actor models without taking organizational variables into account. Being interested in both organizational and conflict theories, I decided to build a bargaining model of two large organizations,(1) and to evaluate the effect of organizational variables by comparing the mathematical solution of my model with those of conventional "individual-actor" models.

As I soon found out, the task was far more difficult than I expected. The meager literature in the field provided virtually no well-accepted hypotheses connecting organizational variables and the bargainers' behavior, which were absolutely necessary in constructing a model. Perhaps the task was premature in view of the rudimentary state of the field. My progress ground to a halt.

Invaluable aid came from the professional advice of Professors Edgar H. Schein and John van Maanen, who guided me into the empirical literature. I was soon overwhelmed by the richness of the field, and began to reformulate my original topic into a more manageable and empirically meaningful one. Since knowledge about the organizational effect on conflict was non-existent in the field, the most fruitful approach seemed to be that of empirically generating "grounded" hypotheses through a detailed case study.

Evolution of the Research Design

The process of choosing the appropriate research design was described in Chapter II in detail. In this process Professor D. Quinn Mills provided me with a long list of unions and their brief history to facilitate my case-sampling.

Actual Research I: Documentary Study

1. Data Collection

My academic environment was exceptionally propitious for the kind of study on which I had embarked. A number of scholars with whom I was associated at MIT and Harvard were dedicated, well-informed and extremely helpful. The Dewey Library at MIT has not only an extensive and meticulously filed collection of industrial relations materials, but also exceptionally competent librarians. I also used the Baker and Littauer Libraries of Harvard University, the Boston Public Library, and in the later stages the Brown University Library and the Library of Congress. Baker Library has a special microfilm reader-printer machine, one of the few in Boston, which I sometimes occupied continuously for more than three weeks, probably to the great inconvenience of the Harvard community.

In a hypothesis-generation study, one should not apply any a priori criteria in choosing "relevant" data, but should go through all the available data and gradually identify what is important. Accordingly, I read all the available documents and put them into the form of cards, which were classified into three categories: data cards, theory cards, and methodology cards. All of them were filed according to subject.

The reliability of the data was carefully checked. Archival data inevitably have distortions of some kind, which can be eliminated only by careful cross-examination of several different sources. All the contradictory statements from various sources were recorded, compared and interpreted on methodology cards. The following general criteria were used in this process.

(1) Data from unknown sources were discarded.

(2) If an anti-union (pro-union) source reported a "fact" unfavorable (favorable) to the union, the qualitative implication of the "fact" was used.

(3) All the apparently biased sources other than (2) were cross-checked with the other sources. If they showed contradictions, I looked for an explanation. If I could find a reasonable explanation which enabled

me to choose one source over another, I adopted it. If not, the data were abandoned.

(4) The primary sources were used without extensive cross-checking.

(5) The accounts in "neutral" newspapers and magazines (such as the New York Times, Newsweek, Business Week,, US News and World Report and The Wall Street Journal) were relatively generously used except for the interpretative parts of the articles.

2. Description of the Union's Organization and Behavior

When I finished collecting data for each period, I got hold of as large a desk as possible so that I could spread out all the relevant cards and materials and then construct a story that was consistent with all the data displayed on the desk. Since the purpose of these sections was to establish the characteristics of the organization and its behavior (rather than to show how such characteristics came into existence), the reasons for the emergence of such characteristics were discussed rather sketchily.

One of the most serious problems I encountered in these two sections was the difficulty of establishing organizational characteristics from the kind of data I had. For example, how could I show that the miners' interest changed from wage increase in the 1940's to job security and safety in the 1960's, when the only relevant data at hand were more than 30,000 local resolutions? A thorough reading of all the resolutions would probably convince most people, but it would be impractical to ask them to do so. Illustrative examples would not be enough because of the possibility of arbitrarily picking non-representative cases favorable to my position. At this point I took to heart the admonition: "If you have qualitytive data, quantify as far as possible. If you have quantitative data, qualify as far as possible."(2) The most straightforward application of this strategy was simply to count the number of resolutions on each issue and make an inter-temporal comparison. Table A-1, which was used at various places in the text, was the result.

This quantification method was used in many other places. In order to compare the degree of democracy in the different administrations, for example, I simply calculated the average number (per day) of rank-and-file members who were allowed to speak in the conventions, and measured the proportion of time allocated to their speeches by the proportion of space devoted to them in the minutes (Table 7-3).

It should be noted in this regard that many quotations in the text were meant to be supplementary to these quantitative data and therefore should be taken as illustrative rather than as evidential.

3. Analysis

In the analysis section I used a few custom-made procedures. The first was the extensive utilization of cards. As in 2., I spread out all the relevant cards and materials on the largest desk in the library (sometimes occupying as many as three large desks), and tried to find links among them. When I came up with some ideas, I wrote them down on theory cards, which gradually accumulated to a fairly large number. I then classified and compared the theory cards, searching for inconsistencies and going back to the raw data cards whenever necessary. The criteria I used in evaluating alternative explanations were (a) consistency (with all the cards I had) and (b) comprehensiveness (to cover all the cards). Playing with many interesting and unpolished ideas was rather enjoyable.

In parallel with the above procedure I was constantly surveying all the extant literature in social sciences relevant to the topic in a search for applicatble theories. I found such areas as sociological and political theories of leadership (particularly those of charisma), theories of mass society, theories of democracy, the communications literature, the literature on information processing, application of cybernetics in social sciences, studies of organizational corruption, those of leadership career and of succession, particularly useful. The analysis section was a product of the continual shuttling among these three processes.

Actual Research II: Interview in Washington

The latter part of the Boyle period and the Miller period were still too current and controversial to rely solely on the documental data. I decided to conduct an interview study to supplement them.

There were serious difficulties in this effort. First, the only time my schedule allowed for the trip was the worst time of all, just one and a half months before the union's presidential election in 1977. There were numerous defections of prominent leaders. Miller reportedly had become paranoid and fired virtually everyone. Violence was often reported. In such a chaotic atmosphere of fear and suspicion, one cannot expect much cooperation. I was afraid that the trip might not be worth the effort at all.

The second difficulty was that this union traditionally had very little contact with the academic world or the government (except for the investigation of irregularities), and that even my well-known and influential advisors had absolutely no official contact with the union.

The third difficulty was the time constraint. My schedule allowed only three to four weeks, which might prove too short for any meaningful research. One or two weeks might pass quickly before I even learned how to get by. Many of the field methodology books suggested that one spend as long as several months just in getting the feel of the place before the start of actual research. As I look back, I am now strongly convinced that extensive preparation can substantially increase the effectiveness and efficiency of field research.

The first obvious preparation was to study all the available documents in detail before the departure. I made a long list of all the questions that I could not answer solely from the documents, and tried to think of all the possible alternative explanations for them. My purpose was to use a substantial part of the interviews to test such hypothetical explanations. For each hypothesis, I formulated a few questions whose answers would enable me to evaluate its validity. This large list of questions proved extremely helpful in the field.

Secondly, I tried to find as many names of potential informants as I could, and to get in touch with them if possible. I asked Professor Myers to write to the research director, Tom Bethel. I also asked Professor Piore to write to his former student who, I accidentlly heard, had taken a research post in the UMW. One of innumerable friends who were generous enough to listen to my research problems told me that her friend used to be an attorney for the Department of Labor, and knew many lawyers who investigated the UMW's election irregularities in 1969. She also mentioned that another friend's husband was an accountant for the UMW. Naturally I asked her help, which turned out to be quite useful.

Although I faced a great deal of unexpected difficulties in the field, the preparation I made was undoubtedly helpful. For example, after I reached Washington, I found that Miller had closed down the research department and locked the door with chains and nails. All the researchers had left there, and none of my advisors' letters had reached them. The long list of names I had prepared earlier saved me from this first crisis, which otherwise could have jeopardized the research completely. I found their telephone numbers from directory assistance and called them at home. Many of them declined to meet me, but I was able to expand my contacts from the few people I met by asking these to introduce me to further appropriate contacts.

I found the newspaper correspondents very helpful. Mr. Ben Franklin of the New York Times, a top priority on my list, impressed me with his sharp observation and broad knowledge. At his suggestion I attended a press conference of Lee Roy Patterson, which opened new sources for my research. I then began visiting the campaign offices of Patterson and Harry Patrick. Campaign workers in both camps were highly involved in the election and took the stranger who began shuttling between both offices as a symbolic target for their competition. They became very enthusiastic in persuading me, giving many examples and arguments. My frequent shuttle escalated their excitement, which brought me a massive amount of data. Although much of the information I received from them was too biased to be used directly, I obtained a great number of hints and clues from it.

During the course of my research, the fashionable, sophisticated methodology which every American doctoral student has to master in his graduate program, turned out to be of virtually no use. From my perspective, the recent enthusiasim for quantitative methodology in American social sciences often looked pathological. Methodology is prophylactic in its essence. Just as hygene can save us from contagion but cannot ensure health, methodology can only warn us of pitfalls but is powerless in developing new ideas. In the atmosphere of methodological enthusiasm, many young scholars, fearful of offending the powerful establishment and of putting their "professional" reputation at stake, avoid controversial theses, and work on rather trivial questions with "methodological perfection". A great deal of effort and time have been devoted to "rigorously proving" something which everyone seems to have known for years. In Andreski's words, these scholars resemble the carpenter who became so obsessed with keeping his tools clean that he could not cut the wood.(3)

In the United States, social scientists usually become experts in one particular method and apply it throughout their careers. Since a method, like any tool or skill, is suited only to a particular phenomenon, this one-man-one-expertise tendency unduly confines what each social scientist can do. After all, no social phenomenon is so conveniently demarcated as to be amenable to analysis by only one method. The result is a flood of trivial "findings" or careless application of an inappropriate method to the wrong phenomenon. Probably what is needed is training in several different methods and in the ability critically to compare and choose the most appropriate multi-method combination, depending on the research topic. Methodology of choosing methods is what I felt was seriously needed throughout my research.

FOOTNOTES

Chapter I:

(1) Bok, D. C. and Dunlop. J. T. , Labor and the American Community, New York, Simon and Schuster, 1970, p. 207.

(2) op. cit.

(3) Simkin, W. E., "Refusals to Ratify Contract", Industrial and Labor Relations Review, July, 1968, pp- 518-540.

(4) Hansen, A., "Cycles of Strikes", American Economic Review, 1921, pp. 612-621.

(5) Griffin, J. I., Strikes: A Study in Quantitative Economics, New York: Columbia University Press, 1937.

(6) Yoder, D., "Economic Changes and Industrial Unrest in the United States", Journal of Political Economy, Vol. 2, 1940, pp. 222-237.

(7) Jurhat, E. H., and Jurhat, D. G., "Economic Functions of Strikes", Industrial and Labor Relations Review, Vol. 19, 1966, pp. 231238.

(8) Rees, A., "Industrial Conflict and Business Fluctuations", Journal of Political Economy, Vol. 60, 1952, p. 373.

(9) Weibtraub, A., "Prosperity versus Strikes: An Empirical Approach", Industrial and Labor Relations Review, Vol. 19, 1966, pp. 231-238.

(10) O'Brien, F. S., "Industrial Conflict and Business Fluctuations: A Comment", Journal of Political Activity, Vol. 73, 1965, pp. 650-654.

(11) Ashenfelter, O., and Johnson, G. E., "Bargaining Theory, Trade Unions and Industrial Strike Activity", American Economic Review, Vol. 59, 1969, pp. 35-49.

(12) Ashenfelter and Johnson's original hypothesis was that:

> "The parties were less likely to agree prior to conflict the greater the acceptable wage increase (y_o) and the speed at which the membership's expectations are reduced during a strike ( ); the parties are the more likely to agree the greater is the ratio of the preagreement profit level to the wage bill ( ), firms discount rate (r), and the minimum acceptable wage increase (y*)"
> (Ashenfelter and Johnson, op. cit., p. 40)

They then constructed an operational regression model, which predicts:

> (1) the greater the civilian unemployment rate, the less likely the strike will be;
> (2) the greater the annual percentage rate of change of money wages, the less likely the strike will be;
> (3) the greater the annual percentage rate of change of consumer prices, the more likely the strike will be; and
> (4) the more the ratio of corporate profits after taxes to total compensation, the more likely the strike will be.

(13) Pencavel, J. H., "An Investigation into Industrial Strike Activity in Britain", Economica, Vol. 37, 1970, pp- 239-256.

(14) Skeels, J. W., "Measure of U. S. Strike Activity", Industrial and Labor Relations Review, Vol. 24(4), July, 1971, pp. 515-525.

(15) Hibbs, D. A., Jr., Industrial Conflict in Advanced Industrial Societies, Cambridge, Center for Political Studies, Massachusetts Institute of Technology, 2974.

(16) Harbison, F. H., and Coleman, J. R., Goals and Strategy in Collective Bargaining, New York, Harper, 1951.

(17) Knowles, K. G. J. C., Strikes: A Study in Industrial Conflict, Blackwell, Oxford, 1952.

(18) Kerr, C., and Siegel, A., "The Inter-Industry Propensity to Strike - An International Comparison", in Kronhauser, A., Dubin, R. and Ross, A. M. (eds.), Industrial Conflict, New York, McGraw Hill, 1954, pp. 89-212.

(19) Revans, R. W., "Industrial Morale and Size of Unit", in Galeson, W. and Lipset, S. M. (eds.), Labor and trade Unionism, New York, Wiley, 1960, pp. 295-300.

20) Horvath, W. J., "A Statistical Model for the Duration of Wars and Strikes", Behavioral Sciences, Vol. 13 (1), January, 1968, pp. 19-28.

(21) Ingham, G. K., "Plant Size, Political Attitude and Behavior", Sociological Review, Vol. 17 (2) (New Series), July, 1969, pp. 235-249.

(22) Eisele, C. F., "Plant Size and Frequency of Strikes", Labor and Law Journal, Vol. 21 (12), December, 1970, pp- 779-786.

(23) Eisele, C. F., "Organization Size, Technology and Frequency of Strikes", Industrial and Labor Relations Review, Vol. 27 (4), July, 1974, pp. 560-571.

(24) Sayles, L. R., and Strauss. G., The Local Union: Its Place in the Industrial Plant, 1st Ed., New York, Harper, 1953, p. 8.

(25) Lester, R. A., As Unions Mature: An Analysis of the Evolution of American Unionism, Princeton, N.J., Princeton University Press, 1958.

(26) Harbison, F. H., and Coleman, J. R., op. cit.

(27) Ross, A. M., and Hartman, P., Changing Patterns of Industrial Conflict, New York, Wiley, 1960.

(28) Snyder, D., "Institutional Setting and Industrial Conflict: Comparative Analysis of France, Italy and the United States", American Sociological Review, Vol. 40, June, 1975, pp. 259-278.

(29) Tannenbaum, A. S., "Unions", in March, J. G. (ed,), Handbook of Organizations, Chicago, Rand McNally and Company, 1965, pp. 710-763.

(30) Ross, A. M. and Hartman, P., op. cit.

(31) Britt, D. and Galle, O., "Industrial Conflict and Unionization", American Sociological Review, 37, 1972, pp. 46-57.

(32) Definitions of various aspects of strike activities were as follows:

Volume of Conflict

$$= \frac{\text{The number of man-days lost from strikes and walkouts}}{\text{The number of workers employed}} \times 1000$$

Proneness to Conflict

= The number of work stoppages

Intensity of Conflict

$$= \frac{\text{The number of workers involved} \quad \times 1000}{\text{The number of work stoppages x the number of workers employed}}$$

Extensity of Conflict

$$= \frac{\text{The number of man-days idle}}{\text{The number of workers involved}}$$

(33) Tannenbaum, A. S., and Kahn, R., "Organizational Control Structure: A General Descriptive Technique as Applied to Four Local Unions", Human Relations, Vol. 10, 1957, pp- 127-140.

(34) Roomkin, M., "Union Structure, Internal Control, and Strike Activity", Industrial Labor relations Review, Vol. 29 (2), January, 1976, pp. 198-217.

(35) Tannenbaum, A. S., op. cit. p. 731.

(36) It may be unfair to completely negate the value of the research on economic factors solely on this basis. Many of the studies in this category are originally interested in the Inter-temporal variation of the overall strike activities, and do provide valuable information on this issue.

(37) Bok, D. C. and Dunlop, J. T., op. cit.;
Walton, R. E., and McKersie, R. B., A Behavioral Theory of Labor Negotiations: An Analysis of a Social Interaction System, New York, McGraw Hill, 1965.

(38) Bok, D. C., and Dunlop, J. T., op. cit., p. 233.

(39) Rees, A., op. cit., p. 381.

Chapter II

(1) Bailyn, L., "Research as a Cognitive Process: Implications for Data Analysis", Quality and Quantity, 11 (1977), pp. 97-117.

(2) Lipset, S. M., Trouw, M. A., and Coleman, J. S., Union Democracy: the Internal Politics of the International Typographical Union, Glencoe, Ill., Free Press, 1956.

(3) Glaser, B. G., and Strauss, A. L., The Discovery of Grounded Theory: Strategies for Qualitative Research, Chicago, Aldine Publ. Co., 1967.

(4) The author would like to acknowledge his debt to Professor D. Quinn Mills for helpful suggestions in this exploratory survey of the unions.

(5) Although it was 1963 when W. A. Boyle actually became president, it is better for the purposes of this study to classify 1960-1972 as one period. Thomas Kennedy, who succeeded Lewis in 1960, was in ill health and delegated most of his essential power to the then Vice President Boyle.

Chapter III

(1) Rostow, E. V., "Bituminous Coal and the Public Interest", Yale Law Journal, Vol. 50, 1941, pp. 543-594.

(2) Berquist, F. E., and Associates, Economic Survey of the Bituminous Coal Industry under Free Competition and Code Regulations, Washington, U. S. National Recovery Administration, 1936.

(3) Stentham, I. C. F., Coal Mining, New York, Philosophical Library, 1956.

(4) Baratz, M. S., The Union and the Coal Industry, New Haven, Conn., Yale University Press, 1955, pp. 2-3.

(5) Baratz, M. S., op. cit., p. 4.

(6) Henderson, J. M., and Quandt, R. E., Microeconomic Theory: Mathematical Approach, 2nd Edition, New York, McGraw Hill, 1971.

(7) Keynes, J. M., The General Theory of Employment, Interest and Money, New York, Harcourt, Brace, 1936, p. 70.

(8) Baratz, M. S., op. cit., p. 5.

(9) Baratz, M. S., op. cit., p. 6.

(10) A personal letter to Dr. Baratz from G. H. Seal, Vice President of C. H. Sprague & Son Coal Co., May 11, 1951, in Baratz, op. cit., p. 4.

(11) Baratz, M. S., op. cit., p. 6.

(12) Bituminous Coal Association, Bituminous Coal Annual, 1951, Washington, 1952.

(13) Hamilton, W. H., and Wright, H. R., The Case of Bituminous Coal, New York, MacMillan Co., 1925, pp. 263-264. The table was originally reported in U. S. Coal Commission, Relief from Irregular Operation and Over Development, Part I, 1923, and U. S. Geographical Survey, Weekly Report of the Production of Bituminous Coal, Anthracite and Beehive Coke, 1922-24.

(14) Theoretically, capacity is defined as the amount of production if the equipment is used most efficiently. It is very difficult to obtain an accurate estimate of this figure. In this table, capacity is defined as the tonnage the mines would have produced if they had operated 308 days in the year. While this definition makes the calculation far simpler, the apparent arbitrariness of the assumption is its major defect.

(15) Bituminous Coal Association, op. cit.

(16) Evans, M. K., Macroeconomic Activity: Theory, Forecasting and Control, An Econometric Approach, New York, Harper & Row, 1969.

(17) National Coal Association, Bituminous Coal Data, 1974 Edition, Washington, 1975.

(18) Coleman, A., op. cit., p. 57.

(19) Coleman, A., op. cit., p. 68.

(20) Alinsky, S. D., John L. Lewis: An Unauthorized Biography, Vintage Books, 1949, p. 13.

(21) Alinsky, S., op. cit., p. 41.

(22) Coleman, A., op. cit., pp. 157-158.

(23) Alinsky, S., op. cit., p. 148.

(24) Lantz, H. R., People of Coal Town, New York, Columbia University Press, 1958, pp. 145-146.

(25) Lantz, H. R., op. cit., pp. 145

(26) Gouldner, A. W., Wildcat Strike,. Yellow Spring, Ohio, Antioch Press,1954.

(27) Lantz, H. R., op. cit., p. 146.

(28) The following description is based on Alinsky, op. cit.; Arble, M., "Notes from a Coal Mine", The New York Times Magazine, January 12, 1974; Arble, M., The Long Tunnel: A Coal Miner's Journal, New York, Athaneum, 1976; Coleman, M., Men and Coal, New York, Farrar and Rinehart, 1946; Peterson, B., Coaltown Revisited: An Appalachian Notebook, Chicago, Henry Regnery Company, 1972; Vecsey, G.: One Sunset a Week: The Story of a Coal Miner, Saturday Review Press, 1974; and Wechsler, J. A., Labor Baron: A Portrait of John L. Lewis, New York, William Morrow and Company, 1944.

(29) U. S. Department of Labor, Bureau of Labor Statistics, Injury Rates By Industry, 1970, BLS Report No. 406, 1972.

(30) Vecsey, G., op. cit., p. 19.

(31) Ibid.

(32) Lantz, H. R., op. cit., p. 130.

(33) Ibid.

(34) Ibid., p. 142.

(35) Ibid., pp. 142-143.

(36) Ibid., p. 133.

(37) Ibid., p. 132.

(38) Coleman, M., op. cit., Chapters 1-3.

(39) Zweig, F., Men in the Pits, London, Victor Gollaney, Ltd., 1948, pp. 100-101.

(40) Lilienthal, D., "The Meaning of Unionism: A Study of Members of the Plumbers' Union, of the United Mine Workers, and of the United Automobile Workers of America", unpublished Ph.D. thesis, University of Chicago, 1956.

(41) Lantz, H. R., op. cit., pp. 257-258.

(42) Newsweek, July 4, 1976, p. 4.

(43) Peterson, B., op. cit., p. 72.

(44) Coleman, M., op. cit.

(45) Ibid., p. 288.

(46) Ibid.

(47) Zweig, F., op. cit., pp. 8-19.

(48) Vecsey, G., op. cit., p. 246.

(49) Lantz, H. R., op. cit., p. 147.

(50) Korson, G., Coal Dust on the Fiddle: Songs and Stories of the Bituminous Industry, Philadelphia, University of Pennsylvania Press, 1943, pp. 128-129.

(51) Lantz, H. R., op. cit., p. 129.

(52) Fortune, March, 1947, pp. 97-98.

(53) Alinsky, S., op. cit., p. 4.

(54) Hardman, J. B. S., "John L. Lewis, Labor Leader and Man: An Interpretation", Labor History, Winter, 1960, Volume 2, No. 1, p. 8.

(55) Newsweek, July 4, 1976, p. 42.

(56) Lantz, op. cit., p. 144.

(57) Ibid., p. 143.

(58)Peterson, B., op. cit., p. 25.

(59) Ibid., p. 35.

(60) Korson, G. G., op. cit., pp. 321-322.

(61) Lilienthal, D., op. cit., pp. 140-141.

(62) Karsh, B., and London, J., "The Coal Miners: A Study of Union Control", Quarterly Journal of Economics, Vol. 68 (3), August, 1954, p. 431.

(63) Korson, G. G., op. cit., pp. 331-332.

(64) Wechsler, op. cit., pp- 8-9.

(65) Zweig, F., op. cit., p. 108.

(66) Lantz, H. R., op. cit., p. 261.

(67) Ibid.

Chapter IV

(1) Constitution of the International Union, United Mine Workers of America, 1932. In the following discussion, "Constitution" refers to the above material.

(2) Constitution, Article XI, Sections 1 and 2.

(3) Constitution, Article VII.

(4) Constitution, Article III, Section 1, and Article XII, Section 1.

(5) Constitution, Article XII, Section 2.

(6) Constitution, Article III, Section 1 and Article IX, Section 13.

(7) The United Mine Workers of America, Proceedings of the 38th International Convention of The United Mine Workers of America, 1944, Volume 1, p. 301.

(8) New Republic, April 14, 1949.

(9) Before 1942, the membership dues were $1.00 a month, out of which 15¢ went to the local, 15¢ to the district, and the remaining 70¢ to the international. The Cincinnati Convention of 1942 raised the dues to $1.50 with 30¢ to the local, 30¢ to the district and 90¢ to the international.

(10) The United Mine Workers of America, Proceedings of the International Convention of the United Mine Workers of America, 1942, Vol. 2, p. 14.

(11) Karsh, B. and London, J., "The Coal Miners: A Study of Union Control", Quarterly Journal of Economics, August, 1954, Vol. 69 (3), p. 145.

(12) According to Article VII of the Constitution, "International Officer" included International Executive Board Members.

(13) Weber's definition will be adopted in this study:

> ... the term "charisma" shall be understood to refer to an extraordinary quality of a person, regardless of whether this quality is actual, alleged, or presumed. "Charismatic authority", hence, shall refer to a rule over men, whether predominantly external or predominantly internal, to which the governed submit because of their belief in the extraordinary quality of the specific person. (Gerth, H. H., and Mills, C. W., p. 295).

(14) Dow, T. E., "The Theory of Charisma", Sociological Quarterly, Vol. 10, Summer, 1969, pp. 306-318.

(15) Tucker, R. C., "The Theory of Charismatic Leadership", Daedalus, Volume 97, Summer, 1968, pp. 731-755.

(16) Bord, R. J., "Toward a Social-Psychological Theory of Charismatic Social Influence Processes", Social Forces, March, 1975.

(17) Ake, C., "Charismatic Legitimization and Political Leadership", Comparative Studies in Society and History, Vol. 9, October, 1966, pp. 1-13;
Fagen, R., "Charismatic Authority and the Leadership of Fidel Castro", Western Political Quarterly, Vol. 18, 1965;
Friedland, W., "For a Sociological Concept of Charisma", Social Forces, Vol. 43, October, 1964, pp. 18-26.
Wolpe, H., "A Critical Analysis of Some Aspects of Charisma", Sociological Review, Vol. 16, November, 1968, pp. 305-318.

(18) U. S. Senate, Committeee on Education and Labor, Hearings before the Senate Subcommittee on Labor, 1949.

(19) The United Mine Workers of America, Proceedings of the International Conventions of the United Mine Workers of America, 1942, Vol. 1, pp. 233-244.

(20) The United Mine Workers, of America, John L. Lewis and the International Union, p. 119.

(21) The New York Times, December 29, 1949. Mr. Denham was then General Council of the NWLB.

(22) Raskin, A. H., "John L. Lewis - A Glorious Anachronism", The New York Times Magazine, February 13, 1955.

(23) The United Mine Workers, of America, Proceedings of the International Union, p. 280.

(24) The United Mine Workers of America, Proceedings of the International Conventions of the United Mine Workers of America, 1942, Vol. 1, p. 233.

(25) Karsch, B., and London, J., op. cit.

(26) Alinsky, S., op. cit., p. 281; The New York Times, June 17, 1942.

(27) Coleman, M., op. cit., pp. 214-216.

(28) Mills, C. W., "The Case for the Miners", New Republic, May 24, 1943, Vol. 103, No. 21.

(29) The New York Times, January 10, 11, 12, 13, 14, and 16, 1943.

(30) The New York Times, January 20, 21 and 23, 1943.

(31) The New York Times, March 11, 1943.

(32) Alinsky, S., op. cit., p. 286.

(33) Ibid., p. 228.

(34) The New York Times, March 20, 1943.

(35) Ibid., April 23, 1943.

(36) Ibid., April 25, 26, 28 and 29, 1943.

(37) Ibid., May 3, 1943.

(38) Ibid., May 15, 1943.

(39) Ibid., May 26, 1943.

(40) Ibid., June 1 and 2, 1943.

(41) Ibid., June 3, 1943.

(42) Ibid., June 2, 1943.

(43) Alinsky, S., op. Cit., pp. 310-311; Coleman, M., op. cit., p. 258.

(44) Alinsky, S., op. cit., p. 311.

(45) The New York Times, June 4, 1943.

(46) Ibid, June 5, 1943.

(47) Ibid., June 8, 1943

(48) Ibid., June 10, 1943.

(49) Ibid., June 19, 1943.

(50) Ibid., June 20 and 21, 1943.

(51) Ibid., June 23, 1943.

(52) Ibid., July 21, 1943.

(53) Ibid., July 22, 1943.

(54) Ibid., August 17, 1943.

(55) Ibid., August 26, 1943.

(56) Ibid., September 24, 1943.

(57) Ibid., October 27, 1943.

(58) Ibid., October 30, 1943.

(59) Ibid., November 3, 1943,

(60) Ibid., November 4, 1943.

(61) Ibid., November 21, 1943.

(62) Ibid., November 5, 1943, p. 18.

(63) Coleman, M., op. cit., pp. 199-278.

(64) For example, John L. Lewis reportedly said:

> I had learned the bitter lesson that as long as the great mass of workers was unorganized, so long would if be impossible for organized labor to achieve its legitimate goals. When unions neglect to organize the unorganized they pay the penalty of their own neglect. I was never permitted to forget that lesson because every year as we sat down to negotiate with the coal operators, they would begin by denying unreasonable positions by citing the lower wage of the unorganized steel workers. The coal operators would then declare that since the mine workers were earning more money than the steel workers, we should be satisfied. The low pay of the steel workers was a drag on the wage scale of the United Mine Workers. It became increasingly clear that the mine workers could never really win a just wage until the steel workers were organized and their miserable wages raised to a human decent standard. This seemed to be a simple elementary, economic fact and it applied not only to the miners but also to other organized union groups.
> (Cited by Alinsky, S., op. cit., p. 64)

(65) Alinsky, op. cit., p. 2; Hardman, op. cit.

(66) The United Mine Workers of America, Proceedings of the International Convention of the United MineWorkers of America, 1944, Vol. 1.

(67) Business Week, October 5, 1946, pp. 95-100.

(68) A study of UMWA financial records discloses that $3,024,956 was spent on District 50 from December, 1940, to June, 1943. (Wesler, J. A., Labor Baron: A Portrait of John L. Lewis, New York, Marrow, 1944.)
Business Week also commented:

> UMW spent a hell of a lot of money and man-power for organizing the District 50. No figures have been available on how much the parent organization spent, but there is little doubt that UMW paid one of the heaviest organization labor costs in labor history. (Business Week, October 5, 1946, pp. 95-100)

(69) The New York Times, September 10, 1941.

(70) Ibid., September 12, 13, 14, 16, 21, 23, 25, 28, 29, 30, and October 5, 1941.

(71) The United MineWorkers of America, *Proceedings of the International Convention of the United Mine Workers of America, 1942*, Vol. 1.

(72) Ibid., p. 122.

(73) For example, one delegate revealed his difficulty in persuading the young rank-and-file who began to leave the union because of the lack of autonomy:

> ... In the fight that we are carrying on at home, it is pretty hard to convince them of principles of the United Mine Workers (i.e. instrumental efficiency argument) ... today back home we are losing many members on account of that one thing, because they feel that International officers and the Executive Board are the dominating part of the United Mine Workers ... Where you have 100% organized men in your district it is all right to feel that you don't want autonomy, but we have young fellows in our district who insist on the principle of democracy (whom I cannot persuade without autonomy). Delegate Label from Social Union No. 4047, District 31, *Proceedings of the International Convention of the United Mine Workers of America, 1942*, Vol. 1, p. 209.

(75) Arendt, H., *The Origin of Totalitarianism*, New York, Harcourt, Brace, 1951;
de Tocqueville, A., *Democracy in America*, Vols. 1 and 2, New York, Knopf, 1945;
Kornhauser, W., *Politics of Mass Society*, New York, Free Press, 1959;
Lipset, S. M., *Political Men*, London, Heineman, 1960.

(76) Kornhauser, W., *op. cit.*; Selznick, P., *Organizational Weapon*, New York, McGraw Hill, 1952.

(77) Selznick, P., *op. cit.*, pp. 293-294.

(78) Arendt, H., *op. cit.*;
Kornhauser, W., *op. cit.*

(79) Kornhauser, W., *op. cit.*, p. 45.

(80) Blumer, M. I. A., "Sociological Models of the Mining Community", *The Sociological Review*, Vol. 23 (1), February, 1975.

(81) Kerr, C., and Siegel, A., *op. cit.*, p. 193.

(82) Cartwright, D., and Zander, A., *Group Dynamics*, 2nd Edition, New York, Harper and Row, 1953;
Festinger, L., and Thibaut, J., "Interpersonal Communication in Small Groups", *Journal of Abnormal and Social Psychology*, Volume 46, 1951, pp. 92-99.

(83) Polalsov, W. N., "Sufficient unto Himself in Coal Digger: Why the Miners Behave the Way They Do - A Social Portraiture of the Nation's Most Vital, Least Known Labor Force", *Labor and Nation*, May-June, 1947, Vol. 3, No. 3.

(84) Keer, C. and Siegel, A., "The Interindustry Propensity to Strike - An International Comparison", in Kornhauser, A., Dubin, R., and Ross, A. M. (eds.), Industrial Conflict, New York, McGraw Hill, 1954, pp. 189-212.

(85) Coser, L., The Functions of Social Conflict, New York, Free Press, 1956, p. 62.

(86) Ibid., pp. 68-69;
Malinowski, B., "An Anthropological Analysis of War", in his Magic, Science and Religion, Glencoe (Ill.), Free Press, 1948, pp. 277-309;
Simmel, G., Conflict, Glencoe, Free Press, 1955.

(87) Alinsky, S., op. cit.

(88) Ibid., pp. 283-284.

(89) Gerth, H. H., and Mills, C. W., From Max Weber: Essays in Sociology, New York, Oxford University Press, 1958, p. 246.

(90) Ibid., pp. 246-247.

(91) Ibid., p. 249.

(92) Alinsky, S. op. cit.; Hardman, J. B. S., op. cit.

(93) Hardman, J. B. S., op. cit.

(94) Polasov, W. N., op. cit.

(95) Alinsky, S., op. cit.

Chapter V:

(1) The New York Times, September 22, 1950.

(2) Ibid., January 19, 1951.

(3) Ibid., July 23, 1952.

(4) Ibid., August 24, 1952.

(5) Ibid., September 21, 1952.

(6) Therefore, this new agreement was not in the form of a new contract but in the form of an "amendment" of the still valid 1952 contract.

(7) Fox succeeded Moses as President of the BCOA in 1956 after Moses' sudden death.

(8) Business Week, October 4, 1958.

(9) The United Mine Workers of America, Proceedings of the International Convention of the United Mine Workers of America, 1956, Vol. 1, p. 309.

(10) The United Mine Workers Journal, Sept. 1, 1954, p. 10.

(11) Business Week, October 4, 1958. p- 108.

(12) Ibid., May 8, 1954.

(13) The New York Times, June 9, 1953.

(14) The United Mine Workers of AMerica, Proceedings of the International Convention of the United Mine Workers of America, 1952, Vol. 1, p. 267.

(15) Finley, J. E., The Corrupt Kingdom, the Rise and Fall of the United Mine Workers, New York, Simon and Schuster, 1972.

(16) The Walsh-Healey Act required companies which had a direct transaction with the government to adopt the prevailing wage scale in the area. The new entrepreneurs, however, successfully escaped from paying the union wage by establishing a string of "paper" companies. A trucking company created separately from the mining company, owned by the same man, "bought" the dog-hole coal and then sold it to a tipple corporation, also owned by the same man. The tipple company, which hired only a small number of employees, could easily pay the union wage, and sold the coal to the TVA.

(17) U. S. Court of Appeals: Osborne Mining Co., Inc. vs. The United Mine Workers of America, Labor Relations Reference Manual, Vol. 46, p. 2380f. and p. 2065f.

(18) E.g., USCA, 6th Cir., Gilchrist, W. G., Jr., vs. The United Mine Workers of America, 290 F.2d, p. 36;

USCA, 6th Cir.: *Snyder and Randolph, Inc. vs. The United Mine Workers of America*, 290 F.2d, p. 36;
USCA, 6th Cir.: *Tennessee Consolidation Coal Co. vs. The United Mine Workers of America*, *Labor Relations Reference Manual*, Vol. 62, p. 2312f.;
USC, E. Dist. Tennessee: *Pennington vs. The United Mine Workers of America*, *Labor Relations Reference Manual*, Vol. 62, p. 2604f.;
USC, E. Dist. Tenn.: *Ramsey vs. The United Mine Workers of America*, *Labor Relations Reference Manual*, Vol. 64, p. 2498.

(19) *The New York Times*, March 17, 1959.

(20) Ibid., March 18, 1959.

(21) *Ramsey*, *op. cit.*, p. 2498.

(22) *The New York Times*, April 1, 1959.

(23) Ibid., April 18, 1959.

(24) *The New York times*, November 10, 1959.

(25) Finley, J. E., *op. cit.*, p. 152.

(26) *The New York Times*, March 8, 1959.

(27) USCA, 6th Cir.: *White Oak Coal Company vs. The United Mine Workers of America*, 318 F. 2d, p. 599.

(28) *The New York Times*, March 28, 1959.

(29) *White Oak Coal Company*, *op. cit.*, p. 599.

(30) The basis for this time estimate is that in early 1949, Barnum L. Colton, an acquaintance of Lewis, was made president, and A. D. Lewis, John Lewis' brother and president of the UMWA's District 50, became one of the directors.

(31) *Ramsey*, op. cit., p. 2498.

(32) *U. S. News and World Report*, June 29, 1956, p. 59.

(33) Finley, J. E., *op. cit.*, p. 162.

(34) *Ramsey*, *op. cit.*

(35) Caldwell, N., and Graham, G. S., "John L. Lewis and Cyrus Eaton", *Harper's*, Dec., 1961

(36) *Ramsey*, p. 2623.

(37) Ibid.

(38) Caldwell, N., and Graham, G. S., *op. cit.*

(39) Pennington, op. cit., p. 2604f.

(40) Ramsey, op. cit. op. cit., p. 2498.

(41) Ibid.

(42) Caldwell, N., and Graham, G. S., op. cit., p. 28.

(43) Ramsey, op. cit.

(44) The United Mine Workers of America, Proceedings of the International Convention of the United Mine Workers of America, 1964, Vol. 1.

(45) Pennington, op. cit., p. 2624.

(46) The United Mine Workers of America, op. cit.

(47) Coal supply was often interrupted by labor disputes.

(48) Finley, J. E., op. cit., p. 169.

(49) Ibid.

(50) Baratz, M. S., The Union and the Coal Industry, New Haven, Yale University Press, 1955;
The New York Times, Sept. 22, 1950.

(51) U. S. News and World Report, June 29, 1956, p. 16.

(52) The United Mine Workers Journal, Feb. 1, 1960.

(53) Ibid., Vol. LXI, No. 6, March 15, 1960, p. 21.

(54) Ibid., Vol. 60, No. 19, p. 14.

(55) Karsh, B., and London, J., op. cit.; Finley, J. E., op. cit.

(56) The United Mine Workers of America, Proceedings of the International Convention of the United Mine Workers of America, 1952, 1956 and 1960.

(57) Machiavelli, N., The Chief Work and Others, Vol. 1, 2, and 3 (transl. A. Gilbert), Durham (N. C.), Duke University Press, 1965.

(58) Boulding, K. E., Beyond Economics: Essays on Society, Religion and Ethics, Ann Arbor, University of Michigan Press, 1968.

(59) Finley, J. E., op. cit., p. 187.

(60) Karsh, B. and London, J., op. cit.

(61) An insight of Machiavelli suggests that this finding may be more general than in the UMWA case:

> Injuries are to be done all together, so that, being savored less, they will anger less; benefits are to be conferred little by little, so they will be savored more. (Machiavelli, The Prince, in The Chief Works and Others, Vol. 1, p. 38)

(62) The United Mine Workers of America, Proceedings of the International Convention of the United Mine Workers of America, 1948, Vol, 1, p. 346.

(63) During the long 1943 negotiations, the 200-member policy committee was asked to stay in Washington for prompt consultations at any time.

(64) Declining importance of the Scale Committee can be seen in the following resolution:

> Whereas, Reports on obtaining a new Contract can be made directly to the members of each and every Local Union; and
> Whereas, they would also know exactly in between contracts, what conditions exist at the mines at that present time; therefore, be it
> Resolved, that the "Scale Committee" from the rank and file for the drawing up and approving of the United Mine Workers' Contract be restored. (Convention Proceedings, 1956, Vol. 1, p. 51, from Local Union No. 4731, Crucible, Pa.).

(65) The United Mine Workers of America, Proceedings of the International Convention of the United Mine Workers of America, 1952, Vol. 2, p. 21.

(66) Won and Yamamura reported the same phenomena in a different industry. Won, G., and Yamamura, D., "Career Orientation of Local Union Leadership: A Case Study", Sociology and Social Research, Vol. 52, No. 2, January, 1968, pp. 243-252.

(67) Lipset, S. M., "The Political Process in Trade Unions: A Theoretical Statement", in Galenson, W., and Lipset, S. M. (eds.), Labor and Trade Unions in N.Y., Wiley, 1960.

(68) The United Mine Workers of America, Proceedings of the International Convention of the United Mine Workers of America, 1956, Vol. 1.

(69) Somers, G. G., Grievance Settlement in Coal Mining, West Virginia University, Business and Economic Studies, Vol. 4, No. 4, June, 1956.

(70) Coser, L, The Function of Social Conflict, Glencoe (Ill.), The Free Press, 1959.

Chapter VI:

(1) The United Mine Workers Journal, December 15, 1959.

(2) The New York Times, December 23, 1959.

(3) The total numbers of miners and of the UMWA membvership declined from 461,991 and 595,100 in 1942 respectively to 143,822 and 151,500 in 1962. Source: the National Coal Association, Bituminous Coal Data, 1974 edition, Washington, 1975; and Troy, L., Trade Union Membership 1897 - 1962, National Bureau of Economic Research 1965, Occasional Paper 92.

(4) This practice was started by John Lewis in the late 1950's.

(5) The figures were calculated from Tables A-2 and A-3.

(6) The New York Times, December 23, 1959.

(7) Obviously, the personal quality of a charismatic leader cannot be inherited. Charismatic authority, however, is not based on the actual quality of the leader but on the members' belief in it. In this regard, it is possible that the followers accept a new leader at the beginning, the authority of this new leader chosen by their retiring hero based on their belief in his word that the successor is equally extraordinary and capable. This initial belief is referred to as inherited charismatic authority. It will not free the new leader from the pressure to prove his quality, but it will at least allow him to do without the most difficult immediate outstanding achievements required of his first-generation charismatic forerunner to establish his authority at the outset.

(8) Hume, B, Death and the Mines: Rebellion and Murder in the United Mine Workers, New York, Grossman, 1971, p. 57.

(9) Finley, J. E., op. cit., p. 238

(10) Ibid.

(11) The United Mine Workers Journal, March 1 to June 15, 1969.

(12) Hodgeson vs. UMWA, 80 LRRM 2145-2158. The U. S. District Court of the District of Columbia found that in five issues between June 15 and December 15, there were no less than 166 references to Boyle, most of them in bold face type, with 16 pictures, but that absolutely no mention of Yablonski was made.

(13) U. S. Senate, The Subcommittee on Labor of the Committee on Labor and Public Welfare, op. cit., p. 172.

(14) Hume, B., op. cit., p. 51.

(15) Armbrister, T., Act of Vengeance: The Yablonski Murders and their Solution, New York, Saturday Review Press, 1975, pp. 69-70.

(16) Ibid., p. 68.

(17) Ibid.; Hume, B., op. cit., p. 68.

(18) Proceedings of the International Convention of the United Mine Workers of America, 1964, Vol. I, p. 23.

(19) Senate Subcommittee on Labor, op. cit., p. 123.

(20) Proceedings, op. cit., p. 28-29.

(21) Ibid., pp. 322-323.

(22) Ibid., pp. 323-336.

(23) U. S. Senate, Subcommittee on Labor and Public Welfare, Hearings on Investigation of Mine Workers' Election - 1970, p. 10; Joseph L. Rauh, Jr., letter to Secretary of Labor Schulz, July 18, 1969.

(24) Senate Subcommittee on Labor and Public Welfare, op. cit., pp. 11, 110111, and 143-144.

(25) Ibid., pp. 57 and 378-455.

(26) In order to seek investigation by the Department of Labor, it was required that all internal measures be exhausted first (Landrum-Griffin Act). USC, District of Columbia, Hodgeson, op. cit.

(27) Ibid., pp. 2149-2150.

(28) The Board of Trustees consisted of three trustees, one of them neutral, one representing the union and one the industry. Decisions were made by majority voting.

(29) The New York Times, July 16, 1969.

(30) Senate Subcommittee, op. cit., pp. 164-206.

(31) U. S. Department of Labor, Office of Labor-Management and WelfarePension Reports, "Memorandum from Leonard J. Lurie (Acting Director) to W. J. Usery, Jr. (Assistant Secretary of Labor)", November 26, 1969, p. 3, Senate Subcommittee, op. cit., pp. 38-103.

(32) Hume, B., op. cit., p. 197.

(33) Ibid.

(34) Senate Subcomittee, op. cit., pp. 378-455.

(35) Armbrister, T., op. cit., p. 8.

(36) May 29 was the day when Yablonski announced his candidacy.

(37) Finley, J. E., op. cit., pp. 259-261.

(9) There were two important cutoffs in the 1950's: one in 1952 in which the eligibility rule of twenty years service in the industry was modified to further require that it had occurred within the thirty years prior to the application, and the one in 1954, where aids for the disabled and widows were terminated. Despite these important cutbacks, complaints were seldom heard in the Lewis reign.

(40) The New York Times, November 28 and December 6, 1962.

The anthracite miners, who were entitled to only $30 a month for pensions, were even more angry. They organized the Class of Pensioned Anthracite CoalMiners and Widows of Deceased Pensioned Anthracite Coal Miners in 1961, and sued the Fund for its failure to demand royalty payments into the Fund. (The New York Times, March 12, 1963

(41) For example, Raph Nader and students working voluntarily for him, as well as Joseph Rauh and Congressman Hechler, were prominent examples of the outsiders.

(42) Armbrister, T., op. cit., p. 106.

(43) The dissident group's claims to membership ranged from 25,000 to 45,000, about one tenth to one fifth of the whole UMW membership (The Wall Street Journal, June 16, 1970). The expanded strength of the dissident movement was clearly shown in the presidential election of District 5 in 1970. An insurgent leader, Louis Antal, who had been defeated by a clear margin of two-to-one in 1966, almost won the election in 1970. Before 1192 absentee ballots, mostly from retired or pensioned miners, were counted, Antal was leading the pro-Boyle incumbent, Michael Budzanoski, by 4436 to 3922. The result became a very strong threat which the international could hardly ignore (The Wall Street Journal, December 10, 1970).

(44) The Wall Street Journal, June 16, 1970.

(45) E.g., Trbovich vs. UMWA, USSC, 79 LRRM 2193; Yablonski vs. UMWA, USC, Dist. of Columbia, 80 LRRM 3435, etc.

(46) The clause was revised from:

> 1. Seniority in principle and practice shall be recognized in the industry.
> 2. In all cases where the working force is to be reduced, employees in each job classification at a mine with the least service, shall be laid off first.
> (Convention Proceedings, 1964, Vol. 1, p. 45)
>
> to:
>
> 1. Seniority at the mine shall be recognized in the industry on the following basis: length of service and qualification to perform the work.
> (Convention Proceedings, 1964, Vol. 1, p. 45)

Many discontented miners suspected that the qualification provision above would have the same effect as the classification provision and would not improve their job security (The Wall Street Journal, April 9, 1969).

(47) (The New York Times, April 9, 1969; (The Wall Street Journal, April 9, 1969.

(48) The New York Times, April 25, 1969.

(49) Proceedings of the International Convention of the United Mine Workers of America, 1968, Vol. 1, pp. 49-76.

(50) The New York Times, April 30, 1966; The Wall Street Journal, May 8, 1966.

(51) The Wall Street Journal, July 18, 1968.

(52) Ibid., October 7, 1968.

(53) The local resolution in the 1964 and 1968 International Conventions showed that the graduated vacation schedule had been one of the most important demands of the rank-and-file. (Proceedings of the International Convention of the United Mine Workers of America, 1964 and 1968, Vol. 2.

(54) The Wall Street Journal, October 15, 1968.

(55) The New York Times, October 2, 1971.

(56) The New York Times, October 21, 1971; The Wall Street Journal, October 21, 1971. The immediate cause of the Boyle outburst was the operators' proposal that they pay the wage increases every six months for three years only to those miners who did not participate in an illegal strike during the preceding six-month period. Having been attacked strongly by the dissenting members, Boyle found this demand totally unacceptable.

(57) The New York Times, November 5, 1971.

(58) The Wall Street Journal, November 2, 1971.

(59) The Wall Street Journal, November 15, 1971.

(60) Proceedings of the International Convention of the United Mine Workers of America, 1964, Vol. 1, p. 171.

(61) Ibid., 1968, Vol. 1, p. 12.

(62) Business Week, April 23, 1966, p. 132; The New York Times, April 11, 1966-

(63) The New York Times, April 13, 1966.

(64) Ibid., April 16, 1966.

(65) Ibid., October 2, 1971.

(66) Wiener, N., Cybernetics, or Control and Communication in the Animal and the Machine, 2nd ed., Cambridge, Mass., M. I. T. Press
__________, The Human Use of Human Beings: Cybernetics and Society, New York, Avon Books, 1967.

(67) Asby, W. R., Design for a Brain: the Origin of Adaptive Behavior, 2nd ed. rev., London, Chapman and Hall, 1966.
__________, An Introduction to Cybernetics, New York, Wiley, 1963.

(68) Beer, S., Brain of the Firm: the Managerial Cybernetics of Organization, London, Penguin, 1972.
__________, Cybernetics and Management, 2nd ed., London, English University Press, 1967.
__________, Decision and Control: the Meaning of Operational Research and Management Cybernetics, London, New York, Wiley, 1966.

(69) Boulding, K. E., op. cit.
__________, The Organizational Revolution: A Study in the Ethics of Economic Organization, Chicago, Quadrangle Books, 1968.

(70) Deutsch, K. W., The Nerves of Government: Models of Political Communcation and Control, Glencoe, Free Press, 1963.

(71) Williamson, O. E., Corporate Control and Business Behavior: an Inquiry into the Effects of Organization Form on Enterprise Behavior, Englewood Cliffs (N. J.), Prentice-Hall, 1970.

(72) This specification is exactly the same as Herbert Simon's conceptualization of the organizational goal, which is better accepted in organizational literature. Simon, H. A., "On the Concept of Organizational Goal", Administrative Science Quarterly, June, 1964, Vol. 9, p. 1-22.

(73) Boulding, K. E., 1968, op. cit.; Deutsch, K. W., op. cit., p. 147.

(74) Boulding, ibid.; Deutsch, ibid., p. 258.

(75) Ashby, W. R., 1966, op. cit., pp. 131-132.

(76) "A change in degree" and "a change in kind" are rather ambiguous terms. They can be regarded as the same as Simon's routinized problem solving, which does not require a change in existing programs of an organization and non-routinized problem solving, which can be done only by creating a new program. (Simon, H. A., The New Science of Management Decision, New York, Harper, 1960.

(77) In the following, the rank and file's rebellion is regarded as a part of the environment. This is because the purpose of this section is to analyze the leaders' decision-making performance.

(78) The Wall Street Journal, August 27, 1965.

(79) The question was whether the company could order a crew to drive an entry for an airshaft and portal on a day when the full mine was idle. (The Wall Street Journal, September 13, 1965.)

(80) Ibid.

(81) Ibid., September 20 and 24, 1965.

(82) For example, Festinger (1950) has pointed that the structuring of groups into hierarchies automatically introduces restraints against free communication and aggressively-toned comments by low-status members towards those in higher-status positions. Back et al. (1950), Kelley (1951), and Thibaut (1951) have shown that selective screening of information from low- to high-status members is a characteristic of communication in social groups, and serves as a "psychological substitute" for actual movement upward on the part of aspiring low-status members. (Festinger, L., "Informal Social Communication", Psychological Review, Vol. 57, 1950. p. 217-282; Back, K., Festinger, L., Hymovitch, B., Kelley, H. H., Schachter, S., and Thibaut, J., "The Methodology of Studying Rumor Transmission", Human Relations, Vol. 3, 1950, pp. 307-312; Kelley, H. H., "Communication in Experimentally Created Hierarchies", Vol. 4, 1951, pp. 39-56; Thibaut, J., "An Experimental Study of the Cohesiveness of Underprivileged Groups", Human Relations, Vol. 3, 1950, pp. 251-278.

(83) Simon, H. A., Administrative Behavior, New York, Free Press, pp. 162-163.

(84) Cohen, A. R., "Upward Communication in Experiementally Created Hierarchies", Human Relations, 1958, Vol. 11, pp. 41-53.

(85) For example, Hurwitz, H. I., Zander, A. F., and Hymovitch, B., "Some Effects of Power on the Relations among Group Members", in Cartwright, D., and Zander, A. (eds.), Group Dynamics, Evanston, Ill., Row Peterson, 1953.

(86) This proposition was validated by Read, W. H., "Upward Communication in Industrial Hierarchies", Human Relations, Vol. 15 (1), February, 1962, pp. 3-12.

(87) Hume, B., op. cit., pp. 177-178.

(88) Ibid., pp. 55, 62, 81-82.

(89) Armbrister, T., op. cit., p. 70.

(90) Miller, J. G., "Information Input Overload", in Yovits, M. C., Jacobi, G. T., and Goldstein, G. D. (eds.), Self-Organizing Systems, Washington, D. C., Spartan, 1962, pp. 61-78.

(91) Baker, H., Ballantine, J. W., and True, J. M., Transmitting Information through Management and Union Channels, Princeton University, Department of Economic and Social Institutions, Industrial Relations Section, 1949.

(92) Downs, A., Inside Bureaucracy, Boston, Little, Brown and Company, 1967, pp. 112-132.

(93) Geutzdow, H., "Communications in Organization"., In March, J. (ed.), Handbook of Organizations, Chicago, Rand McNally, 1965.

(94) Gaus, J. M., and Walcott, C. O., Public Administration and the United States Department of Agriculture, Chicago, 1940.

(95) March, J. G., and Simon, H. A., Organizations, New York, John Wiley & Sons, Ind., 1958.

(96) For the concept of incremental decisions, see Braybrooke, D., and Lindblom, C. E., A Strategy of Decision: Policy Evaluation as a Social Process, New York, The Free Press, 1963.

(97) In some other unions, the leader can take a very different career path. For example, the International Typographical Union was found to have a large number of social and sport clubs which were autonomous from the union hierarchy and that most of the union's officials were products of such club acivities. In many unions in which local leaders are responsible in negotiating a contract with the local company and are elected by their constituency on the basis of their contract achievement, very different skills may be required to clumb up the hierarchy from those required in the case of the UMW. (Lipset, Martin and Trow, op. cit.)

(98) In the case of the Typographic Union, in order to become a high official of the union, an informal leader of a social club has to show a variety of abilities from managing a club to organizing various activities including semi-autonomous union activities.
In a union where locals have more autonomy, local leaders have to obtain a sizeable gain in contract negotiations and win grievances in order to become prominent enough to be elected to a higher office. In this process, the leaders are required to have a broad view of conditions in the industry and the members' desires, and must be capable of incorporating them into his policy.

(99) Hume, B., op. cit., p. 59, and Armbrister, T., op. cit., p. 73.

(100) Armbrister, T., p. 73.

(101) Downs, A., op. cit., pp. 112-132.

Chapter VII:

(1) The New York Times, May 29, 1972.

(2) Some close observers considered Mike Trbovich, who had been a close associate of the late Yablonski and the National Chairman of the Miners for Democracy, had the better edge, and that Karl Kaften of Moundsville, West Virginia, and Lou Antol of Arnold, Pennsylvania, could have been stronger candidates than the Miller-Trbovich ticket. Kaften and Antol withdrew from the race, and Trbovich was defeated by Miller with a small margin. There is no evidence, however, that this unexpected result was caused by behind the scenes political maneuvering. According to Mr. Ben Franklin of the New York Times, who had been closely associated with the UMW leaders, Kaften and Antol independently reached the conclusion that the reformist movement would not be able to win the election and that for the time being they could serve better as district leaders, which they were certain to be elected, than as defeated presidential candidates. (From an interview with Mr. Franklin, May, 1977.)

(3) The United Mine Workers Journal, January 1, 1973, p. 6.

(4) The New York Times, December 23, 1972; The Wall Street Journal, December 23, 1972.

(5) Bureau of National Affairs, Daily Labor Report, February 1, 1973, 22: A-16.

(6) op. cit.

(7) Article XIX, Section 2 of the 1973 Constitution.

(8) Ibid., Section 4.

(9) Ibid., Section 3.

(10) Ibid., Section 4.

(11) Ibid., Section 4.

(12) Ibid., Section 5.

(13) Ibid., Section 7.

(14) Whether the opposition in the IEB was purely political and destructive or not is a debatable question. The important point here is the fact that Miller regarded it as destructive.

(15) Proceedings of the International Convention of the United Mine Workers of America, 1976, p. 250.

(16) In fact, the divisions reports to the International Conventions had been carbon copies of the preceeding years for more than a decade.

(17) Bureau of National Affairs, Daily Labor Report, May 24, 1973, 101: A-18.

(18) The safety training had been conducted solely by the federal and state governments.

(19) The department was established as the "Research and Marketing Department" in 1957, when the industry was in constant decline. The major emphasis had been "marketing" for the industry. (From an interview with one of the staff members of the UMW.)

(20) For obvious reasons, the author cannot disclose the informant's name, position and background, which are necessary for the reader in order to evaluate the validity of his statement. One may at least make the vague remark that he was a former miner who occupied a rather high post in the international union, which made possible his familiarity with the IEB operation; he was neither an IEB member, nor a member of the staff departments.

(21) Article XVIII, Sections 2, 3 and 4.

(22) Interview with a union staff member, whose name must remain anonymous.

(23) In 1977, the number of anti-Miller members of the IEB grew from six in 1973 to fourteen or fifteen. (From an interview with a union staff member,)

(24) This anti-Miller "group" was not tightly controlled. Many of them voted rather independently on many issues, but were fairly consistent in being against Miller.

(25) As will be illustrated in the text, Miller was indeed very sincere, candid and democratic. It is obviously debatable whether he deliberately chose his style from several possible alternatives. This controversial issue aside, interviews with his aides suggested that they had been well aware of this limitation in style and had made conscious efforts to conform to it.

(26) The United Mine Workers, Proceedings of the International Convention of the United Mine Workers of America, 1976, pp. 237-242.

(27) The New York Times, December 1, 1974.

(28) Miller's performance in the 1977 contract negotiations gives a very different image of his leadership. The situation in 1977 was exceptionally chaotic and can be considered as an idiosyncratic case.

(29) It is probably unfair to explain their defection solely in terms of their political self-interest. Many relatively neutral informants told the author that Miller was a sincere but hopeless administrator. He often disappeared for as long as several days, unexpectedly and without leaving any message. He is reported sometimes to have taken terribly stupid moves in the IEB meetings (details unknown). All of these mistakes and his unpredictable behavior gradually made his supporters wonder whether they should continue to leave union operations to him.

(30) The United Mine Workers, The Year of the Rank and File, 1973: Officers' Report to the United Mine Workers of America, 46th Constitutional Convention, pp. 89-90.

(31) Vice President Trbovich continued to be cooperative with the Miller administration at least publicly until 1974. After the contract negotiations, he became increasingly irritated by Miller's leadership and finally began attacking him publicly.

(32) <u>Proceedings of the International Convention of the United Mine Workers of America, 1976</u>, pp. 59-60.

(33) The UMWA, <u>Officers' Report to the 47th Constitutional Convention of the United Mine Workersof America</u>, September, 1976, p. 2.

(34) According to the Department of Labor, only eight unions had a bigger percentage increase during that period, and the increase of at least five of those unions resulted mainly from mergers.

(35) UMWA, <u>Officer's Report 1976</u>, p. 2.

(36) <u>The Wall Street Journal</u>, December 18, 1972.

(37) <u>The New York Times</u>, December 5, 1975.

(38) <u>The Wall Street Journal</u>, December 7, 1973.

(39) This and all the rest are based on <u>The Wall Street Journal</u>, December 11, 1973.

(40) <u>The New York Times</u>, August 20, 1974.

(41) Ibid., August 13, 1974.

(42 Ibid., August 25, 1974.

(43) <u>The Wall Street Journal</u>, August 28, 1974.

(44) Ibid., September 20, 1974.

(45) <u>The New York Times</u>, October 15, 1974.

(46) Ibid.

(47) <u>The Wall Street Journal</u>, October 15, 1974.

(48) Ibid., October 23, 1974.

(49) <u>The New York Times</u>, November 3, 1974.

(50) Ibid., November 4, 1974.

(51) <u>The Wall Street Journal</u>, November 4, 1974.

(52) <u>The New York Times</u>, November 5, 1974.

(53) Ibid., November 6, 1974.

(54) Ibid., November 7, 1974.

(55) Ibid., November 9, 1974. Although the expiration date was November 12, the 9th and 10th fell on a weekend and the 11th was Veterans' Day. Traditionally, miners walk out early in such cases.

(56) The Wall Street Journal, November 11, 1974.

(57) The New York Times, November 12, 1974.

(58) For example, The Wall Street Journal accused the negotiators for both parties in its editorial of November 13, 1974.

(59) The New York Times, November 13, 1974.

(60) Ibid.

(61) The Wall Street Journal, November 14, 1974.

(62) The New York Times, November 14, 1974.

(63) The Wall Street Journal, November 14, 1974.

(64) 49.7% was the figure calculated by the UMW. The industry's estimate was 62.8% (The New York Times, November 14, 1974), while The Wall Street Journal used the 8% inflation rate and estimated 53% (The Wall Street Journal, November 18, 1974).

(65) The New York Times, November 14, 1974; The Wall Street Journal, November 14, 1974.

(66) The New York Times, November 16, 1974.

(67) The New York Times,November 16, 17, 18, 19, 20, 1974; The Wall Street Journal, November 16, 18, 19, 20, 1974.
The Two-week vacation in the previous contract was split into one week in summer and one week in winter. Since absenteeism was extremely high at Christmas time anyway, miners regarded this new split vacation as a reduction from two weeks to one.

(68) The Wall Street Journal, November 20, 1974.

(69) The New York Times, November 21, 1974.

(70) Ibid., November 22, 1974.

(71) Ibid., November 23, 1974.

(72) Some council members told Miller that even an 18% pay increase would not be enough.

(73) The New York Times, November 24, 1974.

(74) Ibid., November 25, 1974.

(75) Ibid., November 26, 1974.

(76) Ibid., November 27, 1974.

(77) Corporate Report of the Kennecott Copper Co., 1974.

(78) Corporate Report of Continental Oil Co., 1974.

(79) Corporate Report of Occidental Petroleum Co., 1971.

(80) Corporate Report of the Pittson Co., 1974.

(81) Daily Labor Report, December 3, 1973.

(82) The United Mine Workers Journal, Vol. 87, No. 15, September 1, 1976, p. 6-7

(83) The Wall Street Journal, August 28, 1974.

(84) Ibid., December 31, 1973.

(85) Business Week, December 15, 1973.

(86) Ibid.

(87) UMWA, The Year of the Rank and File, 1973, p. 7.

(88) An interview with a union staff member.

(89) The New York Times, November 10, 1974.

(90) Ibid., November 6, 1976.

(91) This hypothesis was originally suggested by Mr. Ben A. Franklin of The New York Times, (November 4, 1974), and confirmed by the author's interview with union officials.

(92) Interview with union staff members who should remain anonymous.

(93) The New York Times, November 20, 1974.

(94) An interview with a union staff member who must remain anonymous.

(95) Karl Kafton, for example, was reported to have said, "Some of the package should be reconsidered and re-evaluated," The New York Times, November 19, 1974.

(96) It may be debatable whether or not all 37 members were genuinely opposed to the agreement. Many neutral or pro-agreement members, who found the opposition making up the majority, might decide to vote along with them on the ground that the unaninous vote would strengthen the union negotiator's position in the second round of bargaining. Nevertheless, the margin of 37-1 seemed to be large enough to make the factional-fight theory less persuasive.

(97) The reason for the failure is not clear.

(98) An interview with a council member whose name cannot be disclosed.

(99) The New York Times, November 23, 1974.

(100) The Wall Street Journal, November 18, 1974.

(101) The New York Times, November 19, 1974.

(102) Ibid., November 15, 1974.

(103) Interview with a union staff member.

Appendix 2:

(1) Takamiya, M., "A Pure Theory of Inter-Organizational Conflict", Alfred P. Sloan School Working Paper, No. 747-74, November, 1974.

(2) Bailyn, L., "Research as a Cognitive Process: Implications for Data Analysis", Quality and Quantity, 11 (1977), pp. 97-117.

(3) Andreski, S., Social Sciences as Sorcery, New York, St. Martin Press, 1973.

BIBLIOGRAPHY

Adams, K. C., "What the Miners Want", American Federationist, April, 1946, Vol. 53, No. 4.

Aiken, E., and Bleiberg, R. M., "Full Disclosure for Whom?", Barrons, 54:7, August 5, 1974.

Ake, C., "Charismatic Legitimatization and Political Leadership", Comparative Studies in Society and History, Vol. 9, October, 1966, pages 1-13.

Alinsky, S. D., John L. Lewis: An Unauthorized Biography, Vintage Books, 1949.

Althouse, R., Work, Safety and Life Style Among Southern Appalachian Coal Miners: A Survey of the Men of Standard Mines, Morgantown, Office of Research and Development, Division of Social and Economic Development, Appalachian Center, West Virginia University, 1974.

American Druggist, "Archambault named by UMW to bring rational prescribing to its members", 165, January 10, 1972, page 39.

American Federationist, "The Miners Ask Only for Justice", January, 1947, Vol. 54 (1), pages 4-5.

American Iron and Steel Institute, Annual Statistical Report, 1945, New York, 1946.

Andreski, S., Social Science as Sorcery, New York, St. Martin's Press, 1973.

Angle, P. M., Bloody Williamson: A Chapter in American Lawlessness, New York, Knopf, 1952.

Arble, M., "Notes from a Coal Mine", The New York Times Magazine, January 12, 1974.

____________, The Long Tunnel: A Coal Miner's Journal, New York, Atheneum, 1976.

Arendt, H., The Origins of Totalitarianism, New York, Harcourt, Brace, 1951.

Arbrister, T., Act of Vengeance: The Yablonski Murders and their Solution, New York, Saturday Review Press, 1975.

Ashby, W. R., An Introduction to Cybernetics, New York, Wiley (Science Editions), 1963.

____________, Design for a Brain: The Origin of Adaptive Behavior, 2nd. ed. rev., London, Chapman and Hall, 1966.

Ashenfelter, O., and Johnson, G. E., "Bargaining Theory, Trade Unions and Industrial Strike Activity," American Economic Review, 59 (1969), pp. 35-49.

Back, K., Festinger, L., Hymovitch, B., Kelley, H. H., Schachter, S., and Thibaut, J., "The Methodology of Studying Rumor Transmission", Human Relations, Vol. 3, 1950, pages 307-312.

Bailyn, L., "Research as a Cognitive Process: Implications for Data Analysis", Quality and Quantity, 11, 1977, pages 97-117.

Baker, H., Ballantine, J. W., and True, J. M., Transmitting Information through Management and Union Channels, Princeton University, Department of Economics and Social Institutions, Industrial Relation Sections, 1949.

Baker, R. H., The National Bituminous Coal Commission, Baltimore, Johns Hopkins Press, 1941.

Baratz, M. S., The Union and the Coal Industry, New Haven, Yale University Press, 1955.

Bedolis, R. A., "UMW and the Antitrust Law", Conference Board Record, 1, December, 1964, pages 28-33.

Beer, S., Decision and Control: the Meaning of Operational Research and Management Cybernetics, New York, Wiley, 1966.

__________, Cybernetics and Management, 2nd ed., London, English University Press, 1967.

__________, Brain of the Firm: the Management Cybernetics of Organization, London, Allen Lane, Penguin, 1972.

Berish, F. E., and Associates, Economic Survey of the Bituminous Coal Industry under Free Competition and Code Regulation, Washington, U. S. National Recovery Administration, 1936.

Billings, D., "Culture and Poverty in Appalachia: A Theoretical Discussion and Empirical Analysis", Social Forces, Vol, 53, December, 1974, pages 315323.

Bituminous Coal Association, Bituminous Coal Annual, 1951, Washington, 1952.

Blan, P., "Critical Remarks on Weber's Theory of Authority", American Political Science Review, Vol, 57, 1963, pages 305-316.

Bleiberg, R. M., "Long Cold Winter? The United Mine Workers Seem Set to Strike", Barrons, 54:7, October 14, 1974.

Bok, D. C., and Dunlop, J. T., Labor and the American Community, New York, Simon and Schuster, 1070.

Boorstin, D., "Coal Negotiations", Editorial Research Reports, October 25, 1974, Vol. 11, No. 16.

Bord, R. J., "Toward a Social-Psychological Theory of Charismatic Social Influence Process", Social Forces, March, 1975.

Boulding, K. E., The Organizational Revolution: A Study in the Ethidx of Economic Organization, Chicago, Quadrangle Books, 1968.

__________, Beyond Economics: Essays on Society, Religion and Ethics, Ann Arbor, University of Michigan Press, 1970.

Bowers, E. W., "Coal Pact Question: Just What are the Effects", Iron Age, 214:64-5, November 5, 1974.

Braybrooke, D., and Linblom, D. E., A Strategyx of Decision: Policy Evaluation as a Social Process, New York, The Free Press, 1963.

Britt, D., and Galle, O., "Industrial Conflict and Unionization", American Sociological Review, 37, 1972, pages 48-57.

Brophy, J., A Miner's Life, An Autobiography, Madison, University of Wisconsin Press, 1964.

Brown, M. B., "What Will the Miners Do Now?" New Society, Vol. 10, November 23, 1964.

Bulmer, M. E. A., "Sociological Models of the Mining Community", The Sociological Review, Vol. 23, No. 1, February, 1975, pages 61-92.

Business Week, "Lewis Triumph: Miners' Chieftain Wrung Some Concessions...", May 29, 1943, page 14.

____________, "At Stake in Coal Fight", October 30, 1943, pages 15-17.

____________, "Lewis Bids Again. Soft Coal Strike Notice Seen as First Strategic Move for Real Showdown", March 3, 1945, pages 17-18.

____________, "Coal Strategy. Mine Owners and Workers, Worried over Peacetime Future of their Industry, May Speed Compromise Settlement", March 10, 1945, pages 16-17.

____________, "AFL and Lewis Bid for Power", February 2, 1946, page 86.

____________, "Lewis Strategy, Mine Workers Submit Nine General Proposals on Wages and Work Conditions, Leaving First Move to Operators", March 16, 1946, page 102.

____________, "Labor Catchall: John Lewis' Big District 50", October 5, 1946, pages 95-98.

____________, "Lewis' Third Labor Movement", December 20, 1947.

____________, "New Union Drive. Ohio's Non-Union Strip Mines", May 27, 1950.

____________, "UMW Acts to Swell Treasury", February 10, 1951.

____________, "UMW's Silence: Calm Before the Storm", February 23, 1952.

____________, "Coal: Soft Market, Hard Bargaining?" May 17, 1952, page 2.

____________, "62 Years of UMW: Strife, Strikes and Strength", June 7, 1952.

____________, "Lewis Must Play Politics", August 2, 1952, page 98.

____________, "Coal Talks Start Amiably", August 9, 1952, page 101-104.

____________, "Spread the Work, Lewis Asks", September 13, 1952, page 158.

____________, "Lewis Wins the Hard Way", September 27, 1952, page 138.

__________, "Southern Coal Men Go Along With Lewis' Terms", October 4, 1952, page 158.

__________, "Miners Dig Democrats Out of a Hole", November 1, 1952, page 144.

__________, "Coal Hearing Ends in Warning", November 22, 1952, pages 173-174.

__________, "In Coal, New Kind of Wage Deal?", July 4, 1953, pages 104-105.

__________, "Hints of a McDonald-Lewis Tie", July 4, 1953, pages 105-106.

__________, "In Coal, UMW Feels the Heat", May 8, 1954, pages 132-134.

__________, "Coal: No Demands for Now", August 7, 1954, pages 90-91.

__________, "Stalemate over Miners' Pay", November 20, 1954, page 172.

__________, "Bite on Miners. Lewis Slaps a Special $20 Levy on Men with Jobs to Beef Up the UMW's Already Sizeable Treasury", October 1, 1955, page 160.

__________, "Lone Wolf May Rejoin the Pack", June 16, 1956, pages 165-167.

__________, ""Why Coal Men Threaten to Sail Their Own Ships", June 23, 1956, pages 26-27.

__________, "Forever Lewis", October 6, 1956, pages 70-74.

__________, "Lewis is Still the Strong Man Behind UMW Policies and Practices", October 20, 1956, pages 103-104.

__________, "Trouble for UMW's District 50", November 3, 1956, pages 162-163.

__________, "John L. Lewis Goes to Bat Again", October 4, 1958, pages 97-100.

__________, "Mines at Odds", November 1, 1958, page 73.

__________, "UMW Near the End of the Era", February 14, 1959, pages 83-84.

__________, "New Threat in 'Bloody' Harlan", March 14, 1959, page 124.

__________, "Violence Lingers in Kentucky", April 25, 1959, page 48.

__________, "New Mine Head Seeks Peace", January 23, 1960, page 114.

__________, "District 50's Independence from UMW is a Problem to Both", September 23, 1961.

__________, "UMW on the Griddle in Court and Coal Field", November 3, 1962, pages 49-51.

____________, "UMW Gives Nod to Boyle", January 26, 1963, page 70.

____________, "UMW Seeks Job Security, Safety", January 4, 1964, page 68.

____________, "Miners' New Leader Wokrs Another Seam", March 28, 1964, pages 121-122.

____________, "Troubles Pile Up for Most Sued Union"., April 18, 1964, pages 121-124.

____________, "UMW Faces Miners' Revolt", August 15,1964, page 70.

____________, "Miners Want the Vote", September 19, 1964, page 152.

____________, "Miners Gear for Double Trouble", December 5, 1964, page 99.

____________, "Union Chiefs Face Double Trouble", December 12, 1964, page 99.

____________, "Miners Start Pushing", January 22, 1966, page 98.

____________, "Coal Strike Leaves Discord in UMW Ranks", May 7, 1966, page 122.

____________, "Battle for Miners", April 8, 1967, pages 100-101.

____________, "Striking Miners Foggy Over Issues", April 23, 1966, page 132.

____________, "UMW's Family Fight Moves to Court Room", May 3, 1969, page 96.

____________, "UMW Battle Heats Up", May 10, 1969, page 51.

____________, "Leadership Fight Looms Among Miners", June 7, 1969, page 122.

____________, "Lewis Heir Faces Revolt", November 15, 1969, page 110.

____________, "Mine Workers: Can They Survive Reform?", December 20, 1969, page 32.

____________, "Yablonski's Death Stirs Up Miners", January 10, 1970, page 35.

____________, UMW vs. Jack Yablonski's Ghost", May 2, 1970,page 38.

____________, "Years of Trial for the UMW", February 6, 1971, page 88.

____________, "Coal Walks Out Before It Bargains", June 19, 1971, page 37.

____________, "Bombshell From the Yablonski Trial", June 26, 1971, page 30.

____________, "Boyle's Troubles Have Just Begun", April 8, 1972, pages 25-26.

____________, "Boyle's Opponents Gain Real Strength", May 13, 1972, pages 52-53.

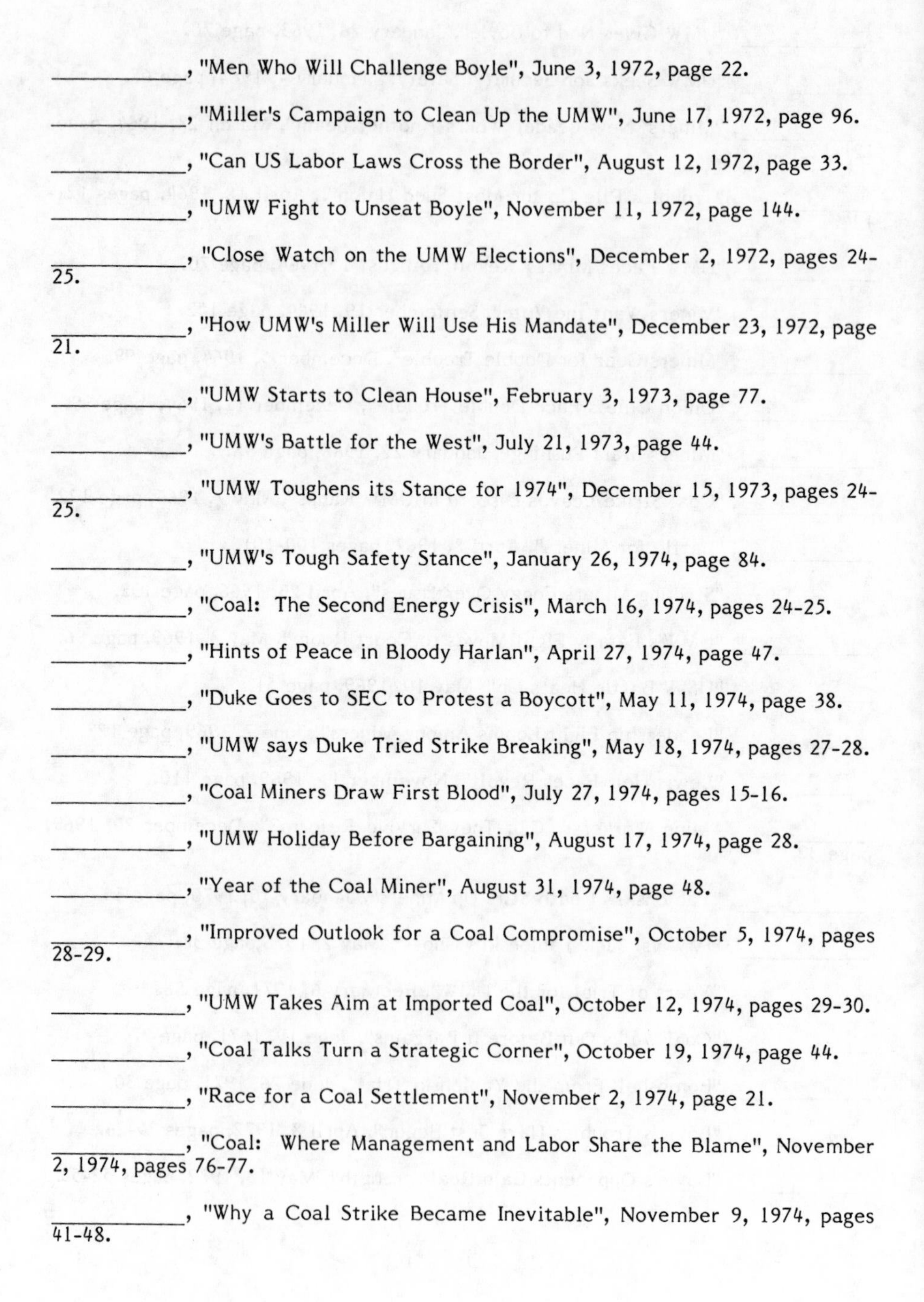

___________, "Men Who Will Challenge Boyle", June 3, 1972, page 22.

___________, "Miller's Campaign to Clean Up the UMW", June 17, 1972, page 96.

___________, "Can US Labor Laws Cross the Border", August 12, 1972, page 33.

___________, "UMW Fight to Unseat Boyle", November 11, 1972, page 144.

___________, "Close Watch on the UMW Elections", December 2, 1972, pages 24-25.

___________, "How UMW's Miller Will Use His Mandate", December 23, 1972, page 21.

___________, "UMW Starts to Clean House", February 3, 1973, page 77.

___________, "UMW's Battle for the West", July 21, 1973, page 44.

___________, "UMW Toughens its Stance for 1974", December 15, 1973, pages 24-25.

___________, "UMW's Tough Safety Stance", January 26, 1974, page 84.

___________, "Coal: The Second Energy Crisis", March 16, 1974, pages 24-25.

___________, "Hints of Peace in Bloody Harlan", April 27, 1974, page 47.

___________, "Duke Goes to SEC to Protest a Boycott", May 11, 1974, page 38.

___________, "UMW says Duke Tried Strike Breaking", May 18, 1974, pages 27-28.

___________, "Coal Miners Draw First Blood", July 27, 1974, pages 15-16.

___________, "UMW Holiday Before Bargaining", August 17, 1974, page 28.

___________, "Year of the Coal Miner", August 31, 1974, page 48.

___________, "Improved Outlook for a Coal Compromise", October 5, 1974, pages 28-29.

___________, "UMW Takes Aim at Imported Coal", October 12, 1974, pages 29-30.

___________, "Coal Talks Turn a Strategic Corner", October 19, 1974, page 44.

___________, "Race for a Coal Settlement", November 2, 1974, page 21.

___________, "Coal: Where Management and Labor Share the Blame", November 2, 1974, pages 76-77.

___________, "Why a Coal Strike Became Inevitable", November 9, 1974, pages 41-48.

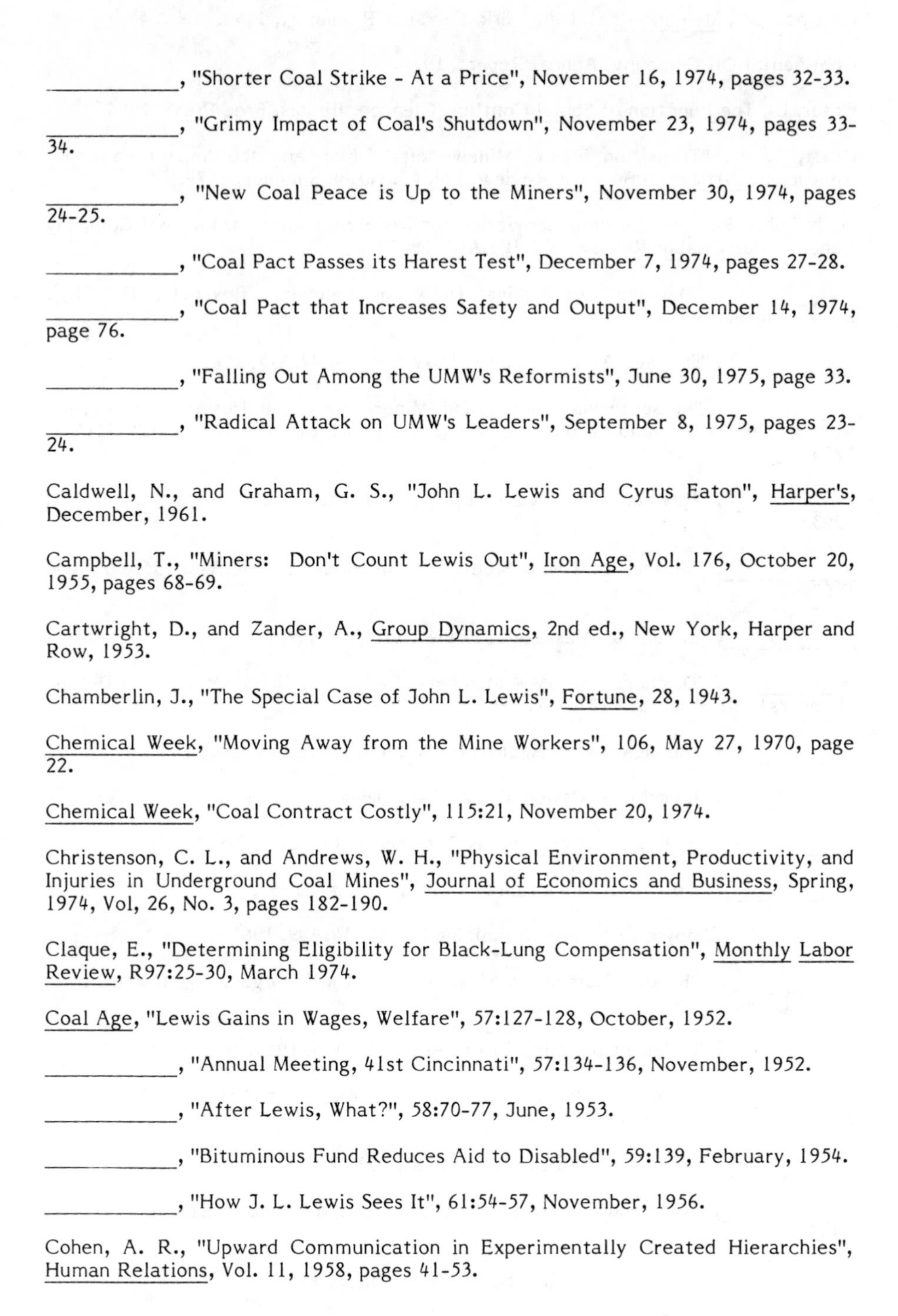

____________, "Shorter Coal Strike - At a Price", November 16, 1974, pages 32-33.

____________, "Grimy Impact of Coal's Shutdown", November 23, 1974, pages 33-34.

____________, "New Coal Peace is Up to the Miners", November 30, 1974, pages 24-25.

____________, "Coal Pact Passes its Harest Test", December 7, 1974, pages 27-28.

____________, "Coal Pact that Increases Safety and Output", December 14, 1974, page 76.

____________, "Falling Out Among the UMW's Reformists", June 30, 1975, page 33.

____________, "Radical Attack on UMW's Leaders", September 8, 1975, pages 23-24.

Caldwell, N., and Graham, G. S., "John L. Lewis and Cyrus Eaton", Harper's, December, 1961.

Campbell, T., "Miners: Don't Count Lewis Out", Iron Age, Vol. 176, October 20, 1955, pages 68-69.

Cartwright, D., and Zander, A., Group Dynamics, 2nd ed., New York, Harper and Row, 1953.

Chamberlin, J., "The Special Case of John L. Lewis", Fortune, 28, 1943.

Chemical Week, "Moving Away from the Mine Workers", 106, May 27, 1970, page 22.

Chemical Week, "Coal Contract Costly", 115:21, November 20, 1974.

Christenson, C. L., and Andrews, W. H., "Physical Environment, Productivity, and Injuries in Underground Coal Mines", Journal of Economics and Business, Spring, 1974, Vol, 26, No. 3, pages 182-190.

Claque, E., "Determining Eligibility for Black-Lung Compensation", Monthly Labor Review, R97:25-30, March 1974.

Coal Age, "Lewis Gains in Wages, Welfare", 57:127-128, October, 1952.

____________, "Annual Meeting, 41st Cincinnati", 57:134-136, November, 1952.

____________, "After Lewis, What?", 58:70-77, June, 1953.

____________, "Bituminous Fund Reduces Aid to Disabled", 59:139, February, 1954.

____________, "How J. L. Lewis Sees It", 61:54-57, November, 1956.

Cohen, A. R., "Upward Communication in Experimentally Created Hierarchies", Human Relations, Vol. 11, 1958, pages 41-53.

Coleman, M., Men and Coal, New York, Farrar & Rheinhart, 1943.

Continental Oil Company, Annual Report, 1974.

Coser, L., The Function of Social Conflict, Glencoe, Illinois, Free Press, 1956.

Craft, J. A., "Transition in the Mineworkers' Union and the Impact on Labor Relations", Pittsburgh Business Review, Vol. 45, No. 4, Summer, 1976.

Daily Labor Review, "Alaimo Conviction for Receiving Money from Coal Company Upheld", Daily Labor Review, (CA3) 3:A-1, 1962.

____________, "Damage Suit Against UMW for Secondary Boycott", (DC Eky), 231:A-2, 1962.

____________, "Damage Awards Against UMW", (CA6) 37:A-4, 1963.

____________, "Presbyterian Church and Miners Memorial Hospital Association Reached an Understanding on Sale and Transfer of the Ten Hospitals", 85:A-9, 1963.

____________, "Raymond O. Lewis Elected Vice President of the UMW", 114:A-4, 1963.

____________, "Federal Coal Mine Safety Act Amendment", 154:A-8. 155:A-7, A-8, 1963.

____________, "Labor Day Message of Boyle", 170:A-s, 1963.

____________, "Discharge of UMW Members, Refusal of Union Officers to Defend Members", (Ill. App. Ct.) 232:A-7, 1963.

____________, "Damage Award Against UMW", (CA6) 246:A-1, D-1, 1963-

____________, "Election of Officers", 223:A-15, 1964.

____________, "Boyle, Lewis and Owens Returned to Office", 229:A-3, 1964.

____________, "Antitrust Conviction of UMW", 170:A-7, 1965.

____________, "Boyle Asks New Organizing Drive", 14:A-9, 1965.

____________, "Kmetz Named as Head of the UMW Organizing Committee", 23:A.11, 1965.

____________, "Federal Coal Mine Safety Act", 113:A-3, 1965.

____________, "Public Works and Economic Development Act of 1965, Boyle's Statement", 91:A-6, 1965.

____________, "Welfare and Retirement Fund", 153:BB-1, 1965 and 170:A-2, 1965.

____________, "Raymond O. Lewis Retiring as the UMW Vice President", 187:A-6, 1965.

____________, "Federal Coal Mine Safety Act", 8:A-7, 1966.

____________, "Titler Chosen to Succeed Lewis as the UMW Vice President", 11:A-9, 1966.

____________, "Coal Contract Negotiations", 31:A-11, 1966, and 35:A-5, 1966.

____________, "Peabody Coal Co. and Two Other Firms Sign New Wage-Fringe Agreements with UMW", 69:A-10. 1966.

____________, BCOA and Southern Coal Producers Sign New Wage-Fringe Agreement with UMW", 82:A-10, 1966.

____________, "Welfare Fund, Increase in Widows Benefits, Coverage of Hospital and Medical Benefits for Miners' Children", 13:A-18, 1967.

____________, "Soft Coal Miners, Monthly Pension Increased", 91:A-6, 1967.

____________, "Penalty Clause in Labor Agreement Held Unlawful" (NLRB), 120:A-1, E-1. 1967.

____________, "The Welfare Fund", 155:A-4, 1967, and 165:A-5, 1967.

____________, "District 50 Expelled", 51:A-3, 1968, and 59:A-3, 1968.

____________, "Strike Violence, District 30 and Eastern Kentucky Strike Leaders Held in Civil Contempt", (CA6) 80:A-4, 1968.

____________, "Fight Between UMW and District 50", 86:A-6, 1968, and 101:A-6, 1968.

____________, "Welfare and Retirement Fund Payments, 1967-68", 141:A-4, 1968.

____________, "UMW Put Trusteeship in District 1", 162:A-12, 1968.

____________, "Federal Coal Mine Health and Safety Act of 1968", 178:AA-1, 1968, and 180:A-6, E-1, 1968.

____________, "Coal's Three Year Contract", 201:A-8, 1968.

____________, "Stronger Legislation Proposed by Udall, Discussion at Conference on Code Mine Safety Act", 242:A-8, 1968.

____________, "Comprehensive Coal Mine Health and Safety Program Introduced into Congress", 16:A-10, 1969, and 27:A-11, 1969.

____________, "House General Labor Subcommittee Hearings on Mine Safety Bill", 33:A-9, 1969.

____________, "Senate Hearings on Mine Safety Bill", 35:A-1; 39:AA-1, E-1; 42:A-8, F-1, CT-1; 45:A-10; 48:A-1, D-1, E-1., F-1; 53:A-14; 54:A-19, A-21; 58:A-9, F-1; and 59:A-16.

____________, "Pension for Soft Coal Miners Raised", 121:A-8, 1969.

____________, "UMW Election Dispute", 139:A-11; 142:A-12; 142:A-5; 144:A-10;

154:A-10; 156:A-11; 161:A-11; 165:A-10, F-1;167:A-7; 167:A-9; 168:A-11, F-1; 169:A-1, A-2, D-1; 178:A-10; 185:A-9; 204:A-12, A-13; 207:A-11, A-12; 216:A-15, A-16; 221:A-14; 231:A-8, E-1; 234:A-11, A-22; 235:A-5, A-8; 238:A-10, 240:AA-2; 241:A-9; 242:A-19; and 250:A-13, 1969.

____________, "BCOA President Resigning as Industry Trustee of the Welfare Fund", 135:A-6, 1969.

____________, "UMW Welfare Fund", 149:A-3; 150:A-10; and 164:A-7, 1969.

____________, "Boyle's Statement on Anthracite Negotiations", 213:A-3, 1969.

____________, "Miller Makes Step-by-Step Changes", 22:A-16, 1973.

____________, "Miller Receptive to Reaffiliation with AFL-CIO, Major Organizing Drive Planned", 87:A-5, G-1, 1973.

____________, "Labor's Non-Partisan League, Nelson Named Director", 94:A14, 1973.

____________, "Convention Called for December 3-14 in Pittsburgh", 97:A-8, 1973.

____________, "Safety Division, Craft Named Executive Director", 101:A-18, 1973.

____________, "Miller Joins Committee for National Health Insurance", 144:A-10, 1973.

____________, "Appointments, Personnel Changes - Huge Appointed Union Trustee on Welfare Fund", 160:A-9, 1973.

____________, "Duke Power Co., UMW Declare War", 164:A-11, 1973.

____________, "Welfare and Retirement Fund", 200:A-7; 204:A-2; 222:A-6, 1973.

____________, "UMW Demands Impeachment", 217:A-6, 1973.

____________, "Miller on Energy Shortage in the Convention", 232:A-15, 1973.

____________, "Democracy Stressed, Grievance Procedure Considered", 233:A-1, 1973.

____________, "Anthracite Industry and Mine Safety, Trbovich in the Convention", 233:A-9, 1973.

____________, "1974 Negotiations, Hard Bargaining Expected", 234:A-6, 1973.

____________, "Bargaining Demand Adopted, Strike Fund Rejected", 242:A-12, 1973.

____________, "Miller Urges Early Bargaining", 7:A-13, 1974.

____________, "Bituminous Coal Operators' Association Agreed to Negotiate Early", 13:A-8, 1974.

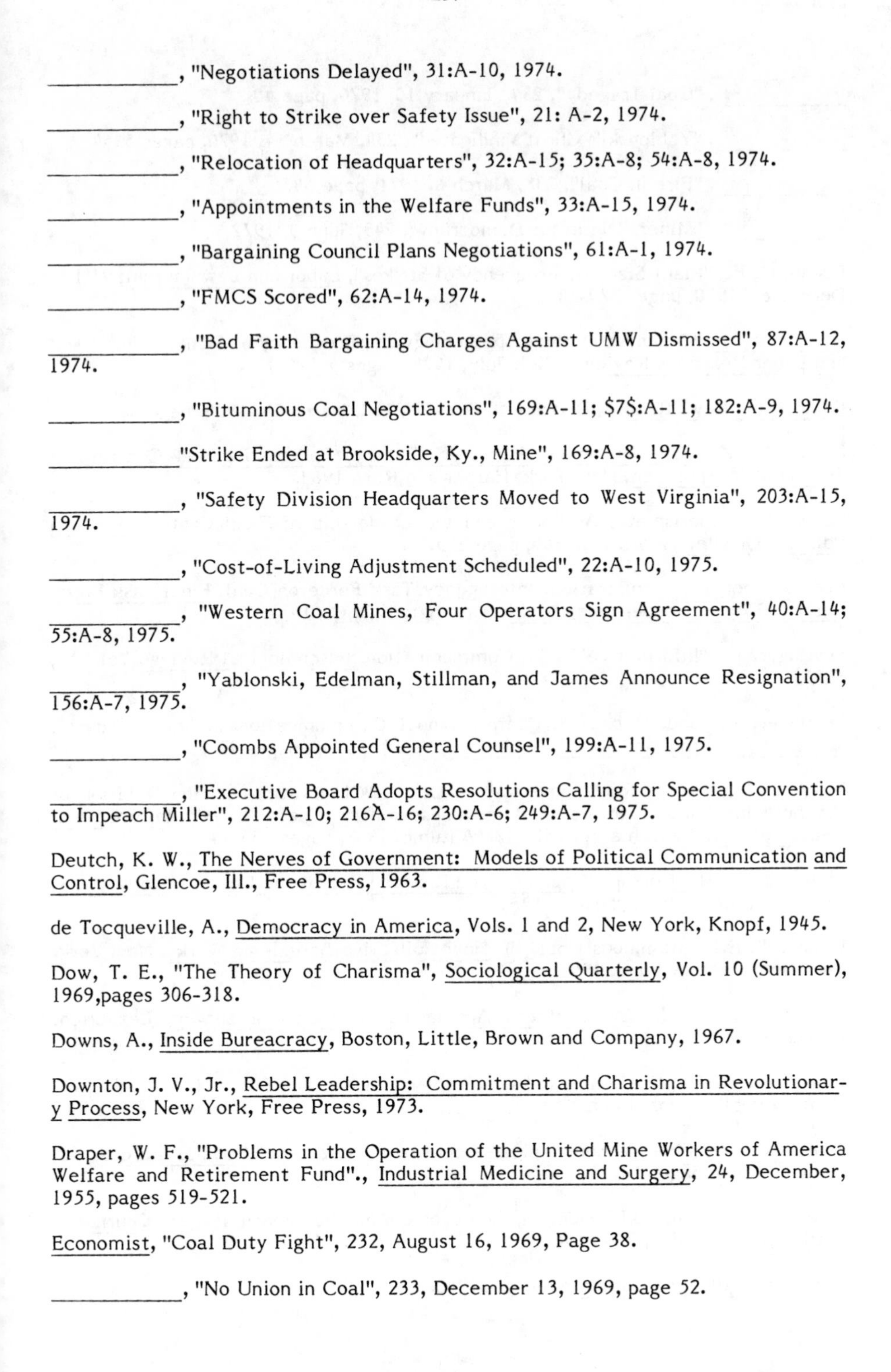

____________, "Negotiations Delayed", 31:A-10, 1974.

____________, "Right to Strike over Safety Issue", 21: A-2, 1974.

____________, "Relocation of Headquarters", 32:A-15; 35:A-8; 54:A-8, 1974.

____________, "Appointments in the Welfare Funds", 33:A-15, 1974.

____________, "Bargaining Council Plans Negotiations", 61:A-1, 1974.

____________, "FMCS Scored", 62:A-14, 1974.

____________, "Bad Faith Bargaining Charges Against UMW Dismissed", 87:A-12, 1974.

____________, "Bituminous Coal Negotiations", 169:A-11; 7:A-11; 182:A-9, 1974.

____________"Strike Ended at Brookside, Ky., Mine", 169:A-8, 1974.

____________, "Safety Division Headquarters Moved to West Virginia", 203:A-15, 1974.

____________, "Cost-of-Living Adjustment Scheduled", 22:A-10, 1975.

____________, "Western Coal Mines, Four Operators Sign Agreement", 40:A-14; 55:A-8, 1975.

____________, "Yablonski, Edelman, Stillman, and James Announce Resignation", 156:A-7, 1975.

____________, "Coombs Appointed General Counsel", 199:A-11, 1975.

____________, "Executive Board Adopts Resolutions Calling for Special Convention to Impeach Miller", 212:A-10; 216A-16; 230:A-6; 249:A-7, 1975.

Deutch, K. W., The Nerves of Government: Models of Political Communication and Control, Glencoe, Ill., Free Press, 1963.

de Tocqueville, A., Democracy in America, Vols. 1 and 2, New York, Knopf, 1945.

Dow, T. E., "The Theory of Charisma", Sociological Quarterly, Vol. 10 (Summer), 1969,pages 306-318.

Downs, A., Inside Bureacracy, Boston, Little, Brown and Company, 1967.

Downton, J. V., Jr., Rebel Leadership: Commitment and Charisma in Revolutionary Process, New York, Free Press, 1973.

Draper, W. F., "Problems in the Operation of the United Mine Workers of America Welfare and Retirement Fund"., Industrial Medicine and Surgery, 24, December, 1955, pages 519-521.

Economist, "Coal Duty Fight", 232, August 16, 1969, Page 38.

____________, "No Union in Coal", 233, December 13, 1969, page 52.

___________, "Coal Tragedy", 234, January 10, 1970, page 40.

___________, "Yablonski's Ghost Vindicated", 234, March 14, 1970, pages 5354.

___________, "Fire in Coal", 238, March 6, 1971, page 54.

___________, "Miners Dig In for Democracy", 243, June 3, 1972.

Eisele, C. F., "Plant Size and Frequency of Strikes", Labor and Law Journal, 21(12), December, 1970, pages 779-786.

___________, "Organization Size, Technology and Frequency of Strikes", Industrial and Labor Relations Review, 27(4), July, 1974, pages 560-571.

Engineering News Record, District 50 Ousted", 180, March 14, 1958, page 88.

Evans, M. K., Macroeconomic Activity: Theory, Forecasting and Control, an Econometric Approach, New York, Harper and Row, 1969.

Fagen, R., "Charismatic Authority and the Leadership of Fidel Castro", Western Political Quarterly, Vol. 18, 1965, page 275.

Federal Energy Administration, Interagency Task Force on Coal, Final Task Force Report, Project Independence, Coal, Washington, D. C., 1974.

Festinger, L., "Informative Social Communication, Psychological Review, Vol. 57, 1950.

Festinger, L., and Thibau, J., "Interpersonal Communication in Small Groups", Jounal of Abnormal and Social Psychology, Vol. 46, 1951, pages 92-99.

Field, L. W., Weing, R. T., and Wayne, D. M., "Observations on the Relation of Psychosocial Factors to Psychiatric Illness among Coal Miners", International Journal of Social Psychiatry, Vol. 3(2), Autumn, 1957, pages 133-145.

Finley, J. E., The Corrupt Kingdom: The Rise and Fall of the United Mine Workers, New York, Simon and Schuster, 1972.

Fisher, W. E., "Bituminous Coal", in How Collective Bargaining Works, New York, Twentieth Century Fund, 1942.

Ford, T. R (ed.), The Southern Appalachian Region: a Survey, Lexington, University of Kentucky Press, 1962.

Foster, W. E., The Coal Miners, Their Problems in War and Peace, New York, New Century Publications, 1945.

Friedland, W., "For a Sociological Concept of Charisma", Social Forces, 43, October, 1964, pages 18-26.

Friedrich, C., "Political Leadership and Problem of Charismatic Power", Journal of Politics, Vol. 23, February, 1961.

Department of Agreiculture, Chicago, 1940.

Gaus, J. M., and Walcott, C. O., Public Administration and the United States Department of Agriculture, Chicago, 1940.

George, H., Blood and Coal, Philidelphia, Dorrane, 1950.

Gerth, H. H., and Mills, C. W., From Max Weber: Essays in Sociology, New York, Oxford University Press, 1958.

Gifford, A., "An Application of Weber's Concept of Charisma", Berkeley Publications in Society and Institutions, Vol. 1, April, 1955, pages 40-49.

Glaser, B. G., and Strauss, A. L., The Discovery of Grounded Theory: Strategies for Qualitative Research, Chicago, Aldive Publishing Company, 1967.

Glasser, C., "Union Wage Policy in Bituminous Coal", Industrial and Labor Relgaions Review, July, 1948.

Gouldner, A. W., Wildcat Strike, Yellow Spring, Ohio, Antioch Press, 1954.

Green, A., Only a Miner: Studies in Recorded Coal Mining Songs, Urbana, University of Illinois Press, 1972.

Griffin, J. J., Strikes: a Study in Quantitative Economics, New York, Columbia University Press, 1937.

Guetzkow, H., "Communication in Organizations", in March, J. (ed.), Handbook of Organizations, Chicago, Rand McNally & Company, 1965.

Hackamack, L. C., "Cooperation-Conflict in Labor-Management Relations: a Study of Contrasting Cases (Women's Garment Industry and Bituminous Coal Industry)", Ann Arbor, University of Michigan Microfilm.

Hamilton, W. H., and Wright, H. R., The Case of Bituminous Coal, New York, MacMillan Company, 1925.

Habsen, A., "Cycles of Strikes", American Economic Review, 1921, pages 612-621.

Harbison, F. H., and Coleman, J. R., Goals and Strategy in Collective Bargaining, New York, Harper, 1951.

Prospective Labor History, Winter, 1960, Vol. 2, pages 3-29.

Haynes, W. W., Present and Prospective Market for West Kentucky Coal, Lexington, University of Kentucky Business Research Bulletin No. 30, 1955.

Henderson, J. M., and Quandt, R. E., Microeconomic Theory: Mathematical Approach, 2nd. ed., New York, McGraw Hill, 1971.

Hibbs, D. A., Jr., Industrial Conflict in Advanced Industrial Societies, Cambridge, Center for Political Studies, Massachusetts Institute of Technology, 1974.

Horvath, W. J., "A Statistical Model for the Duration of Wars and Strikes", Behavioral Sciences, 13(1), January, 1968, 19-28.

Hudson, H. D., The Progressive Mine Workers of America: A Study in Rival Unionism, Urbana, Ill., University of Illinois, 1952.

Hume, B., Death and the Mines: Rebellion and Murder in the United Mine Workers, New York, Grossman Publications, 1971.

Hurwitz, J. I., Zander, A. F., and Hymovitch, B., "Some Effects of Power on the Relations Among Group Members", In Cartwright, D., and Zander, A. F. (eds.), Group Dynamics, Evanston (Ill.), Row Peterson, 1953.

Industry Week, "Coal Firms Still Sizing Up Mine Union's New Leaders", 176:16-17, February 12, 1973.

__________, "Miners Set Tough Stance for 1974 - and Beyond", 179:15-16, December 10, 1973.

__________, "Fears Mount over Coal Supplies", 183:15-17, November 4, 1974.

__________, "Industry Could Handle a Short Coal Strike", 183:12, November 11, 1974.

__________, "No Quick Settlement in Coal", 183:7-8, November 25, 1974.

__________, "Western Coal Mines Draw UMWA Interest", 184:9, March 10, 1975.

__________, "Union Fight May Stall Coal Labor Stability", 186:16-17, July 14, 1975.

International Labor Office, Mechanization in Coal Mines and Its Social Consequences, Geneva, 1970.

Ingham, G. K., "Plant Size, Political Attitude and Behavior", Sociological Review, 17(2) (new series), July, 1960, pages 235-249.

Iron Age, "Yablonski Slaying Leaves Coal Fields, UMW Uneasy", January 10, 1970, page 35.

__________, "UMW Presents: A Modern-Day Morality Play", 209, May 18, 1972.

Jurhat, E. H., and Jurhat, D. B., "Economic Functions of Strikes", Industrial and Labor Relations Review, 2(1949), 527-545.

Karsh, B., and London, J., "The Coal Miners: A Study of Union Control", Quarterly Journal of Economics, August, 1954, Vol. 68 (3), 415-436.

Kennecot Copper Company, Annual Report, 1974.

Kerr, C., and Siegel, A., "The Inter-Industry Propensity to Strike - An International Comparison", in Kornhauser, A., Dublin, R., and Ross, A. M. (eds.), Industrial Conflict, New York, McGraw Hill, 1954, pages 189-212.

Keynes, J. M., The General Theory of Employment, Interest and Money, New York, Harcourt Brace, 1936.

Klock, J. J., Jr., and Palzer, D., "Democracy in the UMW", Labor Law, 625-631, October, 1974.

Knowles, K. G. J. C., Strikes: A Study in Industrial Conflict, Blackwell (Oxford), 1952.

Kornhauser, W., Politics of Mass society, New York, Free Press, 1959.

Korson, G. G., (ed.), Songs and Ballads of the Anthracite Miner: A Scan of Folklore Which Once Ran Through Life in the Hard Coal Fields of Pennsylvania, New York, Hitchcock, 1927.

___________, Coal Dust on the Fiddle, Philadelphia, University of Pennsylvania Press, 1943.

___________, Black Rock: Mining Folklore of the Pennylvania Dutch, Baltimore, Johns Hopkins Press, 1960.

___________, Minstrels of the Mine Patch, Hatboro (Penn.), Folklore Associates, 1964.

Kramen, D., "Follow the Leader", New Republic, April 14, 1965, Vol. 116, No. 15.

Kruger, D. H., "Arbitration and Its Uses in 36 Firms in Wisconsin", Labor Law Journal, Vol. 6, No. 3, March, 1955, pages 165-181.

Lantz, H. R., People of Coal Town, New York, Columbia University Press, 1958.

Lester, R. A., As Unions Mature: An Analysis of the Evolution of American Unionism, Princeton, Princeton University Press, 1958.

Lewis, J. L., "Not Guilty", Collins, June 15, 1944.

___________, Statement of John L. Lewis on the Determination of Prevailing Minimum Wages for the Bituminous Coal Industry Under the Walsh-Healy Public Contract Act, Vol. 1, U. S. Department of Labor Wage, Hour and Public Contract Division, February, 1955.

___________, The John L. Lewis Paper, 1897-1969, Madison, State Historical Society of Wisconsin, 1970 (microfilm).

Lilienthal, D.,"The Meaning of Unionism: A Study of Members of the Plumbers' Union, of the United Mine Workers, and of the United Automobile Workers of America", unpublished Ph.D. Thesis, University of Chicago, 1956.

Lipset, S. M., "The Political Process in Trade Unions: A Theoretical Statement", in Galenson, W., and Lipset, S. M. (eds.), Labor and Trade Unionism, New York, Wiley, 1960, pages 216-244.

___________, Political Men, London, Heineman 1960.

Lipset, S. M., Trow, M. A., and Coleman, J. S., Union Democracy: The Internal Politics of the International Typographical Union, Glencoe (Ill.), Free Press, 1956.

Lucas, R. A., Men in Crisis: A Study of a Mine Disaster, New York, Basic Books, 1969.

Klock, J. J., Jr., and Palzer, D., "Democracy in the UMW", Labor Law, 625-631, October, 1974.

Knowles, K. G. J. C., Strikes: A Study in Industrial Conflict, Blackwell (Oxford), 1952.

Kornhauser, W., Politics of Mass society, New York, Free Press, 1959.

Korson, G. G., (ed.), Songs and Ballads of the Anthracite Miner: A Scan of Folklore Which Once Ran Through Life in the Hard Coal Fields of Pennsylvania, New York, Hitchcock, 1927.

__________, Coal Dust on the Fiddle, Philadelphia, University of Pennsylvania Press, 1943.

__________, Black Rock: Mining Folklore of the Pennylvania Dutch, Baltimore, Johns Hopkins Press, 1960.

__________, Minstrels of the Mine Patch, Hatboro (Penn.), Folklore Associates, 1964.

Kramen, D., "Follow the Leader", New Republic, April 14, 1965, Vol. 116, No. 15.

Kruger, D. H., "Arbitration and Its Uses in 36 Firms in Wisconsin", Labor Law Journal, Vol. 6, No. 3, March, 1955, pages 165-181.

Lantz, H. R., People of Coal Town, New York, Columbia University Press, 1958.

Lester, R. A., As Unions Mature: An Analysis of the Evolution of American Unionism, Princeton, Princeton University Press, 1958.

Lewis, J. L., "Not Guilty", Collins, June 15, 1944.

__________, Statement of John L. Lewis on the Determination of Prevailing Minimum Wages for the Bituminous Coal Industry Under the Walsh-Healy Public Contract Act, Vol. 1, U. S. Department of Labor Wage, Hour and Public Contract Division, February, 1955.

__________, The John L. Lewis Paper, 1897-1969, Madison, State Historical Society of Wisconsin, 1970 (microfilm).

Lilienthal, D.,"The Meaning of Unionism: A Study of Members of the Plumbers' Union, of the United Mine Workers, and of the United Automobile Workers of America", unpublished Ph.D. Thesis, University of Chicago, 1956.

Lipset, S. M., "The Political Process in Trade Unions: A Theoretical Statement", in Galenson, W., and Lipset, S. M. (eds.), Labor and Trade Unionism, New York, Wiley, 1960, pages 216-244.

__________, Political Men, London, Heineman 1960.

Lipset, S. M., Trow, M. A., and Coleman, J. S., Union Democracy: The Internal Politics of the International Typographical Union, Glencoe (Ill.), Free Press, 1956.

Lucas, R. A., Men in Crisis: A Study of a Mine Disaster, New York, Basic Books, 1969.

Machiavelli, The Chief Works and Others, 3 Vols., trans. Gilbert, A., Durham (N. C.), Duke University Press, 1965.

Malinowski, B., "An Anthropological Analysis of War", in Magic, Science and Religion, Glencoe, Free Press, 1948.

March, J. G., Handbook of Organizations, Chicago, Rand McNally & Company, 1965.

March, J. G., and Simon, H. A., Organizations, New York, John Wiley and Sons, 1958.

McManus, G. J., "Striking over Shortages - Sense or Nonsense"", Iron Age, 213:32-33, March 25, 1974.

____________, "Orphans of the Earth Flirt with a Strike", Iron Age, 214:37-38, December 4, 1974.

Miller, A. R., "UMWA Recommendation for Black Lung Amendment", Labor Law Journal, 26:199-206, April, 1975.

Miller, H. G., "Information Input Overload", in Yovitz, M. C., Jacobi, G. T., and Goldstein, G. D. (eds.), Self-Organizing Systems, Washington, D. C., Spartan, 1962, pages 61-78.

Miller, J. P., "Pricing of Bituminous Coal: Some International Comparisons", in Friedrich, C. J., and Mason, E. J. (eds.), Public Policy, Cambridge, Harvards University Press, 1940.

Miller, S., "The United Mine Workers: A Study on How Trade Union Policy Relates to Technological Change", Ann Arbor, University of Michigan Microfilm.

Mills, C. W., "The Case for the Miners", New Republic, May 24, 1943, Vo. 103, No. 21.

Monthly Labor Review, "United Mine Workers' Convention, 1944", Vol. 59, No. 6, December, 1944, pages 1195-1202.

____________, "Four Years of Operation under the UMWA Welfare and Retirement Fund", Vol. 74, January, 1952, pages 37-39.

____________, "1952 Convention of UMW", Vol. 75(6), December, 1952, pages 641-643.

____________, "The 43rd Convention of the UMW of A", January, 1961, Vol. 84(1), pages 27-31.

____________, "UMWA Welfare and Retirement Report", October, 1961, Vol. 84, page 1105.

____________, "Mine Worker Upheaval", Vol. 92, October, 1969, page 2.

____________, "Miller Wins Miners' Presidency", Vol. 96, Feburary, 1973, pages 64-65.

____________, "Meeting, 46th, Pittsburgh", Vol. 97, February, 1974, pages 75-76.

__________, "Soft Coal Settles", Vol. 98, January, 1975, pages 82-83.

Morley, F., "Labor and Contracts: UMW Spearheads Growing Union Skepticism about Inflation", Barron's, 31:5, November 12, 1951.

__________, "Mind of John L. Lewis: He Reviews the Mess in Steel and Draws His Conclusions", Barron's 32:5, April 28, 1952.

Myers, R. J., "Further Experience of the UMWA Welfare and Retirement Func", Industrial and Labor Relations Review, 14, July, 1961, pages 556562.

__________, "Mine Workers' Welfare Fund: Fifteen Years Experience", Industrial and Labor Relations Review, 20, January, 1967, pages 265274.

Te Nation, "Why They Follow John Lewis", April 3, 1943, Vol. 156(14).

__________, "John L. Lewis Rides Again", March 10, 1945, Vol. 160, No. 10.

The National Bureau of Economic Research, Report of the Committee on Prices in the Bituminous Coal Industry, New York, 1939.

The National Coal Association, Bituminous Coal Data, 1975, Washington, D. C., 1976.

The National Committee for the Defense of Political Prisoners, Harlan Miners Speak: Report on Terrorism in Kentucky Coal Fields, New York, Da Capo Press,1970.

The New Republic, "Second Class Citizens", May 17, 1943, Vol. 108, No. 20.

The New York Times, 1940-1977.

New York University, Conference on Labor, Proceedings of New York University 26th Annual Conference on Labor, New York, Matthew Bender, 1974.

Newsweek, July 4, 1976, page 4.

O'Brien, F. S., "Industrial Conflict and Business Fluctuations: A Comment", Journal of Political Economy, 73, 1965, pages 650-654.

Occidental Oil Co., Annual Reports, 1971, 1974.

O'Hanlon, T., "Anarchy Threatens the Kingdom of Coal", Fortune, 83, January, 1971, pages 78-82.

Padway, J. A., "Are Royalties Wrong", American Federationist, April, 1945, Vol. 52, No. 4.

Pencavel, J. H., "An Investigation into Industrial Strike Activity in Britain", Economica, 37, 1970, pages 239-256.

Peterson, B., Coaltown Revised: An Appalachian Notebook, Chicago, Henry Regnery, 1972.

Pittson Co., Annual Report, 1974.

Polakov, W. N., "Sufficient unto Himself is the Coal Digger - Why the Miners Behave the Way They Do - Social Portaiture of the Nation's Most Vital, Least Known Labor Force", Labor and Nation, May-June, 1947, Vol. 3(3).

President's Appalachian Regional Commission, Appalachia: A Report by the President's Appalachian Regional Commussion, 1964, Washington, D. C., 1964.

Railway Age, "In a Time of Need, Coal's Outlook is Cloudy", 175:10-11, August 26, 1974.

Raskin, A. H., "Secrets of John Lewis' Great Power", The New York Times Magazine, October 5, 1952.

__________, "John L. Lewis - A Glorious Anachronism", The New York Times Magazine, February 13, 1955.

__________, "Threat of Long Coal Strike and Peril to Energy Plan", The New York Times, April 27, 1977.

Rauh, J., "Internal Union Problem: A Study of the United Mine Workers' Union", 62 LRRM, 2597.

Read, W. H., "Upward Communication in Industrial Hierarchies", Human Relations, Vol. 15 (1), February, 1962, pages 3-12.

Rees, A., "Industrial Conflict and Business Fluctuations", Journal of Political Economy, 60, 195.

Revans, R. W., "Industrial Morale and Size of Unit", in Galeson, W. and Lipset, S. M. (eds.), Labor and Trade Unionism, New York, Wiley, 1960, pages 295-300.

Rimlinger, G. V., "International Differences in the Strike Propensity of Coal Miners: Experience in Four Countries", ILRR, 1959, pages 389-405.

Roomkin, M., "Union Structure, Internal Control, and Strike Activity", Industrial Labor Relations Review, 29(2), January, 1976, pages 198-217.

Ross, A. M., and Hartman, P., Changing Patterns of Industrial Conflict, New York, Wiley, 1960.

Rostow, E. V., "Bituminous Coal and the Public Interest", Yale Law Journal, Vol. 50, 1941.

Saturday Evening Post, "What the Coal Miners Say about John L. Lewis", January 15, 1949.

Sayles, L. R., and Strauss, C., The Local Union: Its Place in the Industrial Plant, New York, Harper, 1953.

Schelling, T. C., "On the Ecology of Micromotives", The Public Interest, Fall, 1971, pages 59-98.

__________, "Hockey Helmets, Concealed Weapons and Daylight Saving: a Study of Binary Choices with Externalities", Journal of Conflict Resolutions, Vol. 17, No. 3, September, 1973.

Schiffer, I., Charisma: A Psychoanalytic Look at Mass Society, Toronto, University of Toronto Press.

Seelbach, W. F., United States Bituminous Coal Market: Trend Since 1920 and Prospect to 1975, Pittsburgh, Three River Press, 1960.

Seltzer, C., "The Unions, How Much Can a Good Man Do?", The Washington Monthly, June, 1974, Vol. 6, No. 4, pages 7-24.

Selznick, P., Organizational Weapon, New York, McGraw Hill, 1952.

Sheppard, M., Cloud by Day: The Story of Coal, Coke and People, Chapel Hill, University of North Carolina Press, 1947.

Simkin, W. E., "Refusals to Ratify Contract", Industrial and Labor Relations Review, 21(4), July, 1968, pages 518-540.

____________, Mediation and the Dynamics of Collective Bargaining, Washington, D. C., The Bureau of National Affairs, 1971.

Simmel, G., Conflict, trans. Wolff, K. H., Glencoe, Free Press, 1955.

Simon, H. A., Administrative Behavior, New York, McMillan, 1947.

____________, The New Science of Management Decision, New York, Harper, 1960.

Skeels, J. W., "Measure of U. S. Strike Activity", Industrial and Labor Relations Review, 24(4), July, 1971, pages 515-25.

Smith, R. C., Human Crisis in the Kingdom of Coal, New York, Friendship Press, 1952.

Snyder, D., "Institutional Setting and Industrial Conflict: Comparative Analysis of France, Italy and the United States", American Sociological Review, 40, 1975, pages 259-278.

Somers, G. D., Experience Under National Wage Agreements, West Virginia University, Business and Economic Studies, Vol. 2(4), 1953.

____________, "The Multi-Employer Proposals and the Coal Operators", Labor Law Journal, May, 1955, pages 296-310.

____________, Grievance Settlement in Coal Mining, West Virginia University, Business and Economic Studies, Vol. 4(4), June, 1956.

Stentham, I. C. F., Coal Mining, New York, Philosophical Library, 1956.

Suchocki, C. J., and Weimer, G. A., "UMW Election: A Good Chance for Reform", Iron Age, 210:19, December 21, 1972.

Takamiya, M., "A Pure Theory of Inter-Organizational Conflict", Alfred P. Sloan School Working Paper No. 747-74, November, 1974.

Tannenbaum, A. S., "Unions", in March, J. G. (ed.), Handbook of Organizations, Chicago, Rand McNally, 1965.

Tannenbaum, A. S., and Kahn, R., "Organizational Control Structure: A General Descriptive Technique as Applied to Four Local Unions", Human Relations, 3:251-278, 1950.

Thompson, D. B., "Key Coal Talk Issues:/ Fewer Wildcat Strikes, More Output", Industry Week, 182:11-13, September 2, 1974.

___________, "Coal Pact May Bring Better Labor-Management Relations", Industry Week, 183:14-16, December 9, 1974.

Thompson, E. T., "Mines and Plantations and the Movement of People", American Journal of Sociology, 37:603-611, 1932.

Trist, E. L., Higgin, G. W., Murray, H., and Pollack, A. B., Organizational Choice: Capabilities of Groups at the Coal Face Under Changing Technologies, New York, Humanity Press, 1965.

Troy, L., Trade Union Membership, 1897-1962, National Bureau of Economic Research, Occasional Paper 92, 1965.

Tucker, R. C., "The Theory of Charismatic Leadership", Daedalus, 97:731-755, Summer, 1968.

The United Mine Workers of America, John L. Lewis and the International Union, 1952,

___________, Proceedings of the International Conventions, Vols. 1 and 2, 1942, 1944, 1946, 1948, 1952, 1956, 1060, 1964, 1968, 1972 and 1976.

___________, Constitutions of the International Union, 1932 and 1973.

___________, Joint Reports of the International Officers, 1942, 1944, 1946, 1948, 1952, 1956, 1960, 1964, 1968, 1972, 1976.

___________, The United Mine Workers Journal, 1940-1977.

U. S. Coal Commission, Relief from Irregular Operation and Over-Development, Part I., 1923.

U. S. Congress, House of Representatives, Committee on Education and Labor, Subcommittee on Labor: Oversight Hearing on Brookside Mine Labor-Management Dispute, July 25, 1974, Washington, D. C.

U. S. Congress, Senate Committee on Labor and Education, Subcommittee on Labor, Hearings Before the Senate Committee on Labor: Mine Safety Legislation, 1949.

___________, Hearings before the Senate Subcommittee on Labor: United Mine Workers' Election, 1970, 1971, 1972.

U. S. Geographical Survey, Weekly Report of the Production of Bituminous Coal, Anthracite and Beehive Coke, 1922-1924.

U. S. National War Labor Board, The Termination Report of the National War Labor Board, Vols 1, 2, and 3, Washington, 1947-1949.

U. S. Office of Price Administration, Preliminary Survey of Operating Data for Commercial Bituminous Coal Mines for the Years 1943, 1944 and 1945.

U. S. News and World Report, "Peace and Prosperity in the Mines Reported from Pittsburgh and Union Town, Pa.", Vol. 25, No. 1, July 2, 1948.

____________, "Eyes on John L. Lewis", Vol. 41(11), pages 129-132, September 14, 1956.

____________, "John L. Lewis - Board Chairman", Vol. 41(15), Page 114, October 12, 1956.

____________, "John L. Lewis, Businessman", Vol. 40(26), pages 58-60, June 29, 1956.

____________, "Lewis' Billion-Dollar Fund Total Soon Will Hit That Mark", Vol. 39(13), page 108, September 23, 1955.

____________, "Miners' Union in New Venture", Vol. 40(25), pages 118-119, June 22, 1956.

____________, "No Coal Strikes - John L. Lewis and the Operators Tell Why", Vol. 45(25), pages 75-77, December 19, 1958.

____________, "A Pension Plan in Trouble", Vol. 36(18), pages 77-80, April 30, 1954.

Vecsey, G., One Sunset a Week: The Story of a Coal Miner, Saturday Review Press, 1974.

Walton, R. E., and McKensie, R. B., A Behavioral Theory of Labor Negotiations: An Analysis of ASocial Interaction System, New York, McGraw Hill, 1965.

The Wall Street Journal, 1940-1977.

Wechsler, J. A., "Is John Lewis Licked?", The Nation, June 13, 1942, Vol. 154(24).

____________, Labor Baron: A Portrait of John L. Lewis, New York, Marrow, 1944.

____________, "John Lewis, Challenger", The Nation, Vol. 160(13), March 31, 1945.

Weibtraub, A., "Prosperity Vs. Strikes: An Empirical Approach", Industrial and Labor Relations Review, 19:231-238, 1966.

Weimer, G. A., and McManus, G. J., "Coal Miners are Very Energetic About Right to Strike", Iron Age, 212:18, December 20, 1973.

Wieck, E. A., The Miners' Case and the Public Interest, New York, Russell Sage Foundation, 1947.

Wiener, Norbert, Cybernetics, or Control and Communication in the Antimal and the Machine, 2nd ed., Cambridge (Mass.), M. I. T., 1948.

____________, The Human Use of Human Beings: Cybernetics and Society, New York, Avon Books, 1967.

Willner, A. R., Charismatic Political Leadership: A Theory, Princeton, Center for International Studies, Princeton University, 1968.

Willner, R., and Willner, D., "The Rise and Role of Charismatic Leaders", Annals, 358:77-78, 1965.

Wolfe, H., "A Critical Analysis of Some Aspects of Charisma", Sociological Review, 16:305-318, 1968.

Won, G., and Yamamura, D., "Career Orientation of Local Union Leadership: A Case Study", Sociology and Social Research, Vol, 52, No. 2, pages 243-252, January, 1968.

Wooley, B., We Be Here When the Morning Comes, Lexington, University Press of Knetucky, 1975.

Yoder, D., "Economic Changes and Industrial Unrest in the United States", Journal of Political Economy, 48:222-237, 1940.

Zweg, F., Men in the Pits, London, Victor Gollancz Ltd., 1948.

The Wissenschaftszentrum Berlin (Science Center Berlin), a non-profit corporation, serves as a parent institution for institutes conducting social science research in areas of significant social concern.

The following institutes are currently operating within the Science Center Berlin:

1. The International Institute of Management,
2. The International Institute for Environment and Society,
3. The International Institute for Comparative Social Research.

They share the following structural elements: a multinational professional and supporting staff, multidisciplinary project teams, a focus on international comparative studies, a policy orientation in the selection of research topics and the diffusion of results.